New Classic Desserts

New Classic Desserts

Andrew MacLauchlan

Van Nostrand Reinhold

An International Thomson Publishing Company

New York • London • Bonn • Boston • Detroit • Madrid • Melbourne • Mexico City
Paris • Singapore • Tokyo • Toronto • Albany NY • Belmont CA • Cincinnati OH

Copyright © 1995 by Andrew MacLauchlan

I(T)P™ A division of International Thomson Publishing Inc.
The ITP logo is a trademark under license

Printed in Hong Kong
For more information, contact:

Van Nostrand Reinhold
115 Fifth Avenue
New York, NY 10003

International Thomson Publishing GmbH
Königswinterer Strasse 418
53227 Bonn
Germany

International Thomson Publishing Europe
Berkshire House 168-173
High Holborn
London WCIV 7AA
England

International Thomson Publishing Asia
221 Henderson Road #05-10
Henderson Building
Singapore 0315

Thomas Nelson Australia
102 Dodds Street
South Melbourne, 3205
Victoria, Australia

International Thomson Publishing Japan
Hirakawacho Kyowa Building, 3F
2-2-1 Hirakawacho
Chiyoda-ku, 102 Tokyo
Japan

Nelson Canada
1120 Birchmount Road
Scarborough, Ontario
Canada M1K 5G4

International Thomson Editores
Campos Eliseos 385, Piso 7
Col. Polanco
11560 Mexico D.F. Mexico

1 2 3 4 5 6 7 8 9 10 CP 01 00 99 98 97 96 95 94

Library of Congress Cataloging-in-Publication Data
MacLauchlan, Andrew.
    New classic desserts / Andrew MacLauchlan.
        p.   cm.
    Includes index.
    ISBN 0-442-01735-9
    1. Desserts.   2. Cookery (Natural foods)   I. Title.
    TX773.M233   1995
    641.8′6—dc20   93-41842
                                                          CIP

Contents

Acknowledgments

I would like to express my appreciation to many people for their support of this project and my development over the years, those who challenged and enlightened me in the trenches and behind the lines. Those whom I worked beside in the heat of moments I'll never forget: Chris Balcer, Ted and Linda Fondulas, Jonathan St. Laurent, Roy Stewart, Barb, Thor, Dermot, Eric, Catfish, Keith, Marko, Mark and Don Monette, Angelo, Nancy, Bill, Luce, Gary, Charlie Trotter, the Trotters, Jeff, Bob, Guillermo, Mitchell, Patricia, Mimi, Larry Stone, Chris, Mark S., Matt, Jason, Renee, Ulysses, Reggie, Vera, Megan, Nellie, Agnes, Paul, and Michele.

A special thanks for the helpful advice and comments from Dee Coutelle, Nancy Silverton, Jacques Torres, Emeril Lagasse, Daniel Boulud, Charlie Trotter, and Robert Scherner.

Thanks to Valrhona Chocolate Co., European Imports, Nature's Wild Rice, Chicago Produce, Tom Cornille, Pelouze Scale Co., Edward Don and Co., and Conservation International for the supplies and equipment needed for recipe testing. The following Chicago-area restaurants graciously contributed their fine plates for our photography sessions: Charlie Trotter's, Café Provencale, Va Pensiero, Gordon, and Ti Amo.

To the staff at VNR whose tremendous support and direction have been my guiding wire: Pam Chirls, Caroline Schleifer, Mike Suh, Patti Brecht, Sherrel Farnsworth, and Amy Shipper.

I would like to thank my parents for the spatulas, saving that hobart mixer for me, and my work ethic.

My photographers, Halley Smith of Command Z Design and Eric Nixon, were a constant creative force through long productive sessions. Dad, thank you for the fantastic line drawings.

At last my partner, Donna, your support has been sustaining at every turn, the wise editing, last-minute copies, help with the computer, artistic advice, and of course your discriminating palate. Most of all, your love inspires like chocolate.

Foreword

Dessert has always been a very important part of the dining experience at Charlie Trotter's. So much so, that every guest experiences at least three different end-of-the-meal preparations. And all our desserts, like the rest of the food, are prepared absolutely to order, as that is the only way to enjoy the purest and cleanest flavors from the extraordinary, fresh foodstuffs that we use.

We have always had wonderful pastry chefs at the restaurant, but over the years I have particularly enjoyed my relationship with Andrew MacLauchlan. When he came to the restaurant at the beginning of 1991, Andrew brought with him an intense, but controlled and refined approach to the art of dessert making. He adapted quickly and fervently to my approach of "less is more," and he immediately began to zero in on highlighting the essential flavors of apricots, strawberries, sapote, carrots, cherries, lemongrass, hazelnuts, rosemary, chocolate, and the myriad of other products that make up our pastry larder. Behind his astute artist's eye is the soul of a chemist, and the utter purity of flavor in his gorgeous desserts will certainly attest to that.

But what really makes Andrew's approach so unique and so relevant to modern cuisine in America is that while he respects and devises ideas from classical pastry preparations, he simultaneously takes a distinctly American approach with regard to inventiveness and health concerns.

Actually, Andrew is a remarkable innovator. I merely mention the words crispness, peaches, custard, and he returns to me a day later with a brilliant peach crème brûlée crispy filo napoleon—visually stunning, totally delicious, perfectly light and delicate. Incredible! This describes a format in which we've worked out countless ideas together. A wonderful collaboration!

In the end, a meal needs to have harmony and balance. The final thing you eat, the fruit sorbet or the lemon tart or the warm chocolate cake, should fit accordingly with what precedes it. Andrew has compiled a tremendous collection of elegant, healthful, and exciting possibilities. You will not only be stimulated and delighted by what you prepare from this book, you will learn a great deal as well.

Charlie Trotter

Preface

It occurred to me a few years ago that in the wide variety of available dessert cookbooks there was a wealth of information, and some excellent books devoted to classical dessert preparations and fundamentals. However, there seemed to be a lack of current information on how to combine tried and true preparations in a refined manner with insistent consideration of a balance of flavors, textures, and degree of sweetness in each individually plated presentation. I thought that many important questions could be answered in a dessert cookbook that demonstrated examples of plated, finished, individually constructed desserts that showcase and explain both classical and new techniques.

Some of the issues that I emphasize in *New Classic Desserts* include the proper pairing of flavors, effectively using dessert sauces and coulis, and creating desserts by combining essential fruits, nuts, or chocolate with classical pastry preparations, such as a rich crème brûlée. I encourage readers to use the techniques, methods, and ideas presented in this book to formulate their own new and original desserts. In addition, I include a "chef's hint" with each recipe that offers ways to simplify the dessert or prepare it in a whole form as an alternative to individually constructed desserts.

At times, things change very fast in the professional kitchen. Ideas are swept away with the ever-changing varieties of seasonal produce and constant efforts to evolve a cleaner, simpler, and healthier approach. At other times, the best desserts become "standards" for the season in which their specific ingredients are available and of good quality, and are often revived year after year when the season returns. I have tried to capture some of these ideas and share them with other chefs as well as with serious home cooks who would like to indulge a special gathering with a show-stopping finale of a dessert.

I learned my craft in essentially two ways: by example and experimentation. I firmly believe in experimentation with dessert themes and flavors, after the rudiments of cooking and pastry making are understood and inculcated, as a way of continued learning and self-advancement. Dessert-making styles are varied and constantly changing just as cooking styles, ideas, and tastes evolve. I truly admire the rustic and classic desserts and pastries of another era and draw ideas and direct influence from an apple charlotte or pumpkin pie, or from faint memories of childhood such as milkshakes, strawberry shortcake, candy bars, ice cream cones, or banana splits. Maybe it's only the memory of those sweets that are special to us now, but I have tried to mature some of these ideas, to borrow the flavors that I most fondly recall, to reassemble and endow a dessert with new heights of excellence. In every dessert, I strive to contain a singular strength of purpose in the overall presentation, the reasoning behind every element, and the deliberate pairing of flavors in an effort to communicate these ideas to the guest. The greatest achievement is to serve what seems to be a simple, beautiful dessert that, as it is consumed, begins to defy its own simplicity with a subtle perfection, bespeaking a lightness of touch and maturity of experience.

Introduction

My challenge as a restaurant pastry chef is to create classic desserts that are modified with fresh ideas and a lighter approach. These desserts celebrate the passing seasons by featuring the brightest fruits in summer and the warmth of chocolate, coffee, and nuts in winter. In this book, I share my philosophies, techniques, and detailed recipes for a new repertoire of desserts that are flavorful, not overly sweet, and visually stunning. With their origins rooted in classic European and American dessert ideas, these creations have evolved to emphasize flavors, eliminate excess sugar, and define an overall appealing composition.

Advance preparation is essential to the creation of successful desserts. These desserts are no exception to the rule, despite the fact that their final assembly is saved for the last possible moment. These "new classic desserts" involve combining the working principles of restaurant line cooking, with the techniques of the French *patissier*, and procedures of baking. The last-minute details should be done quickly so that the dessert's featured flavors, best

temperatures, and finest textures can be showcased. In the restaurant kitchen, accomplishing this *á la minute* service is a matter of hard work, attention to detail, and, above all, careful timing.

The use of flavorful organic fruits and nuts at the height of their natural growing seasons contributes to a dessert's quality, flavor, and appeal. Fruit served alone can be a satisfying dessert, but I prefer to meld it in some way with particular pastry elements, perhaps an ice cream, sorbet, or flavor-infused custard, in order to offer the taste of rich European pastry without overwhelming the integrity of the featured food. In these desserts, I retain familiar and timeless flavor combinations because they are proven and classic, for example, peaches and vanilla, apples and caramel, chocolate and mint.

A dessert does not need to be complex and ornately constructed in order to be flavorful, unique, and satisfying. When creating a new dessert, I focus on flavor. Then I consider its structure, size, and textures. My desserts have been called "an effort in minimalism," in the sense that they highlight flavors rather than unnecessary decorative elements. I have tried to follow this "rule" although I am not puritanical in this regard. There are occasions when a constructed, decorative dessert is appropriate and inspires the pastry chef in a more whimsical direction. Ideas from architecture, the natural world, or even futuristic motifs, can be conveyed with preparations of chocolate, meringue, or tuile cookie. They are all edible and texturally interesting, if done with skill and prudence.

During the summer months, I prefer to shop for local and organic produce at an area farmer's market, where you find the freshest and most flavorful fruit. I base my dessert ideas on the available ingredients of the day or week. When fruits' natural seasons are observed, the flavors are at their peak. As the seasons change, so do the varieties of fruits. Making use of seasonal fruit can expand your understanding of each variety and often inspires new dessert ideas. In the autumn and winter months, apples, pears, chocolate, and coffee become the staple, cooler-weather flavors.

My fascination with pastry is based on the continual building and learning process I experience since the methods and recipes I use are not set in stone. I alter recipes and apply new ideas to the foods I plan to feature. Dessert making is neither a mysterious nor an exact science; it is not disconnected from the flexible and spontaneous methods of good cooking. Good desserts require attention to details, a few commonsense preparation methods, and careful, calculated execution of the final presentation.

In the art of cooking, numerous boundaries, rules, and methods have to be learned, and the cook or chef needs to be familiar and practiced with the tools of the trade. A good chef emerges after a long seasoning in many kitchens and exposure to numerous styles, culinary opinions, and ethnic cuisines. Possessed of a clear, uncompromising vision, forging a personal, specific style based on these influences, a chef achieves confidence and the ability to be creative.

In the United States, the growing pool of talented, young chefs; the availability of high-quality foods; the embrace of varied ethnic influences; and a growing, knowledgable, and sophisticated dining clientele have shaped a unique and exciting culinary movement with deep roots in the culinary history of France. In many ways, dessert making has not kept up with the advances of this movement and with cooking in general. Pastry chefs are only beginning to enjoy the prominence and creative level that many chefs have reached. My goal is to contribute to this effort and to share my vision in *New Classic Desserts*.

How to Use This Book

Have a mental picture of the look and taste of the final presentation. With this constantly in mind, you will see more clearly all the steps leading up to the finished dessert. Before proceeding with a dessert, you should read through the entire recipe and all advance-preparation recipes. You should also study the photographs, illustrations, and measurements in order to visualize the creation and understand what is required in time, ingredients, and equipment. I have tried to be very specific about pan sizes and other measurements, especially with regard to recipes that make 6 to 8 servings. To prepare larger amounts, and to conform to the standard, professional larger-sized sheetpans or terrine molds, you can multiply the recipes by 2, 3, or 4, as needed.

About Presentation

Presentation is a significant factor for chefs and serious home cooks. Ideas for dessert presentation have roots in early culinary history, from before the days of restaurants, when the "grand cuisine" was available only to the nobility and when chefs were found hard at work in the kitchens of palaces. Large architectural pieces made entirely of pastry and sugar are described and illustrated in the writings of the famous chef Antonin Careme. These decorative pieces were placed on banquet tables and surrounded by an enormous variety of sweets and candies. The notions of dessert decoration and presentation have become increasingly more modest today, and yet, there is a sense of inspiration to be felt from the days of architectural spectacle. Current dessert presentation serves not to create an inedible "look," but can contribute valuable flavorful and textural components to the plate. Several methods for the presentation ideas in this book require some practice or familiarity with cooking sugar, molding hot-from-the-oven tuile cookies, or working with a pastry bag. In the recipes contained in Chapters Four and Five, I explain exactly how to create the pictured desserts, including presentation items.

At the end of each seasonal recipe, I have included a chef's hint in which I offer some ideas for simplifing or eliminating presentation items. This allows you to avoid some of the more complex parts of a recipe, yet still keep the essential flavors of the dessert. You should review these hints before beginning a recipe so you will understand the dessert's possibilities and options. For example, a simple mixture of ripe, seasonal berries, warmed with some Riesling wine in a sauté pan, seasoned with a little sprinkle of sugar and a grind of black pepper, mounded in a bowl and topped with two small scoops of pistachio ice cream, can be a flawless, incredible dessert.

I encourage you to use this book as a collection of ideas and recipes that can be modified or intertwined to develop many more desserts or create variations on my themes. The flavors of fruits, nuts, and chocolate should always dominate, but you should also consider the dessert's structure and diverging textures. For example, in many desserts, different fruits can be substituted for the ones I have used, exchanging peaches for nectarines, apricots, and plums or replacing apples with pears. Never believe there is only one way to make any dessert. Try different options with some of the ideas in this book and perfect them in your own style. Many times, a particular fruit may be unavailable, of poor quality, or unripe, prompting the need for creative use of what is on hand. This fact of life is a great opportunity to offer only the very best seasonal desserts to your guests.

I have had many conceptual ideas of desserts that could never quite bridge the gap between thought and reality. I guess those ideas are still out there, free from the natural laws of heat and cold, gravity and balance, humidity and altitude. They are somewhere, perfect and magnificent. A few of these ideas made it through in some form or another, but a dessert always seems to have potential for further evolution. Sometimes it is difficult to say when it is finished and cannot be any better. However, there comes the time when dessert must be served, when every detail and all the steps preceding the final assembly come into play. In the end, for someone, a few seconds crystallize into pleasure, and perhaps a flash of childhood, and flavors that linger into memory.

New Classic Desserts

CHAPTER ONE

Ingredients and Equipment

The ingredients for these recipes can be considered the building blocks of the finished desserts. Their quality will contribute to the dessert's final character. The number of different ingredients in this book is manageable. By changing combinations of the main flavors, fruits, or nuts with certain basic preparations, a large repertoire of very different desserts can be made. Some ingredients, such as nuts, fruits (dried or fresh), and dairy products, should be bought in small amounts in order to maintain freshness and quality. Bulk ingredients—such as sugar, flour, chocolate, and cocoa powder—can be stored for longer periods if they are sealed in canisters and kept in a relatively cool place.

The range of equipment available to amateur and professional pastry chefs is vast: molds and tart tins of all sizes and shapes, and implements for chocolate making and decorative work. Some are intended for an entirely different style of dessert making than presented here and are not necessary for preparing the desserts in this book. The equipment you will need is not much more than would be found in a well-equipped home kitchen. Because nearly every dessert is an individually prepared whole rather than a cut portion, many recipes call for some specific mold sizes. Working knowledge of basic kitchen appliances and continued practice with the hand-held tools will give you the best success with these dessert creations.

A Word About Dairy Products

Although there is extensive concern about the fat content of dairy products and their place in our diets, I have not totally eliminated them from my desserts. However, for the most part, a dairy-product-based item plays a secondary role to the main flavor sources, which are fruits, nuts, or chocolate. Custards, smooth-textured crème brûlée, and ice creams provide a satisfying contrast to fruits or crispy pastry components. The focus of the ice creams, custards, and crème brûlée here is flavor, and some of them are infused with red wine, spices, chocolate, or coffee. Their richness and the intensity of the flavors allow them to be used in small amounts in a dessert. This conveys the feeling of haute cuisine's rich desserts while appealing to contemporary tastes and dietary concerns.

Eggs

For the recipes in this book, the best results will be obtained by using large eggs. Eggs are a very important part of dessert making. They form the foundation of many recipes, providing the structure and leavening for numerous cakes and doughs. The most important role of the egg yolk in dessert making may be that of a binder and thickener in various creams and custards, whereas the whipped egg white adds volume and lightness to mousses and sponge cakes. When whipping egg whites, be sure the whip and bowl are very clean and free from previously mixed ingredients, such as oils or fats, and that the whites are free from bits of yolk, which can inhibit the whipping process. To add sugar while whipping egg whites, sprinkle it in a little at a time after some foaming has occurred. If the sugar is added too quickly, the whites may not rise.

You can make an egg wash for brushing pastry tops to create a shiny surface or for assembling raviolis.

. . . .

Create an egg wash by whisking together 1 whole egg and 2 tablespoons (30 ml) of water.

. . . .

In recipes that use raw egg (mousses; chocolate marquise, p. 44; espresso bavarian, p. 39), be sure to use the freshest available eggs, refrigerated up to the point of use, and take special care to look at each egg as you crack it to make sure it is fresh. Stale egg yolks and whites appear watery and spread out rapidly in a bowl or pan. A fresh egg white holds together somewhat around the yolk; the yolk appears firm.

Milk

Milk is a key ingredient in numerous custard and ice cream recipes. Although I recommend whole milk, lighter 2 percent or lowfat milk may be substituted, if desired. When preparing a recipe with milk, always taste it to be sure it is fresh. A thick-bottom saucepot is best for heating and cooking milk. Stir occasionally and heat it to the point of simmering so that it does not scorch or overflow the pot.

Cream

I use heavy cream or whipping cream in these recipes. For best results, use well-chilled cream for whipping. Watch the cream closely while whipping it to avoid overbeating. If the cream is to be folded into other ingredients, it should be whipped to a point just beyond soft peaks so that it combines with the other ingredients easily without deflating.

Butter

Butter is used in most pastry doughs and many batters and for brushing molds and parchment-lined sheetpans. For these recipes, always use unsalted butter to maintain control over a recipe's amount of salt. Quite often, butter's consistency, which is affected by its temperature, is very important in a recipe. Unless otherwise indicated, butter used in these recipes should come cold (40°F) from the refrigerator.

Crème Fraîche   Crème fraîche is actually cream that has a rich and slightly sour taste. It may be purchased at some markets or specialty food stores. You may use sour cream instead, if you are unable to find crème fraîche. See Chapter Two for a basic recipe for crème fraîche.

Mascarpone   Mascarpone is a rich, smooth cream cheese that has an unequaled melt-in-the-mouth quality. Available in most large markets, it is sold in small tubs.

Chèvre   Goat cheese, or log *chèvre* as it may be called, has an important place in a few of the new classic desserts. Choose the unflavored (no herbs or spices) variety usually sold in a short, vacuum-packed log.

A Word About Flours

For recipes that call for flour, I recommend using unbleached all-purpose flour. I don't find it necessary to use cake or pastry flour, but you may use cake flour in the sponge cake and génoise recipes and pastry flour in the dough section (except in recipes for pasta, phyllo, puff pastry, and brioche). Instead of being chemically treated ("bleached"), unbleached all-purpose flours have been aged naturally after the milling process to improve their baking qualities. Wheat flour contains some amount of gluten, which provides elasticity and strength. With the addition of moisture and kneading, the gluten fibers link together and form an interlocking network that creates desirable characteristics in several pastry doughs. Gluten development helps create flakiness in a simple shortdough, allows for the stretching of thousands of thin layers separated by butter in puff pastry, or traps the carbon dioxide released by active yeast in the bubble structures of a delicate brioche dough. The development of gluten is undesirable in other baking recipes, as with, for example, cake batters or rich shortdough, which by the nature of their assembly, among other factors, avoid gluten activation.

High-Gluten Flour   High-gluten flour is used primarily in bread making, but is useful in the recipe for phyllo dough in order to allow it to be stretched to a very thin sheet.

Semolina Flour   Semolina flour is milled from "hard" or "winter wheat" and is characteristically off-white or yellow in color. It is the flour of choice for pasta making. Medium- or fine-ground semolina will give the best results.

Cornstarch   Commonly used as a thickener, cornstarch is also useful for dusting phyllo and the work surface when you need to stretch a dough very thin.

A Word About Chocolate

For many, the rich, celebrated flavor of good chocolate can be a highlight of the meal. The best chocolate desserts use high-quality chocolate and feature it prominently. On the other hand, it is sometimes best to serve a small amount of chocolate in the form of petit fours after the meal.

For recipes that call for chocolate, use high-quality bittersweet chocolate. Choose real chocolate without artificial flavors or fats other than cocoa butter. Milk and white chocolate have limited practical use in desserts because they are generally oversweet and lack chocolate flavor, but they can add variety and novelty to petit fours. I have used various brands of Valrhona chocolate, including Valrhona Carribe and Manjari (both bittersweet), and Valrhona Guanaja lactée (milk chocolate) and Ivoire (white chocolate).

Melt chocolate in a double boiler. Chop the chocolate before melting and stir occasionally so it melts evenly.

Cocoa Powder

Use unsweetened Dutch-processed cocoa. In these recipes, I have used Valrhona cocoa powder. Cocoa powder should be sifted to remove any lumps. When combining it with other dry ingredients, sift it with them. When combining cocoa powder with a liquid, add some of the liquid to the powder, and, using a spatula, form a smooth paste before adding the remaining liquid.

A Word About Fresh Fruit

Fruits are the focus of nearly every dessert in this book. They are featured in nearly every presentation, provide the main flavor source, and in most cases, are the inspiration for each dessert. Other elements in these new classic dessert compositions—such as pastry preparations, ice creams, sorbets, or nut brittles—often serve to support the fruit, which has been poached, seasoned, or used uncooked when it is perfectly ripe and bursting with flavor. Fruit on its own is at times an excellent, simple dessert. With a few added pastry techniques and embellishments, you can produce stunning results. The importance of fruit in these desserts cannot be overemphasized. Fresh fruit is the only type that should ever be used. Rather than canned or frozen products, use what is available in season. Choose high-quality, organic fruit when possible, and plan ahead so that it may be left unrefrigerated for a time, if necessary, to achieve proper ripeness. For example, pears may need to be left out to ripen for 5 days, whereas peaches may only need 1 day. Observe the seasons and choose fruit accordingly, when flavors are at their peak. If possible, buy fruit from local sources such as farmers markets or specialized fruit markets. Chances are you will find flavors in fresh fruit that you may have forgotten because of the availability of less flavorful fruit that is often picked before it is ripened. Certainly there is some overlap in seasonality, and local sources may often be limited, so I include some fruits—such as bananas—in both the summer and winter recipe chapters. Citrus fruits are usually reasonably consistent in flavor and quality year-round, but some kinds, such as blood oranges, are available only in late winter.

Important Fresh Fruits

In the chart on this page, fruits are listed in alphabetical order, with the times of the year when they have the best flavor.

Fruit	Seasons
Apples (Jonathan, McIntosh, Granny Smith, Red Rome)	Late summer, fall, winter
Apricots	Spring, early to mid-summer
Bananas	Year-round
Bananas, baby	Late winter, spring
Blackberries	Mid- to late summer, early fall
Cantaloupe and muskmelon	Summer
Cherries	Late spring, early summer
Clementines (seedless tangerines)	Winter, early spring
Coconuts	Year-round
Figs	Late spring, early summer, early fall
Gooseberries	Mid- to late summer, early fall
Guavas	Spring, summer
Kumquats	Late winter, spring
Lemons	Year-round
Limes	Year-round
Mangos	Late winter, spring
Melon, honeydew	Spring, summer
Nectarines	Spring, early summer
Oranges	Year-round

Continued on next page

Fruit	Seasons
Oranges, blood	Late winter, spring
Papaya	Winter, spring
Peaches	Mid- to late summer
Peaches, white	Late summer
Pears (Forelli, Seckel, Comice, Anjou)	Late summer, fall, winter
Pineapples	Late winter, spring
Plums	Spring, early summer
Plums, prune	Late summer
Pumpkins	Fall, early winter
Quince	Fall, winter
Raspberries	Mid- to late summer
Rhubarb	Spring, summer
Starfruit (carambola)	Winter, early spring
Strawberries	Late spring, early summer

A Word About Dried Fruits

Dried fruits have a place in some desserts. Their concentrated, rich flavors are a natural sweetening agent, and their appealing texture add interest and contrast. Dried fruit can even appear with its fresh counterpart in the same dessert, such as a compote or strudel, as a way to capture two distinct textures and intensify the flavor. Try to find the unsulfured variety. Dried fruits may be found at most large supermarkets, and are sold in bulk at natural food stores.

Important Dried Fruits

Apricots
Blueberries
Cherries, sour
Dates
Figs, black mission
Papaya
Raisins
Raisins, golden (Sultanese)

Vegetables   Vegetables in pastry? Somehow, 2 found their way into a dessert: carrots make a tasty sorbet and hot peppers—Thai or jalapeños—when candied, retain an interesting "heat."

A Word About Nuts

Nuts are a focal ingredient in many of my recipes. They enhance presentations by providing contrast in texture and complementing fruit or chocolate with rich, robust flavor. Nuts have been used for centuries in pastry preparations, such as marzipan and nougatine, and they have numerous current applications. Some of the best nuts are available in bulk at natural food stores. Buy raw, shelled, organically grown nuts in small quantities to be sure they are fresh; never use salted or flavored nuts. Store them in the refrigerator in airtight containers, and they will remain fresh for several weeks. Roasting nuts enhances their flavor.

. . . .

To roast nuts, spread them on a baking sheet and place them in a preheated 350°F oven for 8 to 10 minutes, stirring them around occasionally so that they brown evenly.

. . . .

Use a food processor to pulverize or finely chop nuts; use a chef's knife to roughly chop them (¼-inch to ⅛-inch pieces).

Important Nuts

Almonds
Brazil nuts
Cashews
Chestnuts
Hazelnuts
Macadamias
Pecans
Pine nuts
Pistachios
Walnuts
Walnuts, black

A Word About Sweeteners

Sweetness is the deciding factor in the distinction between savory and sweet foods, between entrée and dessert. I try to limit sweetening desserts when possible, and use sweeteners only as necessary to augment or heighten the dessert's true flavors. Examples include poaching tropical fruits or lightly caramelizing a crème brûlée custard. Sweeteners must be used precisely and with restraint to maintain a dessert approach based on balanced, clean, unmasked flavors.

Granulated Sugar When sugar is called for, it means granulated sugar unless otherwise noted. Fine or super-fine sugar is the easiest to use.

Powdered Sugar Powdered sugar (confectioners' sugar or 10x) dissolves quickly and is useful for dusting and caramelizing oven-dried fruits and the tops of some desserts.

Honey The flavors of honey are varied and are usually described by the type of flowers used. Tupelo and orange blossom honeys are fine choices.

Molasses Molasses has a unique, rich flavor. It is sometimes used as a sweetener in pastry doughs or when pumpkin is a main ingredient in a recipe.

Caramel

Caramel is the result when sugar is cooked. Its flavor is rich and especially appropriate for winter desserts. Caramel is used in this book in sauces and ice cream, and for an added flavor in the preparation of certain fruits. Use extreme caution when making caramel, as the temperature necessary to melt sugar is very high.

Barley Malt Powder

Barley malt powder or malt sweetener is naturally derived from an extract of sprouted barley malt. It is available at natural food stores and can be used to flavor custards and ice creams. To combine it with a liquid, make a paste with a small amount of the liquid to dissolve the powder. Heating and stirring the mixture gently in a double boiler will also help to dissolve any lumps.

Glucose

Glucose may be available only on a limited basis, but you can successfully replace it with corn syrup in these recipes. Glucose's interesting feature is its ability to replace part of the sugar in certain ice cream and sorbet recipes. It performs the same functions as the sugar in the freezing process and yet does not taste sweet. This allows for a nicely textured, flavorful sorbet that is not too sweet.

Other Important Ingredients

Salt Salt enhances the flavor of pastry doughs and other preparations made with eggs or butter. A few grains of salt can also bring out the flavors of fruits in some of the fruit soups or sorbets.

Gingerroot The flavor of fresh ginger can be infused into custards and ice creams, and candied ginger perfectly complements the flavors of some fruits and chocolate.

Green Tea Powder Green tea powder is available at Japanese or Asian food stores. Its most familiar use in desserts is as an ice cream

flavor. When combining it with a liquid, first make a paste with a small amount of the liquid. This will dissolve the powder so that you can gradually add the remaining liquid.

Apple Cider The fermented drink made from apples is intensely flavorful. Its most obvious use is in some apple dessert recipes.

Liqueurs and Spirits

Some liqueurs are used in very small amounts as flavor enhancers. Red wine and port are sometimes reduced to intensify their flavors, and champagne, Sauternes, Muscat, or Riesling are valued for their subtle, wonderful flavors when poaching fruit. Some of the spirits used in this book's recipes are brandy, rum, Grand Marnier (orange liqueur), hazelnut liqueur, cognac, kirsch, vodka, and bourbon.

Mint

Freshly picked mint can fill a kitchen with its aroma—its outstanding flavor suggests the bounty of spring and summer. Mint can be infused into custards and ice creams or cut into a chiffonnade and sprinkled around some desserts as a garnish.

. . . .

To make a chiffonnade, stack 2 or more mint leaves on top of one another and with a chef's knife, slice the leaves into pieces that are $1/32$ inch to $1/16$ inch thick.

. . . .

Basil Basil, a wonderful herb that can also be cut into a chiffonnade, can be used to garnish and season some desserts.

Vegetable Oil When oils are called for, peanut or grapeseed are best, because of their tolerance to high heat. Safflower oil will also work. Some recipes call for olive oil as well.

Vanilla

Vanilla as a flavor is used extensively in this book. Vanilla beans have a sweet, aromatic fragrance that enhances many preparations, including pastry cream, ice cream, and sauces. The best vanilla beans, which are from Mexico, are vanilla plant pods that contain tiny black seeds in a sticky pulp. To use vanilla, split and scrape the vanilla bean, cut it in half lengthwise, and scrape out the seeds with a paring knife, add both the seeds and the scraped pod to the cooking liquid. The vanilla flavor will infuse into the liquid. The vanilla pods can be removed from the liquid, rinsed and dried, and then sealed in a container with granulated sugar. The sugar will adopt the vanilla flavor and can be used as desired to replace standard sugar for added vanilla flavor in recipes. The beans could also be used to make vanilla extract by steeping them in vodka, rum, or bourbon.

Rice Rice puddings are hearty, traditional desserts that can be a delicious and satisfying end to a meal. I prefer using soft jasmine rice or Thai rice available in the bulk sections of natural food stores and on some supermarket shelves.

Spices Spices have more flavor when purchased whole and ground as you need them in an electric coffee grinder or with a mortar and pestle. The exceptions are cinnamon and dried ginger, which can be purchased ground.

Important Spices

Allspice
Cardamom (pods)
Cinnamon (sticks and ground)
Cloves
Coriander
Ginger (dried, ground)
Nutmeg
Peppercorns, black and white: infused into some ice creams and custards, the ground pepper adds an interesting twist—heat—to some desserts.
Peppercorns, pink: when roasted and ground, pink peppercorns offer an interesting way to spice berry compotes and strawberry/rhubarb desserts.

Gelatin

I do not use much gelatin in this book, as I feel its role in a dessert's structure should be limited, hidden, or avoided, if possible. Gelatin may be used to stabilize mousses and intensely flavored crème anglaise that is lightened with whipped cream or whipped egg whites. Gelatin needs to be soaked in cold water (or "bloomed") before using. My recipes call for gelatin sheets or powdered gelatin.

Coffee and Espresso Coffee and espresso are strong flavors that have a noble place in many good desserts. Coffee paired with chocolate or hazelnuts is a favorite winter combination. Use whole beans, finely ground, or a high-quality instant coffee.

A Word About Equipment

Working with quality equipment is important to the ultimate success of these desserts. I have listed equipment needs in terms of the minimum requirements for preparation by the home chef/dessert enthusiast. This includes common pastry and kitchen tools and appliances used by professional pastry chefs. Many small appliances, molds, tart rings, straight-side loaf pans, and even small ice cream machines can be found at gourmet kitchen-supply stores. If the exact-size mold or pan is unavailable, there is no need to abandon the recipe altogether. Simply try to adapt it as closely as possible to the sizes you have. I suggest reading through the recipe before you begin to determine if you will need to adapt it in any way.

Ovens

The primary concern when using an oven is maintaining an accurate temperature. An oven that is off by 25° can cause some items to burn or not cook properly. Unless you are very familiar with the quirks and temperature range in your oven, I suggest using an oven thermometer to determine the exact temperature at the beginning of heating and during baking times. The length of baking time and temperatures given for these recipes are for a conventional professional or home roasting oven. If you are using a convection oven, reduce the suggested temperature by 25° to 50°. For best results, always preheat the oven and be mindful of items in the oven by periodically checking them—quickly, so as not to release any heat. Sometimes ovens have hot spots, so a sheetpan will need to be turned around halfway through the baking time.

Range/Cooktop

Gas burners are ideal because heat levels are instantaneous, whereas electric burners require time to heat or cool to different levels. In these recipes, I refer to the range of heat levels in terms of from high to low. With gas burners this means a calculated adjustment of the flame level. You will need to adjust electric burners in advance to achieve the required ideal temperatures.

Electric Mixers

For whipping egg whites and creams, an electric eggbeater works well as long as you continually move the beaters to all parts of the bowl. For doughs, the eggbeater can be used to begin the process, but for better results, you will need to finish combining the ingredients or kneading the dough by hand. The most versatile countertop mixers are made by KitchenAid, and they are basically miniature versions of large professional mixers. With the three main attachments—dough hook, paddle, and whip—a large variety of preparations can be produced, from an elastic phyllo dough to a light meringue.

Ice Cream Machines

Ice creams and sorbets are an integral part of many complete desserts. Small professional electric machines are prevalent in modern restaurant kitchens, but the home chef/pastry enthusiast can use small, hand-cranked, 1- or 2-quart units that contain a prefrozen aluminum cylinder. These work quite well, although the product may not be as light or aerated as those produced by an electric machine.

Juicer Sometimes called an extractor, this is a useful machine for juicing some fruits for soups, sorbets, or sauces.

Propane Torch

A propane torch, available at hardware stores, is a surprisingly versatile tool for pastry making. You can use it to caramelize the top of crème brûlée or to melt a super-thin layer of sugar on some crisp, oven-dried fruit. An oven's broiler or salamander can also perform the same task of delivering intense downward heat, although watchful care and turning of the pan are necessary to avoid burning the product. A propane torch may be used whenever a quick application of heat is needed, but be careful—respect its powerful heat—and be sure to keep the tip of the flame slightly above the food product. If the flame touches the food for any significant period, it can produce a burnt flavor.

Blender A blender is a useful appliance for making fruit *coulis* for sauces and for blending sorbet mixtures. A food processor or food mill will also work well.

Coffee Grinder A small electric coffee grinder is an indispensable tool for grinding spices. You could also use a food processor or a mortar and pestle and sift the mixture after grinding.

Food Processor A food processor is important for some recipes, particularly for pulverizing nuts or nougatine into powder. A larger machine is also good for preparing some pastry doughs.

Pasta Machine A small hand-operated pasta machine is necessary for making raviolis in some recipes.

Saucepots/Saucepans A good thick-bottom pot is best for evenly distributing heat when cooking custards, crème anglaise, or sugar. If you are using a pot with a thin bottom, take greater care watching the cooking

process and stirring the mixture. A saucepan or sauté pan is useful for cooking fruit compotes and for caramelizing apples.

Sheetpans/Baking Pans Professional sheetpans come in a standard size of 12 inches by 16 inches. Comparable sizes available to the home chef would be 10 inches by 14 inches or 12 inches by 15 inches. Loaf pans, with straight or sloping sides, and square pans (9 inches by 9 inches) can be found in gourmet kitchen-supply departments and specialty stores.

Stickless Sheetpan A stickless or nonstick pan is indispensable for baking tuile cookies and for oven-drying fruit.

Bowls Although ceramic or plastic bowls are useful in some cases, a stainless-steel bowl is best for conducting heat, when necessary; for example, when creating a double boiler over a pot of hot water for melting chocolate or whipping a *sabayon*. Stainless-steel bowls in a variety of sizes are a practical part of any well-equipped kitchen.

Muffin Pan A muffin pan may be useful for baking brioche.

Spatulas A metal spatula comes in handy for evenly spreading génoise in a pan or tuile batter to a transparent thickness. Rubber spatulas are useful for transferring ingredients and scraping every drop from a bowl.

Knives The most important knives for a pastry chef are a large chef's knife for roughly chopping nuts or dicing fruit; a long, serrated knife for cutting certain pastry components or sponge cake; and a paring knife for cutting fruit and some pastry items. They *must* be sharp and in good condition.

Ladles   Ladles of 4 ounces and 2 ounces are used in this book to form some decorative elements.

Sieve   A small fine-mesh sieve or sifter is the appropriate tool for removing debris or lumps from dry ingredients. Sifting 2 or more dry ingredients together is also a good way to combine them.

Metal Skewer or Serving Fork   These items are used to make decorative lines on top of some desserts by heating them to red hot and applying them to a layer of powdered sugar.

Colander   A colander is handy for rinsing fruits and draining cooked raviolis.

Chinois   A fine chinois is a very finely meshed china cap. Use it for straining cooked custards to remove any tiny bits of cooked egg and for removing the seeds from berry coulis. A few layers of cheesecloth spread over a colander will also give the same result.

Parchment Paper   Kitchen parchment paper is used to line sheetpans for baking. It can also be cut into convenient sizes and used to hold weighed or measured ingredients. The paper can then be lifted from each side and poured into mixtures.

Pastry Cutters   Round pastry cutters of graduated sizes, both straight edge and fluted edge, are essential tools for a pastry chef's collection. They should range in size from about 4½ inches down to ¾ inch or ½ inch in diameter.

Metal Pastry Horn   A metal pastry horn is used as a form for making cone-shaped pastry items.

Pastry Brush   A small, 1-inch-wide, flat pastry brush is best for brushing melted butter or oil on pans and molds and for dusting excess flour from rolled doughs.

Pastry Wheel   A pastry wheel is a circular blade with a handle. Use it for cutting rolled doughs such as pasta or for cutting tuile that is hot from the oven into strips.

Parisienne Scoop   A parisienne scoop, or melon baller, is useful for pulling the pit out of stone fruits and sometimes for scooping the seed pods from apple or pear halves.

Ice Cream Scoops   The best scoops for preparing the desserts in this book are 1 inch and 1½ inches in diameter.

Pastry Bag and Tips   Pastry bags are helpful for transferring or piping ingredients into certain places, such as filling poached fruit. I often prefer using a small spoon, unless I am making a large number of desserts. For some recipes, a pastry bag fitted with the smallest plain tip or a parchment paper coronet is useful for piping tuile butter. I rarely use a pastry bag to decorate desserts in this book, and when I do use the pastry bag, it is only with plain tips.

Steel Rings   Steel rings of 1½ inches height by 2½ inches in diameter, or similar size, are essential for some desserts.

Tart Rings   Tart rings or flan rings with a rolled rim and vertical sides approximately ½ inch high by 2½ inches in diameter are ideal for some recipes. Fluted or straight-rimmed tart tins with sloping sides of the same size may also be used.

Timbale Molds   Metal timbale molds or thimble-shaped molds approximately 1½ inches and 2¼ inches tall are used in this book.

Rolling Pin   You should use the type of rolling pin with which you feel most comfortable. I prefer a straight, no-handle, single-piece rolling pin, although some have handles or are tapered.

Spoons   A small spoon is helpful for making egg-shaped ice cream or sorbet quenelles that are used to finish some desserts. A smaller version of a spoon called a demitasse can also be used to make quenelles. A slotted spoon is good for retrieving items from hot water or other liquids.

Scale   Use a gram scale to obtain the most accurate measures and for compounding recipe amounts.

Chocolate Thermometer   A thermometer for reading chocolate temperatures should have a range of 80°F to 130°F.

Measuring Cups and Spoons   A transparent, plastic, 1-quart (500 ml) measuring cup and a set of measuring spoons are necessary for proper portioning of ingredients. Graduated-size measuring cups will also work reasonably well.

Whisk   A fine piano-wire whisk is best for most pastry techniques.

Peeler   A quality stationary peeler is sturdier than the swivel type. It also seems to make apple and pear peeling faster and easier.

Corer   An apple corer is essential for some recipes. You should be able to cut cores in diameters of ¾ inch to ⅞ inch.

Grater   A grater is useful for shredding fresh coconut.

CHAPTER TWO

Foundation Recipes

Doughs
Cakes and Batters
Custards and Creams
Chocolate Preparations
Nut Preparations
Sauces and Coulis
Miscellaneous Preparations

This chapter contains all the basic foundation recipes called for throughout the book. These recipes are of enormous value as the basis for thousands of potential desserts. This chapter will prove indispensable over time as a reference tool for fine-tuning or supplementing your current repertoire of basic preparations or, it is hoped, inspiring the continued creation of desserts utilizing the guidelines of *New Classic Desserts*. I have been adopting, modifying, or inventing recipes and methods for many years, refining the very best and concentrating on those used most. This collection represents the best of tried and true classical methods, as well as ideas utilizing current techniques. The yields for these preparations are quite small, usually 6 to 8 servings. In this way, you can avoid storing unused portions, thereby maintaining freshness in your finished products. The yields for the sauces and coulis are enough for the main recipes in which they are used. When quantities of unused preparations remain, they may be stored according to the instructions and used another time for a different dessert— or as the beginning of a new dessert creation.

Doughs

Working with Doughs

Doughs are essentially made of a fat, combined in one of many ways with flour and a liquid to bind the mass together, along with salt or other flavor enhancers such as cocoa or nuts. The various methods for combining these ingredients make a great range of doughs—from the simplest shortdough to an incredible puff pastry. They have numerous and very often different applications. The following are some important points to remember when working with doughs.

Temperature

Temperature is crucial in more places than just the oven. The following items' temperatures also affect the final dough:

- *Room temperature*   Generally mid-sixties Fahrenheit is ideal for working with doughs.

- *Work surface temperature*   It is best to keep your work surface cool. For example, if you have just removed a hot pan from the work surface where you intend to roll a butter mixture into puff pastry, the result could be warm butter oozing out from between dough layers, rather than evenly spreading between them.
- *Butter temperature*   Combined cold with flour, it breaks into small bits, helping to create flakiness. Used at room temperature (65°F to 70°F), it becomes more malleable, allowing it to be combined into a supple dough, such as brioche.

Roll Out

- *Always continuously* dust the work surface, dough, and rolling pin with all-purpose flour to keep the dough from sticking. (I can't stress this hint enough!)

- Dust the dough off later, if necessary, with a dry, clean towel or a dry pastry brush.

If the dough does stick to the work surface, simply slide a metal pastry spatula or long knife underneath it, angled slightly to the work surface.

Picking Up or Moving Dough

You might need to move rolled dough in order to redust the work surface, or to place it on a sheetpan. The following procedure is the best way to do this:

- Hold one edge of the dough against a rolling pin.
- Roll it up around the pin.
- Move as needed.

With this technique, and a little practice, the most delicate and crumbly doughs can be moved as necessary.

Brioche

Yields 1 pound, 4 ounces (570 g)

A rich, supple, yeast-leavened bread that is classically baked in round or braided loaves, or fluted tins. Brioche is widely known as a breakfast bread, served with croissants or other pastries. I have found that its delicate texture and richness make it a good partner for the bright flavors of fruits. One recipe in this book calls for rolling the chilled dough very thin and wrapping it around a stuffed, poached pear. Another makes French toast with round slices of brioche, served with fruits and ice cream.

1 teaspoon (10 g) Honey

2 teaspoons (10 ml) Water

1½ teaspoons (3 g) Yeast, dry-active

1 tablespoon (15 g) Sugar

1 teaspoon (3 g) Salt

1¾ cups (220 g) Flour

3 Eggs

¾ cup (170 g) Butter, room temperature, cut into 1-inch cubes

In a small bowl, stir together the honey, half the water, and the yeast. In a separate bowl, combine the sugar, salt, and remaining water. Set aside.

Place the flour in a mixing bowl equipped with a dough hook, add the yeast mixture, and begin mixing on low speed. Add the eggs and mix until the dough mass begins to form.

Add the sugar and salt mixture and continue to mix for 5 to 8 minutes, or until the dough is smooth. Add the butter and continue mixing until it is completely incorporated.

Scrape the sides of the bowl down with a plastic scraper or spatula and mix for 5 minutes, or until the dough appears smooth and elastic. Wrap the dough in plastic wrap and chill, allowing it to rest for at least 1 hour before use.

Brioche can be refrigerated for 24 hours, or frozen for 1 week.

Puff Pastry

Yields 4, 12-inch by 15-inch by ⅛-inch-thick sheets

Although there are many methods for making puff pastry, this recipe has always been dependable for me. When prepared properly, this puff pastry rises very well in the oven and is incomparably flaky and palatable. Making the dough into a butterfly shape and folding the "wings" over themselves around the butter serve to encase the butter and avoid its squeezing out in the early stages of rolling. To ensure success, before beginning the rolling process, be certain that both the butter mixture and dough are at the same temperature and therefore have similar consistency. If the butter mixture is softer than the dough, you should refrigerate it briefly in order to bring it to the same consistency.

Dough

⅓ cup (70 g) Butter, cut into ½-inch cubes
4 cups (560 g) Flour
2½ teaspoons (10 g) Salt
½ cup + 1 tablespoon (130 ml) Milk
½ cup + 1 tablespoon (130 ml) Water
2 Egg yolks

Combine the flour, butter, and salt in a mixing bowl equipped with a dough hook. Begin mixing on low speed.

In a separate container, mix the milk and water. Whisk the yolks into the milk/water mixture. Add the liquid to the dry mixture and knead for 12 to 15 minutes. Cover it with plastic wrap and set aside, or refrigerate momentarily.

Butter Roll-in

2¼ cups (510 g) Butter
1 cup (140 g) Flour
1 teaspoon (5 ml) Brandy

Combine the butter and flour in a mixing bowl equipped with a paddle, mixing on low speed for 2 minutes. Add the brandy, continue mixing for 30 seconds, then scrape the sides of the bowl down. Mix on medium speed for 1 minute, or until the mixture is smooth and free of any butter lumps.

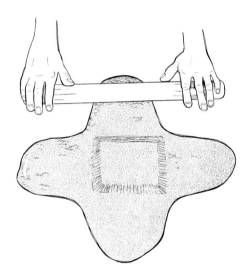

On a floured work surface, roll the dough to 8 inches square by ½ inch in thickness. Roll the corners of the square outward from the center in a butterfly shape to make a 5-inch raised square of dough in its center. Place the butter mixture on the raised square and shape it to the same size. Fold one of the rolled-out corners over the butter square and pat it lightly with a few drops of water. Fold the opposite dough corner over the first corner and press it lightly to make it adhere. Pat it with a few drops of water, and fold a third corner over the center. Repeat the process with the final corner.

Carefully roll the square into a rectangle, a little at a time, so as not to force any of the butter out of the dough. The rectangle should be 14 inches by 7 inches. If butter is oozing

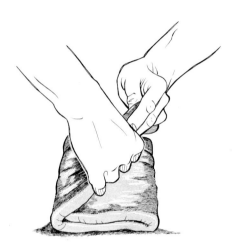

from between the layers, move the dough to a pan, cover it, and refrigerate for 15 minutes before proceeding. Fold 1/3 of the length of the dough over the middle third, then fold the remaining 1/3 over the top of the first third.

Turn the dough 1/4 turn so that you are again facing its longer side. Dust it lightly with flour and roll lengthwise to 18 inches by 9 inches. Dust the excess flour off the dough and repeat the folding procedure. Make 2 small indentations in the dough to represent 2 turns. Wrap in plastic wrap and refrigerate for 1 hour.

Repeat the rolling and turning procedure 2 more times, then make 4 indentations. Wrap the dough and let it rest for 1/2 hour. Repeat the process 2 more times, resting the dough between turns. Rest the dough for at least 2 hours before rolling it into sheets.

Cut the puff pastry in half and roll each half to 12 inches by 30 inches by 1/8 inch thick. Cut the sheets in half, crossways, and stack them, dusting with flour between layers. The puff pastry sheets can be used immediately, refrigerated for 3 days, or frozen for 2 weeks.

Simple Shortdough

Yields 13 ounces (370 g)

This dough works well whenever an unsweetened crust is desirable such as for savory canapes or appetizer tartlets, or for less acidic, sweeter fruits such as bananas, figs, pears, peaches, or blueberries. The smearing and gathering method of mixing the dough produces its flakiness.

½ cup + 1 tablespoon (125 g) Butter, cut
      into ½-inch cubes
1½ cups (200 g) Flour
½ teaspoon (2 g) Salt
Sugar, a dash
¼ cup (60 ml) Ice water

Place the butter in a mixer equipped with a paddle. Sift together the flour, salt, and sugar and add to the butter. Mix on low speed for 1 minute, or until the butter is broken into small bits that are worked into the dry mixture. Add the ice water and pulse so the paddle only goes around twice and the dough still appears unmixed.

Turn the mixture out onto a floured work surface and finish the mixing process by hand, mashing the dough against the work surface with the heel of your hand and alternately gathering it up until the ingredients begin to stick together. Do not overwork, or the finished product will not retain its light, flaky texture.

Wrap in plastic wrap and chill, allowing it to rest for at least 1 hour before use. Shortdough can be refrigerated for 2 days, or frozen for 2 weeks.

Rich Shortdough

Yields 1 pound, 2 ounces (520 g)

This dough is excellent for lining tart pans to make individual or whole fruit tarts. Acidic fruits such as citrus or strawberries pair well with this sweet dough that is reminiscent of a Scotch shortbread cookie.

¾ cup (170 g) Butter, cut into ½-inch cubes
2 cups (275 g) Flour
¼ cup + 1 tablespoon (75 g) Sugar
Salt, a dash
1 Egg
1 Egg yolk

Place the butter in a mixer equipped with a paddle. Sift together the flour, sugar, and salt and add to the butter. Mix on low speed for 2 minutes, or until the butter is broken into small bits that are worked into the dry mixture. Add the egg and egg yolk. Continue mixing just until the dough holds together and the ingredients are thoroughly combined.

Wrap the dough in plastic wrap and chill, allowing it to rest for at least 1 hour before use. Shortdough can be refrigerated for 2 days, or frozen for 2 weeks.

Chocolate Shortdough

Yields 1 pound (450 g)

This recipe, a variation of rich shortdough, can be used to make tarts when a hint of chocolate is appropriate, as for nut fillings or fruits that pair with chocolate, such as oranges or raspberries. This dough also makes excellent chocolate cookies.

½ cup (110 g) Butter, cut into ½-inch cubes
1 cup (140 g) Flour
½ cup (60 g) Cocoa powder
½ cup (100 g) Sugar
Salt, a dash
1 Egg
1 Egg yolk

Place the butter in a mixer equipped with a paddle. Sift together the flour, cocoa powder, sugar, and salt and add to the butter. Follow the instructions above for rich shortdough.

¾ cup (180 ml) Water
2 cups (275 g) Flour, high-gluten
½ teaspoon (2 g) Salt
1 tablespoon (15 ml) Olive oil
Cornstarch, for sprinkling

Pour the water in a mixing bowl equipped with a dough hook. Add the flour and salt and begin mixing on low speed. Knead the dough for 10 minutes, then add the oil and continue kneading for 5 more minutes. Cover with plastic wrap and allow it to rest for ½ hour.

Generously sprinkle cornstarch on a 3-foot by 4-foot working surface. Begin stretching the dough into a circular shape. Hold on to the edge and shake the dough gently to allow gravity and the bouncing motion to stretch it. As it becomes thinner, try to maintain an evenly distributed thickness by stretching the thicker parts of the dough first.

Continue stretching the dough until it is translucent and is about 38 inches by 32 inches. Allow it to dry for about 8 minutes, until it is no longer sticky to the touch.

Use a pastry wheel to cut off the thicker 2-inch edges of the phyllo. Cut the phyllo into 6, 12-inch by 15-inch sheets. Stack the sheets, lightly dusting with cornstarch between layers. Roll up the sheets and wrap them in plastic wrap. Phyllo sheets can be used immediately, refrigerated for 3 days, or frozen for 2 weeks.

Phyllo

Yields 6, 12-inch by 15-inch sheets

Phyllo is widely available in most supermarkets and these products work well for recipes in this book. I find making my own phyllo dough, although challenging when attempted for the first time, to be a rewarding and fascinating process. There is an encouraging sense of accomplishment in successfully stretching the dough into a paper-thin sheet.

Three-Nut Linzer Dough

Yields 2 pounds (900 g)

A linzertorte is a classic European pastry of berry preserves baked in a criss-cross patterned nut dough. I have added some different nuts to the recipe and find it is a very versatile dough for adding a nut influence to various fruit tarts.

2/3 cup (85 g) Almonds, roasted

1 cup (115 g) Powdered sugar

1 Egg white

1 cup (225 g) Butter, cut into 1/2-inch cubes

2 Eggs

1/2 teaspoon (.5 g) Cinnamon

1/2 teaspoon (5 ml) Vanilla extract

1/2 teaspoon (2 g) Salt

1 1/2 cups (200 g) Flour

2/3 cup (85 g) Pistachios, roasted, ground

2/3 cup (85 g) Hazelnuts, roasted, ground

In a food processor, combine the almonds and powdered sugar. Pulverize the mixture, then add the egg white, and process until a smooth paste is formed.

Place the butter in a mixing bowl equipped with a paddle. Add the processed almond mixture and begin mixing on medium speed. Add the eggs and continue mixing for 1 minute. Scrape the sides of the bowl down with a plastic scraper or spatula. Add the cinnamon, vanilla, and salt. Mix for 2 minutes. Add the flour and nuts, mix on low speed for 1 minute, or until the ingredients are thoroughly combined.

The finished dough is very soft and needs to be thoroughly chilled. Wrap in plastic wrap in 2 packages and chill, allowing it to rest for at least 1 hour. Linzer dough can be refrigerated for 2 days, or frozen for 2 weeks.

Vanilla Pasta

Yields 7 ounces (200 g)

I have borrowed pasta from savory cooking, making raviolis to augment a dessert, as in the banana tart with chocolate mousse and walnut raviolis (see p. 229). A single ravioli serves as a dessert on its own in the pumpkin ravioli with candied ginger and roasted caramelized pumpkin broth (see p. 219). The ravioli is a unique vehicle for presenting vibrant dessert flavors.

1 egg

1 teaspoon (5 ml) Vanilla extract

1/2 Vanilla bean, split, scraped

3/4 cup (135 g) Flour, semolina

In a blender, combine the egg, vanilla extract, and the seeds and pulp from the vanilla bean. Blend for 30 seconds.

Pour the egg mixture into a mixing bowl equipped with a dough hook. Add the flour and mix on low speed for 2 minutes, or until the dough comes together. On medium speed, knead the dough for 2 more minutes, until the ingredients are thoroughly combined and the dough is smooth.

Wrap in plastic wrap and chill, allowing it to rest for at least 1/2 hour. The pasta can be refrigerated for 3 days.

Cakes and Batters

Working with Pastry Batters

Most pastry batters' main ingredient is the egg. Within all the different pastry batters, the treatment of the egg(s) in the methods creates the desired structure and characteristics of the finished product. The differences in these finished products can be vast, from the pliable, thin crepe to a crisp, nut-studded meringue. For example, in many batter recipes, the air trapped in whipped whole eggs or in the combination of egg whites and sugar provides the leavening for the cake, or determines the lightness of baked meringue.

Whipping and Folding

Whipping and folding are truly crucial techniques for working with eggs in batters. The following are important points to remember.

- Whip the eggs or egg whites *long enough* so they do not fall and start to turn back into a liquid.
- Fold any whipped eggs or egg whites very gently and *not excessively* so the volume is not reduced.
- Spread finished cake and meringue batters very gently into pans.

Baking

Following the baking temperatures and times for individual cake recipes in this book is important. However, here are some general guidelines on baking temperatures and times:

- For cake batters, 375°F is generally safe.
- For meringues, which are usually baked at low temperatures, 250°F to 275°F for 1 hour is best.

Alternate Baking Method for a Meringue

Use this method for hazelnut meringue (see p. 30).

- Line a sheetpan with parchment or foil.
- Brush with butter, dust with flour.
- Thinly spread hazelnut meringue on the pan.
- Bake at 350°F for approximately 12 minutes (or until lightly, evenly browned).

(See the recipe for poached plum tart on p. 127 for use of this technique.)

Variations of the Classic Pâte à Choux

See the recipes for pistachio popover batter (p. 29) and espresso choux batter (p. 29).

- Bake at 400°F for approximately 15 minutes, then turn the temperature down to 350°F for an additional 5 to 10 minutes to further dry the product.

- Removing pastry puffs too soon from the oven, before they have crisped enough on the outside to stay intact, might cause them to sink. They will not have the hollow centers needed for fillings.

Doneness

Baking times for cakes can vary according to the thickness of the batter in the pan, but there is a good way to tell if a cake is done.

- Delicately touch the cake's surface while it is still in the oven; if the cake is not quite done, it will leave a small impression. If done, it will spring back.

Cooling and Removal from Pan

Allow baked cakes to cool in the pan. To remove a cake from its pan, follow these steps:

- Draw a paring knife around the edge.
- Place another pan (right side up) or cutting board (same size or larger) over the cake.
- Hold the 2 firmly together and turn the pan assembly over. The cake should fall from its pan onto the back of the second pan or the cutting board.

Dobos Sponge Cake

Yields 2, 10-inch by 14-inch cakes

This recipe is named for an Austrian pastry chef who developed the Dobostorte, a classic multilayered pastry. I use the layers to make a unique nut-filled petit four.

½ cup (115 g) Butter, room temperature

1¼ cups (130 g) Powdered sugar

3 Eggs, separated

2 teaspoons (10 ml) Lemon juice

1 teaspoon (5 ml) Vanilla extract

⅔ cup (100 g) Flour

Preheat the oven to 375°F. Prepare 2, 10-inch by 14-inch pans by lining them with parchment, brushing with butter, and dusting with flour.

In a mixing bowl equipped with a whip, place the butter and half of the powdered sugar. Begin mixing on low speed, gradually increasing the speed as the sugar is incorporated into the butter.

Add the egg yolks and whip until thoroughly combined. Scrape the sides of the bowl with a rubber spatula, add the lemon juice and vanilla extract. Whip on high speed for 1 minute, then set aside.

In a separate bowl, sift the remaining powdered sugar. In another bowl, whip the egg whites to soft peaks on high speed. While whipping continuously, add the sifted powdered sugar, a little at a time. Whip to stiff, shiny peaks (approximately 1 minute).

Sift the flour over the egg whites, a little at a time, while gently folding it in with a spatula until it is fully incorporated and smooth. Fold the butter mixture into the egg white mixture until completely smooth and thoroughly combined.

Spread the batter evenly into the 2 prepared pans and bake for 5 to 6 minutes, or until the cake springs back when touched.

Allow the cake to cool. Use immediately or wrap in plastic wrap and store. It can be refrigerated for 2 days, or frozen for 2 weeks.

Chocolate Roulade Sponge Cake

Yields 1, 10-inch by 14-inch cake

This cake, once cooled, remains flexible enough to roll with fruits or fillings and can be drizzled with liqueurs or white wine simple syrup (see p. 54).

2 Egg yolks,   1 Egg
⅓ cup + 2 teaspoons (70 g) Sugar
½ cup (70 g) Flour
¼ cup (30 g) Cocoa powder
3 Egg whites,   1 tablespoon (15 g) Sugar

Preheat the oven to 400°F. Prepare a 10-inch by 14-inch pan by lining it with parchment, brushing with butter, and dusting with flour.

Combine the egg yolks, egg, and sugar in a mixing bowl equipped with a whip. Whip on high speed for 5 minutes. Transfer the mixture to a large bowl.

In a separate bowl, sift together the flour and cocoa powder. Set aside.

In another bowl, whip the egg whites to soft peaks at high speed. Sprinkle 1 tablespoon (15 g) of sugar over them and continue whipping to stiff peaks (approximately 1 minute).

Gently fold ⅓ of the egg whites into the egg yolk mixture. Fold ⅓ of the dry mixture into the egg yolk mixture. Continue folding the rest of the egg whites and the dry mixture into the yolk mixture, alternating each until both are incorporated.

Spread the batter evenly into the prepared pan and bake it for 7 to 8 minutes, or until the cake springs back when touched.

Allow to cool and use it immediately or wrap in plastic wrap and store. It can be refrigerated for 2 days, or frozen for 2 weeks.

Pistachio Sponge Cake

Yields 1, 10-inch by 14-inch cake

This recipe is inspired by the classic French Joconde hazelnut sponge cake. The finished cake has an incomparably light texture. Air that is trapped in the whipped eggs expands in the oven, causing the cake to rise.

½ cup (60 g) Pistachios, lightly roasted
½ cup (60 g) Powdered sugar
3 Eggs
2 tablespoons (15 g) Flour
3 Egg whites
2 tablespoons (30 g) Sugar
2 tablespoons (30 g) Butter, melted

Preheat the oven to 375°F. Prepare a 10-inch by 14-inch pan by lining it with parchment, brushing with butter, and dusting with flour.

In a food processor, combine the pistachios and the powdered sugar and pulverize. Whip the eggs with the sugar and nut mixture at high speed for 8 minutes to double the volume. Sift the flour over the mixture and fold together. Set aside.

In a separate bowl, begin whipping the egg whites on high speed. When they reach soft peaks, sprinkle in the sugar and continue whipping to stiff peaks. Gently fold the whites into the egg and nut mixture until combined. Gentlyfold the butter into the batter.

Evenly spread the batter into the prepared pan. Bake for 12 to 14 minutes, or until the cake springs back when touched.

Allow to cool and use immediately or wrap in plastic wrap and store. It can be refrigerated for 2 days, or frozen for 2 weeks.

Spiced Génoise

Yields 1, 10-inch by 14-inch cake

Génoise is an essential, classic cake recipe that is leavened with air that has been trapped in the whipped eggs expanding in the hot oven. I have found it easier and faster, with equally satisfactory results, to warm the eggs in their own shell rather than warming a whole bowl of eggs over a double boiler.

4 Eggs
½ cup (100 g) Sugar
4 Cloves, whole
1 teaspoon (1 g) Cinnamon, ground
1 teaspoon (3 g) Ginger, ground
½ teaspoon (.5 g) White pepper, ground
½ teaspoon (.5 g) Coriander, ground
4 Cardamom, whole pods
½ cup (70 g) Flour
2 tablespoons (30 g) Butter, melted

Preheat the oven to 375°F. Prepare a 10-inch by 14-inch pan by lining it with parchment, brushing with butter, and dusting with flour.

Place the eggs, shells intact, into a small bowl. Warm by running very warm tapwater over them for about 2 minutes.

Crack the warmed eggs into a mixing bowl equipped with a whip. Add the sugar and whip at high speed for 7 to 9 minutes.

While they are mixing, pulverize the spices in a coffee grinder or by using a mortar and pestle, until they are completely ground. Sift together the spices and the flour. Stir, using a wire whisk, until combined.

When the egg and sugar mixture has tripled in volume, is light in color, and has soft peaks, remove the mixing bowl from the machine and sift ⅓ of the flour and spice mixture over the egg and sugar mixture. Carefully fold together. Sprinkle another ⅓ of the dry mixture over the batter and continue folding. Carefully incorporate the remaining dry mixture.

Fold the butter gently into the mixture.

Evenly spread the batter into the prepared pan. Bake for 16 to 18 minutes, or until the cake springs back when touched.

Allow the génoise to cool and use it immediately or wrap in plastic wrap and store. It can be refrigerated for 2 days, or frozen for 2 weeks.

Chocolate Génoise

Yields 1, 10-inch by 14-inch cake

5 Eggs
¾ cup (150 g) Sugar
⅓ cup (40 g) Cocoa powder
⅓ cup (40 g) Flour
1 tablespoon (15 g) Butter, melted
1 tablespoon (15 ml) Brandy

Preheat the oven to 375°F. Prepare a 10-inch by 14-inch pan by lining it with parchment, brushing with butter, and dusting with flour.

Place the eggs, shells intact, into a small bowl. Warm by running very warm tapwater over them for about 2 minutes.

Crack the eggs into a mixing bowl equipped with a whip. Add the sugar and whip at high speed for 7 to 9 minutes.

While they are whipping, sift together the cocoa powder and flour, stirring with a whisk until combined thoroughly.

When the egg and sugar mixture has tripled in volume, is light in color, and has soft peaks, stop the mixer and sift ⅓ of the dry mixture over them. Turn the mixer speed to low and mix for 5 seconds to gently incorporate. Sift another ⅓ of the dry mixture over the batter, pulsing for 5 seconds. Sift the remaining dry mixture over the batter and mix for 10 seconds.

Remove the bowl from the machine. With a rubber spatula, gently fold the mixture until smooth.

In a bowl, mix together the melted butter and brandy. Fold ⅓ of the batter into it. Gently fold back into the main mixture.

Evenly spread the entire batter into the prepared pan. Bake for 16 to 18 minutes, or until the cake springs back when touched.

Allow to cool and use immediately or wrap in plastic wrap and store. It can be refrigerated for 2 days, or frozen for 2 weeks.

Hazelnut Génoise

Yields 1, 10-inch by 14-inch cake

4 Eggs
¾ cup (150 g) Sugar
½ cup (70 g) Flour
½ cup (60 g) Hazelnuts, roasted
1 tablespoon (15 g) Butter, melted
1 tablespoon (15 ml) Hazelnut liqueur

Preheat the oven to 375°F. Prepare a 10-inch by 14-inch pan by lining it with parchment, brushing with butter, and dusting with flour.

Place the eggs, shells intact, into a small bowl. Warm by running very warm tapwater over them for about 2 minutes. Crack the eggs into a mixing bowl equipped with a whip. Add the sugar and whip at high speed for 7 to 9 minutes.

While they are whipping, pulverize the flour and hazelnuts in a food processor.

When the egg and sugar mixture has tripled in volume, is light in color, and has soft peaks, remove the mixing bowl from the machine. Sprinkle ⅓ of the flour and nut mixture over the eggs and sugar mixture. With a rubber spatula, gently fold together.

Sprinkle another ⅓ dry mixture over the batter and continue folding. Incorporate the remaining dry mixture.

In a bowl, mix the butter and hazelnut liqueur. Fold ⅓ of the batter into it. Gently fold this batter back into the main mixture.

Evenly spread the finished batter into the prepared pan. Bake for 16 to 18 minutes, or until the cake springs back when touched.

Allow to cool and use immediately or wrap in plastic wrap and store. It can be refrigerated for 2 days, or frozen for 2 weeks.

Black Walnut Génoise

Yields 1, 10-inch by 14-inch cake

4 Eggs
¾ cup (150 g) Sugar
½ cup (70 g) Flour
½ cup (60 g) Walnuts, black
1 tablespoon (15 g) Butter, melted
1 tablespoon (15 ml) Brandy

Follow the method for hazelnut génoise with these ingredients. Black walnuts will replace the hazelnuts and brandy the hazelnut liqueur.

Frangipane

Yields 1 pound (450 g)

Frangipane is a classic baked filling that is essentially pastry cream enriched with almonds and eggs. In small amounts, it is delicious when baked with fruits such as figs, pears, peaches, and blueberries.

¼ cup (60 g) Butter
¼ cup (60 g) Sugar
½ recipe Vanilla Pastry Cream—see p. 34
1 Egg white
½ cup (60 g) Almonds, roasted, finely ground
3 tablespoons (30 g) Flour
2 teaspoons (10 ml) Brandy

In a mixing bowl, cream the butter with the sugar. Add the pastry cream and the egg white; mix until smooth.

In a separate bowl, stir together the almonds and flour.

Add to the first mixture, mixing until thoroughly combined. Add the brandy and mix until incorporated.

Frangipane can be used immediately, or refrigerated in a sealed container for 3 days.

. . . .
The remaining vanilla pastry cream can be used in other recipes, or mixed with fresh fruit for a simple, satisfying dessert.
. . . .

Crêpes

Yields 6 to 8 crêpes

Crêpes are a light, thin classical preparation wonderful for encasing vibrant fruits and warm fruit compotes.

¼ cup (60 ml) Water
¼ cup (60 ml) Milk
½ cup (70 g) Flour
Salt, a dash
1 Egg
2 teaspoons (8 g) Butter, melted

In a bowl, combine the water and milk. Whisk in the flour and salt until smooth. Whisk in the egg and butter. At this point, the crêpe batter can be stored in a sealed container, and refrigerated for 3 days. Simply stir it thoroughly before use.

Lightly brush a crêpe skillet or a stickless sauté pan with oil and place it over medium heat for 30 seconds.

Ladle approximately 1 ounce of batter into the center of the hot pan. Quickly turn the pan from side to side to cover the bottom with a thin layer of batter. Cook the crêpe until the surface begins to dry. Turn it over and cook briefly on the other side. Continue making crêpes until all the batter is used.

Pistachio Popover Batter

Yields 1 pound (450 g)

A smaller version of the classic popover is achieved by baking them in a small muffin pan. The resulting hollow center makes a good space to fill with fruits, mousses, ice cream, or sorbets.

¼ cup (60 g) Butter
¾ cup + 2 tablespoons (200 ml) Water
¼ teaspoon (1 g) Salt
⅓ cup (40 g) Pistachios
⅓ cup (40 g) Flour
2 Eggs

Place the butter, water, and salt in a saucepot over high heat.

In a food processor, pulverize the pistachios with the flour.

When the water boils, whisk the nut and flour mixture into it. Lower heat to medium and continue whisking for 1 minute.

Transfer the mixture to a bowl and whisk in the eggs, one at a time. Proceed with the instructions in Chapter Six for baking.

If needed, the batter can be refrigerated in a sealed container for 24 hours.

Espresso Choux Batter

Yields 12 ounces (345 g)

This recipe is drawn from the classic pâte à choux recipe. I have simply replaced the usual water with espresso to give the resulting puffs extra flavor.

¼ cup (60 g) Butter
½ cup (120 ml) Espresso or very strong coffee
Salt, a dash
¼ cup + 2 tablespoons (50 g) Flour
2 Eggs

Place the butter, espresso, and salt in a saucepot over high heat. When the liquid boils, whisk in the flour.

Lower heat to medium and continue whisking for 1 minute.

Transfer the mixture to a bowl and whisk in the eggs, one at a time. See espresso profiteroles in Chapter Six (p. 246) for baking instructions.

If needed, the batter can be refrigerated in a sealed container for 24 hours.

Rainforest Meringue

Yields 1, 10-inch by 6-inch piece

Roasted, tropical nuts make this meringue a good base for a torte of mango, chocolate, and coconut.

2 Egg whites

1/2 teaspoon (2.5 ml) Lemon juice

1/3 cup (60 g) Sugar

1/2 cup (60 g) Powdered sugar

2 teaspoons (5 g) Flour

1/3 cup (40 g) Macadamias, lightly roasted, roughly chopped

1/3 cup (40 g) Cashews, lightly roasted, roughly chopped

1/3 cup (40 g) Brazil nuts, lightly roasted, roughly chopped

Preheat the oven to 275°F.

Prepare a 10-inch by 14-inch sheetpan by lining it with parchment, brushing with butter, and dusting with flour.

Whip the egg whites and lemon juice to soft peaks. Continue whipping to stiff peaks while sprinkling in the sugar (about 3 minutes).

In a separate bowl, sift together the powdered sugar and flour. Mix in each of the nuts. Gently fold 1/3 of the nut mixture into the egg whites, then fold in the remaining nut mixture until combined.

Spread the meringue on the prepared pan to an area of 10 inches by 6 inches. Bake for 1 hour.

Allow it to cool. Use immediately or wrap in plastic wrap and store. It can be stored in a cool, dry place for 2 days.

Hazelnut Meringue

Yields 7 ounces (200 g)

As prepared in the poached plum tart with ginger custard, plum sorbet, and warm plum compote, this hazelnut meringue is meant to be baked in a thin layer, and then cut into shapes when still hot out of the oven. Before they cool, or with a little reheating, the cut shapes can be bent into rings or spirals, or fashioned into cuplike shapes to contain fruits, ice creams, sorbets, or chocolate mousse.

2 Egg whites

2 tablespoons (30 g) Sugar

1/4 cup (35 g) Powdered sugar

2 teaspoons (5 g) Flour

1/2 cup (60 g) Hazelnuts, roasted, finely ground

Whip the egg whites to soft peaks. Continue whipping to stiff peaks while sprinkling in the sugar (about 1 minute).

In a separate bowl, stir together the powdered sugar, flour, and hazelnuts. Gently fold 1/3 of the nut mixture into the egg whites, then fold in the remaining nut mixture until combined.

Proceed with the baking instructions in Chapter Four for poached plum tart (see p. 127).

Tuile Batter

Yields 10 ounces (280 g)

Tuile batter is classically used to make round, thin cookies that are studded with almonds and rolled or bent into half-circle shapes hot from the oven (see spiced tuiles, p. 253). I like to use tuile cookie as a structural and decorative element in many desserts.

½ cup + 2 tablespoons (125 g) Sugar
½ cup + 2 tablespoons (90 g) Flour
2 Egg whites, room temperature
2 tablespoons (30 g) Butter, melted
Salt, a dash

In a mixing bowl equipped with a whisk, combine the sugar and the flour on low speed. Add the egg whites and mix thoroughly. Add the melted butter and salt. Whisk for 1 minute.

This recipe is used as a component of several desserts in Chapters Four and Five. Please proceed with the baking instructions located in these recipes. The tuile batter may be sealed in a container and refrigerated for 1 week.

Honey Wafer Batter

Yields 6 ounces (170 g)

Honey wafers are delicious delicate cookies, perfect for layering with fruits, as in the napoleon of vanilla mascarpone and peaches with white pepper ice cream (see p. 112). They can be formed into shapes while hot from the oven, and also make a good petit four.

2 tablespoons (30 g) Butter
¼ cup (35 g) Powdered sugar
3 tablespoons (60 g) Honey
⅓ cup (40 g) Flour
Cinnamon, a dash
Salt, a dash

Cream the butter with the sugar and honey. Add the flour, cinnamon, and salt; mix until smooth.

Proceed with instructions for baking in Chapter Four. You can also seal the batter in a container and store. It can be refrigerated for 3 days.

Praline Batter

Yields 12 ounces (340 g)

Praline is essentially cooked sugar and nuts. This recipe makes a praline cookie with a crunchy texture that can be formed into shapes while still hot.

½ cup (70 g) Flour

Ginger, ground, a dash

Salt, a dash

¼ cup (60 g) Butter

½ cup (80 g) Brown sugar

¼ cup (90 g) Glucose or corn syrup

½ cup (60 g) Pecans, finely ground

Stir together the flour, ginger, and salt. Set it aside.

Cream the butter, sugar, and glucose until thoroughly combined. Add the nuts and flour mixture. Mix until smooth.

Proceed with the baking instructions in Chapter Four for honeydew melon and pistachio torte with honeydew sorbet and pralines. Seal the batter in a container. It can be refrigerated for 3 days.

Custards and Creams

About Custards and Creams

Of all the items that go into a successful dessert, custards or creams can be pivotal in the way they are prepared. I find satisfaction and a sense of accomplishment every time I make a batch of pastry cream or crème anglaise, and I particularly enjoy making new flavors of ice cream.

Pastry creams may be somewhat easier to make because they are difficult to overcook. This is due to the addition of flour as a thickening agent, which tends to keep the egg yolks from curdling or overcooking. The following are some helpful hints for preparing these items.

Pastry Creams

- Stir them constantly over medium heat to thicken them.
- Allow them to boil for 10 to 15 seconds, constantly stirring.

Crème Anglaise and Ice Cream Bases

- Like pastry creams, these should also be stirred constantly.
- *Do not allow these to boil.*

- In the final moments of cooking, some steam will rise from the surface. At this point, check to see if the cooking process is finished. You can do this by checking the preparation's ability to coat a rubber spatula.
    —Dip the rubber spatula in the anglaise.
    —Pull the spatula out and hold it horizontally over the pot.
    —Slide a finger across the spatula. If the anglaise is done, it will not drip down from that line or will do so very slowly. If it is not done, it will drip down immediately.

Custards

A true custard is made of eggs, milk or cream, and some seasonings or sweeteners. In my crème brûlée custard recipes, I have fused two custard ideas into one in order to obtain the best qualities of each.

Straining and Cooling

- *Straining* Anglaise, pastry creams, and other cooked custards should always be passed through a fine-mesh *chinois* or 2 layers of cheesecloth to strain out any bits of cooked egg or foreign substances.
- *Cooling* When making larger batches especially, it is very important to accelerate the cooling process of the finished product. Do this by standing the container of the warm mixture in a larger container filled with ice or ice water. Refrigerate the mixture immediately for several minutes. *This will eliminate the growth of bacteria.*

Crème Brûlée Custard

I found my classic crème brûlée to be rich and smooth, but too delicate to move around or to stack with fruit and crispy phyllo layers to make a multilayered napoleon. My solution was a melding of two ideas:

- A basic custard mixture based on the ratio of 3 eggs to 1 cup (230 ml) milk or cream.
- Combined in equal parts to the basic crème brûlée before baking.

The basic custard mixture, when baked on its own, is somewhat "eggy" and has an undesirable texture; it is more substantial than needed for a crème brûlée. Fusing the two resulted in a rich and smooth crème brûlée custard just strong enough, when well chilled, to cut into shapes and stack as needed. Make sure that the custard is well chilled before cutting.

Removing Crème Brûlée Custard from the Pan

- Before removing the cooked, almost frozen crème brûlée from the pan, check to see that the custard is very firm but not solid.
- Using a paring knife, cut around the edge of the crème brûlée against the pan sides.
- Invert the pan over a cutting board and apply some heat to the bottom, using either a blow torch in sweeping motions or towel soaked in hot water. The crème brûlée should fall out of the pan onto the cutting board. If it does not, gently pry it from one or more sides with a spatula.
- Peel the plastic off the custard.

Crème Anglaise

Yields 2 cups (460 ml)

This is a central, important recipe for pastry-making. Crème anglaise can be a versatile dessert sauce, served with soufflés or fruits such as berries or as a base for bavarian and other classic pastry inventions. If desired, flavor can be infused into the recipe, added when the milk and cream are placed over heat. A split, scraped vanilla bean, fresh mint, grated ginger, or grated coconut added to the mixture are a few possible variations.

4 Egg yolks
2 tablespoons + 1 teaspoon (35 g) Sugar
1½ cups (360 ml) Milk
¼ cup (60 ml) Heavy cream

In a bowl, whisk together the yolks and sugar until they have a smooth consistency and the color of the yolks has lightened.

In a saucepan, combine the milk and cream over medium heat and bring to a boil. Pour the boiling mixture into the yolks, whisking continuously.

Return the mixture to the saucepan. Cook over medium heat, stirring constantly, until it thickens just enough to coat a spatula. Do not allow to boil.

Pass through a fine chinois or 2 layers of cheesecloth.

Cover loosely and place in refrigerator until needed. Crème anglaise can be refrigerated in a sealed container for 3 days.

Vanilla Pastry Cream

Yields 1¼ cups (280 ml)

This is an essential classic pastry foundation recipe. Infused with particular flavors in the same way as for crème anglaise, pastry creams can add the perfect richness and balance as an element in fruit-flavor-driven desserts.

1 cup (240 ml) Milk
½ Vanilla bean, scraped or ½ teaspoon
      (2.5 ml) Vanilla extract
2 Egg yolks
¼ cup (50 g) Sugar
2 tablespoons (15 g) Flour

In a medium-size saucepan, combine the milk and vanilla bean and bring to a boil over medium heat.

In a bowl, whisk together the yolks and sugar until smooth. Whisk the flour into the yolk and sugar mixture until completely smooth. Pour the boiling milk mixture into the yolks while whisking continuously.

Return the mixture to the saucepan. Cook over medium heat, stirring constantly, as it thickens and begins to boil. Allow it to boil, stirring for 10 seconds.

Pass through a fine chinois or 2 layers of cheesecloth.

Cover loosely and chill quickly by placing the container in an ice-water bath or in the freezer for 15 minutes. It can be used immediately, or refrigerated in a sealed container for 3 days.

Coconut Pastry Cream

Yields 1¼ cups (280 ml)

1 cup (240 ml) Milk
3½ ounces (100 g) Coconut, fresh, finely
    grated
2 Egg yolks
¼ cup (60 g) Sugar
2 tablespoons (15 g) Flour

Follow the method above for vanilla pastry cream, replacing the vanilla bean with 3 ounces (85 g) of coconut.

Roast the remaining coconut in a 350°F oven for 8 to 10 minutes, or until evenly browned.

After straining out the raw grated coconut, fold the roasted coconut into the finished pastry cream.

It can be used immediately, or refrigerated in a sealed container for 3 days.

Ginger Pastry Cream

Yields 1¼ cups (280 ml)

1 cup (240 ml) Milk
2 Egg yolks
¼ cup (60 g) Sugar
2 tablespoons (15 g) Flour
1½ ounces (45 g) Gingerroot, fresh, peeled,
    finely chopped

Follow the method for vanilla pastry cream, except add gingerroot to the milk after adding the yolk–sugar mixture. After straining the cream, whisk 1 teaspoon (4 g) of the strained, chopped ginger back into the pastry cream.

Hazelnut Praline Cream

Yields 1½ cups (340 ml)

Hazelnut Praline
¼ cup (60 g) Sugar
½ cup (60 g) Hazelnuts, lightly roasted

Place the sugar in a saucepan over high heat. When it begins to melt and caramelize, stir with a spoon. When light amber in color and completely melted, immediately remove the sugar from the heat and stir in the hazelnuts.

Pour the mixture out onto a lightly oiled sheetpan and allow to cool.

In a food processor, pulverize the praline until it is very fine and set aside.

Cream
1 cup (240 ml) Milk
2 Egg yolks
2 tablespoons (30 g) Sugar
2 tablespoons (15 g) Flour

Follow the method for vanilla pastry cream without the vanilla bean.

After chilling the cream, fold in the pulverized praline until thoroughly combined. The cream may be used immediately, or refrigerated in a sealed container for 2 days.

Vanilla Custard

Yields 2 cups (460 ml)

This is truly not *a custard since it contains no eggs, but it resembles a traditional custard in texture. It is a modified version of Chef Nancy Silverton's recipe. The bright vanilla flavor pairs well with fruits and berries, as in the napoleon of vanilla custard citrus and raspberries (see p. 115).*

2 sheets or 2 teaspoons powdered (7 g) Gelatin
1¼ cups (290 ml) Heavy cream
½ cup (120 ml) Milk
1 Vanilla bean, split, scraped
2 tablespoons (30 g) Sugar

Bloom the powdered gelatin in 1 teaspoon of cold water or soften the sheets for 10 minutes in enough cold water to cover them.

In a saucepot over high heat, combine the cream, milk, vanilla bean, and sugar. Bring to a boil.

Remove the pot from the heat and whisk in the gelatin.

Pass through a fine chinois or 2 layers of cheesecloth into a container.

Cover loosely and place in refrigerator to use when it is somewhat cooled but has not set.

This recipe is a component of the napoleon recipe in Chapter Four, p. 115. Proceed with these instructions for setting the custard. To store in advance, it can be refrigerated for 2 days. Simply heat it gently to return to a liquid state.

Lemon Custard

Yields 4 cups (920 ml)

Citrus custards are the perfect fillings for tarts served with summertime fruits, as in the lemon tart with blackberries and peppered blackberry coulis (see p. 107).

6 Lemons
6 Eggs
¾ cup (180 ml) Crème fraîche or sour cream
¾ cup (150 g) Sugar

Wash the lemons well. Zest 2 lemons and chop the zest very fine. Juice all the lemons and combine the zest with the juice.

Whisk the eggs into the juice and set aside.

Whisk the crème fraîche with the sugar. Whisk the lemon juice and egg mixture into the crème fraîche, half at a time, until thoroughly combined.

Pour into a thick-bottom saucepan. Cook over medium heat, stirring constantly, until it thickens just enough to coat a spatula. Do not allow to boil.

Cover loosely and place in refrigerator until needed. Proceed with the baking instructions for a lemon tart in Chapter Four, p. 107. It may also be refrigerated in a sealed container for 2 days.

Orange Custard

Yields 1¼ cups (280 ml)

2 Oranges
2 Eggs
¼ cup (60 ml) Crème fraîche or sour cream
2 tablespoons (30 g) Sugar

Follow the above method for lemon custard. This is a foundation recipe for the orange tartlet in Chapter Four, p. 118. Proceed with these baking instructions. This custard can also be refrigerated in a sealed container for 2 days.

Vanilla Crème Brûlée Custard

Yields 2¼ cups (530 ml)

Crème brûlée or burnt cream is a beloved restaurant dessert. Classically, it is baked in a ceramic dish, chilled, and sprinkled with sugar that is caramelized before serving. Each of these four variations is infused with a strong flavor. They have been developed to be baked in a pan, sliced into shapes, and stacked with poached, candied, or ripe fresh fruits and crispy pastry components to make spectacular crème brûlée–fruit combination desserts.

2 Egg yolks
2 tablespoons (30 g) Sugar
1¼ cups (300 ml) Heavy cream
1 Vanilla bean, split, scraped

In a bowl, whisk together the yolks and sugar until they are smooth and the color of the yolks lightens.

In a medium-size saucepan, combine the cream and vanilla bean and bring to a boil over medium heat. Pour the boiling cream into the yolks, whisking continuously. Set aside.

2 Eggs
3 tablespoons (45 g) Sugar
⅓ cup (80 ml) Heavy cream
⅓ cup (80 ml) Milk

Whisk the whole eggs with the sugar for 30 seconds. Add the heavy cream and milk; whisk until combined.

Whisk the vanilla bean mixture into this mixture and pass through a fine chinois or cheesecloth. Proceed with the baking instructions in Chapter Four. It can also be refrigerated in a sealed container for 24 hours.

Chocolate Crème Brûlée Custard

Yields 2¼ cups (530 ml)

2 ounces (60 g) Chocolate, bittersweet, melted
2 teaspoons (2 g) Cocoa powder

Follow the method and ingredients for vanilla crème brûlée custard without the vanilla bean. After whisking the boiling cream into the yolk-sugar mixture, whisk in the chocolate and cocoa powder. Then proceed with the second part of the recipe.

Espresso Crème Brûlée Custard

Yields 2½ cups (580 ml)

2 Egg yolks
2 tablespoons (30 g) Sugar
1⅓ cups (320 ml) Heavy cream
¼ cup (20 g) Espresso, finely ground

In a bowl, whisk together the yolks and sugar until they are smooth and the color of the yolks lightens.

In a medium-size saucepan, combine the cream and espresso and bring to a boil over medium heat. Pour the boiling cream into the yolks, whisking continuously. Set aside.

2 Eggs
3 tablespoons (45 g) Sugar
⅔ cup (160 ml) Heavy cream

Whisk the eggs with the sugar for 30 seconds. Add the heavy cream and whisk until combined.

Whisk the espresso cream into this mixture and pass through a fine chinois or cheesecloth. Proceed with the baking instructions. It can also be refrigerated in a sealed container for 24 hours.

Peppered Crème Brûlée Custard

Yields 2½ cups (520 ml)

1 teaspoon (5 g) White pepper, finely ground

Follow the method and ingredients for espresso crème brûlée custard, except substitute the espresso with white pepper.

Malt Bombe Filling

Yields 2½ cups (575 ml)

When frozen, this light mixture has a unique texture and complements and lightens the richness of ice cream in wonderful ice cream bombe–fruit compote desserts.

2 Egg yolks
2 tablespoons (30 g) Sugar
¼ cup (35 g) Barley malt powder
1 teaspoon (5 ml) Brandy
1 Egg white
½ cup (120 ml) Heavy cream

In a mixing bowl equipped with a whip, whip the egg yolks with half the sugar on high speed until they are light in color and slightly increased in volume.

Sprinkle the malt powder over the egg and sugar mixture. Whip on low speed for 30 seconds. Add the brandy and increase speed to high until the malt powder is thoroughly combined. Set aside. (At this point, if any lumps of malt remain, stir the mixture with a rubber spatula in a bowl placed over some very warm water until they dissolve.)

In a separate bowl, whip the egg white to soft peaks. Sprinkle the remaining sugar over the egg white. Continue whipping to stiff peaks.

In another bowl, whip the heavy cream to stiff peaks. Alternately fold the egg whites and whipped cream into the egg and malt mixture until smooth. Proceed immediately with the instructions for freezing (see hazelnut malt bombe, p. 98).

Espresso Bavarian

Yields 2 cups (460 ml)

Bavarian cream is a classic recipe of crème anglaise lightened with whipped cream and firmed up with a little gelatin. It is good in small amounts in fruit-driven desserts or petit fours.

2 Egg yolks
3 tablespoons (45 g) Sugar
1 cup (240 ml) Milk
3 tablespoons (15 g) Espresso, finely ground
1 sheet or 1 teaspoon powdered (3.5 g) Gelatin
1/2 cup (120 ml) Heavy cream

In a bowl, whisk together the yolks and sugar until they are smooth and the color of yolks lightens.

Combine the milk and espresso in a medium-size saucepan and bring to a boil over medium heat. Pour the boiling milk mixture into the yolks, whisking continuously.

Return to the saucepan and cook over medium heat, stirring constantly, until the mix-ture thickens just enough to coat a spatula. Do not allow to boil.

Pass through a fine chinois or 2 layers of cheesecloth.

Soften the gelatin sheets for 10 minutes in enough cold water to cover them or bloom the powdered gelatin in 2 teaspoons of cold water. Whisk the gelatin into the warm espresso mixture until it is entirely dissolved.

Cover loosely and chill by placing the container in an ice-water bath or in the freezer until it begins to thicken and is cool to the touch.

Whip the heavy cream to soft peaks.

Whisk the espresso mixture, scraping the sides of the container to make sure the mixture is completely smooth. (If it is not smooth, it may be too cool. You will need to reheat it slightly, while stirring, over a saucepot of very warm water.)

When you have obtained a smooth consistency and the mixture is cool to the touch, fold in the whipped cream until the mixture is smooth and thoroughly combined.

Refrigerate it in a sealed container for at least 1/2 hour before using. It can be stored, refrigerated, for 2 days.

Champagne Semifreddo

Yields 1½ cups (350 ml)

This semifreddo (literally, semifrozen) is somewhat like a mousse that hardens only to a certain point in the freezer. It can be flavored with fruit purees or liqueurs and served with fruits or warmed fruit compotes.

1½ cups (360 ml) Champagne
½ sheet or ½ teaspoon powdered (1.75 g)
　　Gelatin
3 Egg yolks
3 tablespoons (45 g) Sugar
½ cup (120 ml) Heavy cream

In a saucepot over high heat, reduce the champagne to ¼ cup (60 ml). Set aside.

Soften the sheet of gelatin for 10 minutes in enough cold water to cover it or bloom the powdered gelatin in 2 teaspoons of cold water.

Create a double boiler by setting a stainless-steel bowl on top of a saucepot half-filled with water over medium heat. When the water begins to simmer, whisk the yolks and the sugar in the bowl of the double boiler. Continue whisking rapidly for 6 minutes, or until the yolks' volume has doubled and their color has lightened.

Whisk the gelatin into the warm champagne. Whisk the champagne into the whipped yolks and place in the refrigerator to cool.

Whip the heavy cream to stiff peaks.

When the champagne mixture is cool to the touch, fold in the whipped cream until smooth and thoroughly combined.

Place the mixture in a sealed container and freeze for at least 2 hours before serving. It may also be stored, covered, frozen, for 2 days.

Chocolate Preparations

Tempered Chocolate

8 ounces (230 g) Chocolate, bittersweet

When chocolate is melted and then rehardens, the cocoa separates from the cocoa butter to some degree, creating a dull or dusty surface. This is a natural occurrence but undesirable when crafting chocolates or other decorative chocolate items. The process of tempering stabilizes the chocolate and keeps it from separating. After tempering, the chocolate will harden to a smooth, shiny surface.

Cut the chocolate into ½-inch pieces, place in a bowl, and melt over a saucepot of hot water over medium heat. Stir from time to time until the chocolate is completely melted. Heat the chocolate to a temperature of 125°F.

Turn the heat off, pour half the chocolate into a separate bowl, and set over the hot water.

Place the first bowl of chocolate over a larger bowl filled with ice water. Stir until the chocolate is cool to the touch (about 82°F) but still in a liquid state.

Stir a small amount of the warm chocolate into the cooled chocolate to bring the temperature up to 87°F. Return the bowl of warm chocolate to the top of the saucepot containing the hot water. The cooled chocolate is now tempered and ready to use for dipping or molding.

As you work with tempered chocolate, it will begin to cool and thicken. Simply stir more of the warm chocolate into the tempered chocolate to maintain it.

Use the tempered chocolate immediately as needed. Any unused chocolate may be stored in a covered container for future use.

Tempered Milk Chocolate

The same method can be used to temper milk chocolate, using lower temperatures. Heat the chocolate to 118°F instead of 125°F. Lower the temperature to 80°F instead of 82°F, and raise the temperature a few degrees to 85°F.

Chocolate Ganache

Yields 10 ounces (280 g)

This is a rich chocolate cream that has numerous uses for delicious chocolate desserts and as a filling for chocolates. It is usually prepared with chocolate, cream, and sometimes butter. I use water instead of either cream or butter. I have found that this produces an equally desirable consistency and pure chocolate flavor without adding unnecessary fat or calories.

8 ounces (230 g) Chocolate, bittersweet, melted
¼ cup (60 ml) Water

In a saucepot, bring the water to a boil. Whisk it into the melted chocolate until thoroughly combined.

Ganache may be used immediately. It can also be refrigerated in a sealed container for 1 week.

Chocolate-Ginger Ganache

Yields 1 pound, 4 ounces (570 g)

With a recipe of chopped candied ginger (see p. 55) folded in, this flavored ganache makes a good filling for ginger chocolates (see p. 247).

4 ounces (115 g) Gingerroot
¼ cup + 2 tablespoons (90 ml) Water
12 ounces (350 g) Chocolate, bittersweet, melted

Peel the gingerroot. Cut into ½-inch pieces. Chop very fine in a food processor. In a saucepot over medium heat, combine the gingerroot with the water.

After the water comes to a boil, pass ginger and water mixture through a fine chinois or 2 layers of cheesecloth.

Whisk the hot water into the chocolate until smooth.

Ganache may be used immediately. It can also be refrigerated in a sealed container for 1 week.

White Chocolate Ganache

Yields 12 ounces (340 g)

In this ganache recipe, I use the slightly sour taste of crème fraîche to counter the sweetness of the white chocolate.

8 ounces (230 g) Chocolate, white, melted
½ cup + 2 tablespoons (145 ml) Crème
    fraîche or sour cream

In a saucepot over medium heat, heat the crème fraîche to a simmer. Whisk into the white chocolate until thoroughly combined.

    Ganache may be used immediately. It can also be refrigerated in a sealed container for 1 week.

Chocolate Mousse

Yields 14 ounces (400 g)

This is a very chocolate-rich chocolate mousse that relies more on egg whites than whipped cream for its volume. It can be served on its own or, as I prefer to use it, as a contributing element in a more elaborate chocolate dessert.

5 ¼ ounces (150 g) Chocolate, bittersweet,
    melted, very warm
1 Egg yolk
1 tablespoon (15 ml) Brandy
1 tablespoon (15 g) Butter, melted
2 Egg whites
1 tablespoon (15 g) Sugar
½ cup (120 ml) Heavy cream

Whisk the egg yolk, brandy, and melted butter into the chocolate.

    Whip the egg whites on high speed. When they reach soft peaks, sprinkle in the sugar. Continue whipping to stiff peaks. Gently fold the whites into the chocolate mixture.

    In a separate bowl, whip the heavy cream to soft peaks. Fold into the chocolate mixture until thoroughly combined.

    Mousse may be used immediately. It can also be refrigerated in a sealed container for 3 days.

White Chocolate Mousse

Yields 13 ounces (370 g)

White chocolate requires more delicate treatment than bittersweet chocolate, as it has a lower tolerance to heat and is more prone to separate. The mousse is excellent served in small amounts with fruits that are compatible to chocolate or as part of a more elaborate chocolate dessert.

½ sheet or ½ teaspoon powdered (1.75 g)
   Gelatin
2 tablespoons (30 ml) Water
1 teaspoon (5 ml) Brandy—optional
6 ounces (165 g) Chocolate, white, melted
1 Egg yolk
1 Egg white
½ cup (120 ml) Heavy cream

Soften the sheet of gelatin for 10 minutes in enough cold water to cover it or bloom the powdered gelatin for 10 minutes in 1 tablespoon (15 ml) of cold water.

In a saucepot, combine the water and brandy. Heat to a boil. Remove from the heat and dissolve the gelatin completely in the hot water.

Whisk the mixture into the white chocolate. Whisk in the egg yolk. Stir over an ice bath until the mixture is cool to touch.

In a separate bowl, whip the egg white to stiff peaks.

In another bowl, whip the heavy cream to soft peaks. Gently fold them alternately into the chocolate mixture until smooth.

Mousse may be used immediately. It can also be refrigerated in a sealed container for 3 days.

Chocolate Marquise

Yields 1 pound, 14 ounces (850 g)

This is a rich, deeply flavored chocolate mousse. Its name refers to its shape, as it is traditionally served in a molded round shape accompanied by crème anglaise. This recipe is excellent served in that way or as an element in a more elaborate chocolate dessert.

4 Egg yolks
½ cup (60 g) Powdered sugar
¼ cup (25 g) Cocoa powder
½ cup (110 g) Butter
8 ounces (230 g) Chocolate, bittersweet,
   melted, warm
1 Egg white
½ cup (120 ml) Heavy cream
½ cup (60 g) Hazelnuts, lightly roasted,
   roughly chopped
¼ cup (60 g) Cherries, dried
¼ cup (60 g) Apricots, dried

Whip the egg yolks with the powdered sugar until the color of the yolks lightens and the mixture doubles in volume. Set aside.

Cream the cocoa powder with the butter, scraping down the sides of the bowl as necessary, until combined. Whisk the chocolate into the butter mixture until thoroughly combined.

Whip the egg white to stiff peaks, set aside.

In a separate bowl, whip the heavy cream to soft peaks. Set aside.

Fold the egg yolks and sugar mixture into the chocolate mixture until completely incorporated. Alternately fold the egg white and whipped cream into the chocolate mixture. Stir in the nuts and dried fruits.

Transfer the mixture to a plastic-wrap-lined rectangular terrine mold or small loaf pan.

Refrigerate sealed in plastic, for at least 1 hour before use. It can also be refrigerated for 4 days.

Praline Chocolate

Yields 10 ounces (280 g)

This recipe of caramel, roasted hazelnuts, and chocolate has a unique crunchy texture. The mixture can be cooled, rolled, and cut into shapes to be served as part of a more complex dessert, as in the chocolate universe (see p. 187), or as a petit four, like the praline moons (see p. 252).

¼ cup (60 g) Sugar

½ cup (60 g) Hazelnuts, whole

5¼ ounces (150 g) Chocolate, bittersweet, melted

Place the sugar in a saucepan over high heat. When it begins to melt and caramelize, stir with a spoon. When the sugar is light amber and completely melted, remove it immediately from the heat. Stir in the hazelnuts.

Pour the mixture out onto a lightly oiled sheetpan. Allow to cool.

In a food processor, pulverize the mixture until very fine. Whisk into the chocolate.

Praline chocolate may be used immediately. It can also be refrigerated in a sealed container for 1 week. Simply melt it over hot water in a double boiler before using.

Nut Preparations

Nut Paste

Yields 10 ounces (280 g)

Rich, flavorful fillings can be made from all varieties of nuts. I use this recipe in desserts and petit fours for intense roasted-nut flavor.

1 cup (120 g) Nuts (hazelnuts, walnuts, or black walnuts), lightly roasted

1 Egg white

¼ cup (35 g) Powdered sugar

½ recipe or ½ cup (120 ml) Vanilla Pastry Cream—see p. 34

1 tablespoon (15 g) Butter, melted

In a food processor, pulverize the nuts. Add the egg white and process for 30 seconds. Add the powdered sugar. Continue to process until smooth. Add the pastry cream and the melted butter. Process until thoroughly combined.

Chill the nut paste and use immediately. It can also be refrigerated in a sealed container for 3 to 4 days.

Nut Brittle

Yields 4 ounces (110 g)

This recipe is more nut than brittle. It is a thin coating of caramelized sugar over lightly roasted nuts. It can be sprinkled over desserts to add to or augment pure nut flavor.

2 tablespoons (30 ml) Water
¼ cup (60 g) Sugar
½ cup (60 g) Nuts—either hazelnuts, pistachios, almonds, macadamias, brazil nuts, or black walnuts

Preheat the oven to 350°F.

Line a sheetpan with parchment paper. Brush the surface with a light coating of vegetable oil.

In a saucepan over medium heat, combine the sugar and water for 1 minute, or until the sugar is dissolved.

Stir the nuts into the sugar syrup. Pour the mixture onto the oiled parchment, spreading out the nuts somewhat. Place the pan in the oven for 8 to 10 minutes, or until the nuts turn light brown.

Store in a sealed container at room temperature. Brittle is best when used within a few days.

Pine Nut Nougat

Yields 7 ounces (200 g)

This is classically an extremely sweet, dense candy traditionally studded with almonds and candied fruit and sold by European pastry shops and confectioners. I have borrowed the idea and altered the recipe to make a filling for baking inside fruits, as in the roasted nectarine and bing cherries with pine nut nougat and bing cherry sorbet (see p. 139).

3 tablespoons (45 g) Sugar
¾ cup (100 g) Pine nuts, lightly roasted
1 tablespoon (20 g) Honey
2 Egg whites

Place the sugar in a saucepan over high heat. When it begins to melt and caramelize, stir with a spoon. When the sugar is light amber and completely melted, immediately remove it from the heat and stir in the pine nuts.

Pour the mixture out onto a lightly oiled sheetpan. Allow to cool.

In a food processor, pulverize the pine nut and caramel mixture until very fine. Set aside.

Whip the egg whites to soft peaks. Continue to whip, drizzling the honey into the egg whites. Whip for 1 minute to stiff peaks. Fold the pine nut mixture into the egg whites until combined.

Use immediately.

Candied Chestnuts

15 candied chestnuts

The flavor of home-candied chestnuts does not compare with that of canned ones. These candied chestnuts and puree can be used to make excellent winter petit fours and desserts.

15 (200 g to 250 g) Chestnuts
2½ cups (600 ml) Water
¼ cup + 2 tablespoons (80 g) Sugar
1½ cups (360 ml) Water

With a paring knife, cut an "X" through the shell of each chestnut. In a saucepot over medium heat, combine the chestnuts with the first amount of water. Boil for 20 minutes. Drain off the water and allow the chestnuts to cool.

Peel off the shells. Peel all the brown paperlike coating from the chestnut meat, being sure to remove it from all the crevices.

Return the peeled chestnuts to the saucepot, adding the sugar and second amount of water. Simmer over low to medium heat for 30 minutes.

The remaining syrup will be reduced and concentrated. It should be reserved with the chestnuts. They can be refrigerated in a sealed container for 2 weeks.

Chestnut Puree

Yields 1 cup (240 ml)

1 recipe Candied Chestnuts (and syrup)—see above
1 tablespoon (15 ml) Water

In a food processor, puree the chestnuts with the syrup and the water until smooth.

Chestnut puree may be used immediately. It can also be refrigerated in a sealed container for 2 weeks.

Roasted Coconut Shavings

30 to 35 shavings

These freshly roasted shavings are excellent for topping tropical desserts and ice creams or sorbets.

1 ounce (30 g) Coconut, fresh, peeled

Preheat the oven to 350°F. Using a very sharp peeler or paring knife, slice coconut pieces as thin as possible. Scatter the shavings on a sheetpan. Place in the oven for 7 to 8 minutes, or until the coconut is lightly and evenly browned.

These shavings are best used within several hours.

Sauces and Coulis

Simple sauces and coulis can take a dessert to new heights of excellence by completing its presentation, providing a way to add vibrant flavor, and boosting the appeal of the central flavor focus. Some of the following sauces are variations of crème anglaise with infusions of various flavors. Sabayon is a classic dessert sauce or accompaniment for berries and other fruits. The chocolate and caramel sauces are lightened by using water rather than cream and butter. Some of the coulis' flavors are complemented with vanilla or pepper, whereas others express the simple bright flavors of fruits and berries.

Vanilla Sauce

Yields 1¼ cup (300 ml)

2 Egg yolks
2 tablespoons (30 g) Sugar
1 cup (240 ml) Milk
½ Vanilla bean, split, scraped

In a bowl, whisk the yolks and sugar until they are smooth and the color of the yolks lightens.

In a saucepan, combine the milk and vanilla bean. Bring to a boil over medium heat. Pour the boiling milk mixture into the yolks, whisking continuously.

Return to the saucepan and cook over medium heat, stirring constantly, until it thickens just enough to coat a spatula. Do not allow to boil.

Pass through a fine chinois or 2 layers of cheesecloth.

Cover loosely and place in refrigerator until needed. Vanilla sauce can be refrigerated for 3 days.

Sabayon

Yields 1½ cup (360 ml)

1 Egg
1 Egg white
¼ cup (60 g) Sugar
1 tablespoon (15 ml) Brandy or cognac

Create a double boiler by setting a stainless-steel bowl on top of a saucepot half-filled with water over medium heat. When the water begins to simmer, whisk the egg, egg white, and sugar in the bowl. Continue whisking rapidly for 9 minutes.

During whisking, pull the bowl off the heat from time to time to be sure the sabayon is not cooking too rapidly. Continue to whip, allowing no part of the sabayon to be still. Add the brandy or cognac and continue whipping for 2 minutes.

The finished sabayon should be tripled in volume. Remove from the heat. You should use it immediately, but it can also be stored in the refrigerator for use within 1 hour.

Bittersweet Chocolate Sauce

Yields ¾ cup (180 ml)

½ cup + 2 tablespoons (145 ml) Water
4 ounces (115 g) Chocolate, bittersweet,
    melted

In a small saucepot, heat the water to a boil. Add it to the chocolate, whisking until the sauce is smooth.

The sauce may be used immediately. It can also be refrigerated in a sealed container for 1 week. If the sauce is chilled, it will need to be melted before being used.

Caramel Sauce

Yields ½ cup (120 ml)

¼ cup (60 g) Sugar
¼ cup + 1 tablespoon (75 ml) Water

Pour the sugar evenly into a saucepan and turn the heat to high. When the sugar begins to melt, stir it gently with a spoon. Turn the heat down to medium. Watch closely as the sugar melts and darkens. When it turns dark amber and lightly smokes, carefully add the water. Stir over the heat until the caramel is dissolved.

Remove the pan from the heat. Adjust the sweetness with additional sugar, to taste.

The sauce can be used immediately. It can also be refrigerated in a sealed container for 1 week.

Caramelized Orange Sauce

Yields ½ cup (120 ml)

2 tablespoons (30 g) Sugar
½ cup (120 ml) Orange juice
White pepper, a dash

Pour the sugar evenly into a saucepan over high heat. When it begins to melt and caramelize, stir gently with a spoon. Continue stirring as it turns light amber color and then continues to darken. When it turns dark amber and lightly smokes, carefully whisk in the orange juice. Add the pepper. Continue to stir until the caramel is completely dissolved.

Remove from the heat. Adjust the sweetness with additional sugar, to taste.

The sauce can be used immediately, or refrigerated in a sealed container for 1 week.

Malt Sauce

Yields ½ cup + 1 tablespoon (135 ml)

1 Egg yolk
1 tablespoon (15 g) Sugar
½ cup (120 ml) Milk
1 tablespoon (10 g) Barley malt powder

In a bowl, whisk the yolk and sugar until they are smooth and the color of the yolk lightens.

Pour the milk into a medium-size saucepan over medium heat and bring to a boil over medium heat.

Pour the boiling milk into the yolk mixture, whisking continuously. Sift the malt powder over the mixture. Whisk briskly into the liquid.

Return the mixture to the saucepan and cook over medium heat, stirring constantly, until it thickens just enough to coat a spatula. Do not allow to boil.

Pass through a fine chinois or 2 layers of cheesecloth.

Cover loosely and chill quickly by placing the container in an ice-water bath or in the freezer for 15 minutes. The sauce may be used immediately. It can also be refrigerated in a sealed container for 3 days.

Raisin Sauce

Yields 1 cup (240 ml)

½ cup (70 g) Raisins
¾ cup (180 ml) Water

In a saucepan over medium heat, combine the raisins and water. Simmer for 5 minutes, then transfer to a blender. Puree for 1 minute.

Pass the sauce through a fine chinois or 2 layers of cheesecloth.

The sauce can be used immediately, or refrigerated in a sealed container for 2 days.

Golden Raisin Sauce

Replace the raisins in the above recipe with golden raisins.

Green Tea Sauce

Yields ½ cup + 1 tablespoon (135 ml)

1 Egg yolk
1 tablespoon (15 g) Sugar
2 teaspoons (7 g) Green tea powder
½ cup (120 ml) Milk

In a bowl, whisk the yolk and sugar until they are smooth and the color of the yolk lightens. Set aside.

Place the green tea powder into a medium-size saucepan and pour in 1 tablespoon of milk. Whisk together. As a paste is formed, gradually add more milk until the paste loosens enough to add all the milk without making any green tea lumps. Place the saucepan over medium heat and bring to a boil.

Pour the boiling milk into the yolk mixture, whisking continuously.

Return the mixture to the saucepan and cook over medium heat, stirring constantly, until it thickens just enough to coat a spatula. Do not allow to boil.

Pass through a fine chinois or 2 layers of cheesecloth.

Cover loosely and chill the mixture quickly by placing the container in an ice-water bath or in the freezer for 15 minutes. The sauce may be used immediately, or refrigerated in a sealed container for 3 days.

Almond Sauce

Replace the brazil nuts in the following recipe with almonds.

Brazil Nut Sauce

Yields 1 cup (240 ml)

2 tablespoons (30 g) Sugar
¼ cup (30 g) Brazil nuts, chopped, roasted

Place the sugar in a saucepan over high heat. When it begins to melt and caramelize, stir with a spoon. When the sugar is light amber and completely melted, immediately remove it from the heat and stir in the brazil nuts.

Pour the mixture out onto a lightly oiled sheetpan and allow to cool.

In a food processor, pulverize the mixture until it is very fine.

1 Egg yolk
1 tablespoon (15 g) Sugar
½ cup (120 ml) Milk

In a bowl, whisk the yolk and sugar until they are smooth and the color of the yolk lightens. Pour the milk into a medium-size saucepan and bring to a boil. Pour the boiling milk into the yolk mixture, whisking continuously.

Return the mixture to the saucepan and cook over medium heat, stirring constantly, until it thickens just enough to coat a spatula. Do not allow to boil.

Pass through a fine chinois or 2 layers of cheesecloth. Stir in the brazil nut mixture.

Cover loosely and chill quickly by placing the container in an ice-water bath or in the freezer for 15 minutes. The sauce may be used immediately, or refrigerated in a sealed container for 3 days.

Hazelnut Sauce

Yields ½ cup (120 ml)

2 tablespoons (30 g) Sugar
¼ cup (30 g) Hazelnuts, chopped, roasted
⅓ cup (80 ml) Water

Place the sugar in a saucepan over high heat. When it begins to melt and caramelize, stir with a spoon. When the sugar is light amber and completely melted, immediately remove it from the heat. Stir in the hazelnuts.

Pour the mixture out onto a lightly oiled sheetpan and allow to cool.

In a food processor, pulverize the mixture until very fine. Add the water and continue to process until smooth.

The sauce may be used immediately, or refrigerated in a sealed container for 24 hours.

Orange Sauce

Yields ½ cup + 1 tablespoon (135 ml)

1¼ cups (300 ml) Juice of approx. 3 oranges
1 tablespoon (15 g) Sugar

In a saucepan over high heat, combine the juice and sugar. Cook for approximately 10 minutes to reduce the volume by half.

It can be used immediately, or refrigerated in a sealed container for 24 hours.

Blood Orange Sauce

Replace the orange juice in the above recipe with juice from blood oranges.

Mango-Vanilla Sauce

Yields ¾ cup (180 ml)

3 ounces (90 g) Mango flesh
¼ Vanilla bean, split, scraped
¼ cup (60 ml) Water
1 tablespoon (15 g) Sugar

Place all ingredients in a blender and puree.

Pass the mixture through a fine chinois or 2 layers of cheesecloth.

It can be used immediately, or refrigerated in a sealed container for 24 hours.

Apricot Coulis

Yields 1 cup (240 ml)

2 (120 g) Apricots, stones removed
½ cup (120 ml) Water
1 tablespoon (15 ml) Sauternes wine
2 tablespoons (30 g) Sugar

Follow the method for mango-vanilla sauce.

Bing Cherry Coulis

Yields ¾ cup (180 ml)

3 ounces (90 g) Cherries, Bing, approximately
   10 to 12, pitted
2 teaspoons (10 ml) Lemon juice
¼ cup (60 ml) Water
1 tablespoon (15 g) Sugar

Follow the method for mango-vanilla sauce.

Honeydew Melon Coulis

Yields ¾ cup (180 ml)

4 ounces (115 g) Honeydew melon,
    approximately 6, 1-inch by 1-inch cubes
2 tablespoons (30 ml) Water
1 tablespoon (15 g) Sugar

Follow the method for mango-vanilla sauce.

Peach Coulis

Yields 1 cup (240 ml)

3.5 ounces (100 g) Peach, approximately 1,
    pitted
2 teaspoons (10 ml) Lemon juice
½ cup (120 ml) Water
1 tablespoon (15 g) Sugar

Follow the method for mango-vanilla sauce.

Pear Coulis

Yields 1 cup (240 ml)

5.5 ounces (150 g) Pear, approximately 1,
    cored, chopped in 1-inch squares
¼ cup (60 ml) Water
1 tablespoon (15 g) Sugar

Follow the method for mango-vanilla sauce.

Peppered Blackberry Coulis

Yields ½ cup + 1 tablespoon (135 ml)

3 ounces (90 g) Blackberries, approximately
    8 to 10 medium-size
¼ cup + 2 tablespoons (90 ml) Water
1 tablespoon (15 g) Sugar
¼ teaspoon (.25 g) Black pepper, ground

Follow the method for mango-vanilla sauce except in regard to the pepper. Whisk this in after straining the other ingredients.

Raspberry Coulis

Yields ¾ cup (180 ml)

3 ounces (90 g) Raspberries, approximately
    18 to 20
¼ cup + 2 tablespoons (90 ml) Water
1 tablespoon (15 g) Sugar

Follow the method for mango-vanilla sauce.

Strawberry Coulis

Yields ¾ cup (180 ml)

3 ounces (90 g) Strawberries, approximately
    6 to 7 medium-size, washed and hulled
¼ cup + 2 tablespoons (90 ml) Water
2 teaspoons (10 g) Sugar

Follow the method for mango-vanilla sauce.

Miscellaneous Preparations

White Wine Simple Syrup

Yields ⅔ cup (160 ml)

Simple syrup is usually made with water and sugar. This version can be used for the same purposes: to sprinkle over génoise and sponge cakes to avoid dryness and add flavor, and for poaching fruits.

½ cup (120 ml) Wine, Chardonnay or
     Sauvignon Blanc
¼ cup (60 g) Sugar

In a saucepot over medium heat, combine the wine and sugar. Simmer for 2 minutes or until the sugar dissolves.

It can be used immediately, or refrigerated in a sealed container for 3 weeks.

Candied Lemon or Orange Zest

Yields ½ ounce (15 g)

When candied, the zest or peel of lemons or oranges adds flavor and an extra decorative touch to many desserts.

½ ounce (15 g) Zest from 1 lemon or orange
¼ cup (60 g) Sugar
¼ cup + 2 tablespoons (90 ml) Water

The zest can be cut from the fruit with a peeler, then sliced into ¹/₁₆-inch-wide strips. In a small saucepot over medium heat, combine all ingredients. Simmer for 7 to 8 minutes, or until the zest appears translucent and no longer tastes bitter.

The zest can be stored in the cooked syrup in a sealed container, refrigerated, for 2 weeks.

. . . .

The zest of citrus fruit is the top, colored part of the rind. It should be removed from its white pulp. To zest a lemon or orange, you can use an ordinary peeler or zester. A zester will give you a finer, thinner peel.

. . . .

Candied Ginger

Yields ½ ounce (15 g)

Candied fresh ginger has a sweet-heat flavor that can be used as an accent to compatible dessert flavors such as pumpkin, apple, plum, or chocolate.

½ ounce (15 g) Gingerroot
1½ cups (360 ml) Water
¼ cup (60 g) Sugar

Peel the gingerroot. Cut it in half lengthwise, then into 1/16-inch-thick slices, and then into 1/16-inch strips. Combine the strips and 1 cup (240 ml) of the water.

Boil for 8 minutes, then drain the water off. Return the strips to the pot with the sugar and the remaining ½ cup (120 ml) of water. Simmer over medium heat for 8 to 10 minutes, or until the strips appear translucent and their flavor is not overpowering.

The candied ginger can be stored in the cooked syrup in a sealed container, refrigerated, for 1 week.

Egg Wash

1 Egg
2 tablespoons (30 ml) Water

In a small bowl, whisk together the egg and water. Use immediately for brushing pastry tops before they are baked.

Egg wash gives a shiny finish to pastry. It is also necessary for assembling raviolis.

Crème Fraîche

Yields 1 cup + 2 tablespoons (270 ml)

1 cup (240 ml) Cream
2 tablespoons (30 ml) Buttermilk

In a saucepot, combine the cream and buttermilk. Bring to a simmer over medium heat. Allow the mixture to sit at room temperature (68°F) for 8 hours.

You can store the crème fraîche covered and refrigerated for 1 week.

CHAPTER THREE

Ice Creams and Sorbets

The first frozen desserts consisted of honey and various fruits mixed with snow, which was often transported to the kitchens of the wealthy ruling classes from nearby mountains. The Chinese invented a method of making sorbet. Their idea was brought to Italy and later spread to France. By the early eighteenth century, a rough version of sorbet sold by vendors in the streets of Paris was gaining in popularity. The quality and increasingly inventive flavors of sorbets continued to evolve through the end of the century, and by 1775, cream and eggs were added to some of the ices to produce the first forms of ice cream. European nobility enjoyed ice creams and sorbets served in the form of *coupes glacées*, parfaits, and elaborately molded bombes following meals and during celebrations.

Today, ice creams and sorbets remain a favorite dessert and an anticipated ending to any meal. They are an essential component in many new classic desserts. Ice cream or sorbet can augment or reinforce the taste of the main flavor of each dessert, also provide instant contrast in temperature and texture. Their rich and intense flavors require a sparing hand when using. A few small scoops or a single egg-shaped *quenelle* is all that is needed for a satisfying finish.

Ice cream or sorbet quenelles are attractive and easy to prepare. You only need a spoon and warm water.

- Make sure the ice cream is somewhat soft.
- Dip the spoon in warm water.
- Place the spoon on the ice cream.
- Draw the spoon toward you at a 45° angle.
- The ice cream should form an egg shape on the spoon.

Some of these recipes have been designed to complement specific desserts; others offer more traditional flavors that can be used with a variety of recipes. I often draw upon traditional regional and ethnic flavor combinations in pairing an ice cream or sorbet with a fruit. For instance, cardamom ice cream served with a date dessert reflects Middle Eastern influences; coconut ice cream with a macadamia tart recalls tropical flavors of the South Seas. Ice creams and sorbets can also be used in more familiar flavor combinations, such as pears with red wine ice cream, or chocolate sorbet with oranges. Many times, I underscore the main flavor of a particular dessert with its own ice cream or sorbet. A good example is warm McIntosh soup with McIntosh sorbet (see p. 207). Using these kinds of guidelines for serving ice creams and sorbets with a dessert will ensure a compatible, refined presentation.

A Word About Storing Ice Creams and Sorbets

After spinning, ice cream should be placed in a covered container and used within several hours. To avoid the icy consistency that may develop after 8 to 12 hours in the freezer, you should melt it down and rechurn it back to a smooth, non-icy consistency.

You can melt down ice cream or sorbet by stirring occasionally over low heat.

Follow the same storage instructions for sorbet, with one exception. Sorbet should generally be respun in *6 to 8 hours,* rather than 8 to 12.

Ice Creams

1¼ to 2 cups (300 to 480 ml)

If more ice cream is needed, simply multiply the ingredient amounts by 4 or 6 as necessary. For even richer ice cream, use equal parts of milk and cream to replace the total volume of milk and cream called for.

Black Sesame Brittle Ice Cream

2 tablespoons (30 g) Sugar
1 tablespoon (7 g) Black sesame seeds

In a small saucepan over medium heat, warm the sugar until it melts and begins to lightly caramelize. Stir in the sesame seeds and pour the caramel onto an oil-coated sheetpan. Set aside to cool.

2 Egg yolks
1 tablespoon (15 g) Sugar
1 cup (240 ml) Milk

In a bowl, whisk together the yolks and sugar until they are smooth and the color of the yolks lightens.

Pour the milk into a medium-size saucepan and bring to a boil over medium heat.

Pour the boiling milk mixture into the yolks, whisking continuously.

Return the mixture to the saucepan and cook over medium heat, stirring constantly, until it thickens just enough to coat a spatula. *Do not allow the mixture to boil.*

Pass through a fine chinois or 2 layers of cheesecloth.

Cover the mixture loosely and quickly chill by placing the container in an ice-water bath or the freezer for 15 minutes.

In a food processor, completely pulverize the sesame brittle. Churn the custard in an ice cream machine according to the manufacturer's instructions. Fold the pulverized brittle into the ice cream. Store for up to 12 hours.

Burnt-Honey Ice Cream

¼ cup (80 g) Honey
2 Egg yolks
2 tablespoons (30 ml) Cream
1 cup (240 ml) Milk
White pepper, a grind

Whisk together half the honey and the egg yolks until they are smooth. Set aside.

In a saucepan over high heat, cook the remaining honey. Watch carefully as the honey bubbles and begins to brown. When it begins to lightly smoke, remove from the heat, add the cream, and stir until the caramelized honey is dissolved.

Add the milk and white pepper, return to medium heat, and bring it to a boil.

Slowly pour the boiling milk and cream into the egg yolks, whisking continuously.

Return the mixture to the saucepan and cook over medium heat, stirring constantly, until it has thickened just enough to lightly coat a spatula or spoon. *Do not allow the custard to boil.*

Pass through a fine chinois or 2 layers of cheesecloth into a container.

Cover loosely and quickly chill by placing the container in an ice-water bath or the freezer for 15 minutes.

Churn in an ice cream machine according to the manufacturer's instructions. Store for up to 12 hours.

Caramel Ice Cream

2 Egg yolks
1 tablespoon (15 g) Sugar

In a bowl, whisk together the yolks and sugar until smooth. Set aside.

2 tablespoons (30 g) Sugar
¼ cup (60 ml) Cream
1 cup (240 ml) Milk

In a small saucepan over medium heat, warm the remaining sugar until it melts and begins to lightly brown. When it is very dark brown and lightly smoking, pour in the cream and stir until the caramel is dissolved. Add the milk and bring to a boil over medium heat.

Pour the boiling milk mixture into the yolks, whisking continuously.

Return the mixture to the saucepan and cook over medium heat, stirring constantly, until it thickens just enough to coat a spatula. *Do not allow the mixture to boil.*

Pass through a fine chinois or 2 layers of cheesecloth.

Cover loosely and quickly chill by placing the container in an ice-water bath or the freezer for 15 minutes.

Churn in an ice cream machine according to the manufacturer's instructions. Store for up to 12 hours.

Cardamom Ice Cream

2 Egg yolks
1 tablespoon + 1 teaspoon (20 g) Sugar
1 cup (240 ml) Milk
1 tablespoon (15 ml) Cream
1 teaspoon (1 g) Cardamom, ground
Black pepper, a grind

In a bowl, whisk together the yolks and sugar until smooth and the color of the yolks lightens.

In a medium-size saucepan, combine the milk, cream, cardamom, and pepper. Bring to a boil over medium heat.

Pour the boiling milk mixture into the yolks, whisking continuously.

Return the mixture to the saucepan and cook over medium heat, stirring constantly, until it thickens just enough to coat a spatula. *Do not allow the mixture to boil.*

Pass through a fine chinois or 2 layers of cheesecloth.

Cover loosely and quickly chill by placing the container in an ice-water bath or the freezer for 15 minutes.

Churn in an ice cream machine according to the manufacturer's instructions. Store for up to 12 hours.

Chèvre Ice Cream

2 Egg yolks
2 tablespoons (30 g) Sugar
1 cup (240 ml) Milk
3 ounces (85 g) Chèvre
Salt, a dash

In a bowl, whisk together the yolks and sugar until they are smooth and the color of the yolks lightens.

Pour the milk into a medium-size saucepan and bring to a boil over medium heat.

Pour the boiling milk into the yolks, whisking continuously.

Return the mixture to the saucepan and whisk in the chèvre until incorporated. Cook over medium heat, stirring constantly, until it thickens just enough to coat a spatula. *Do not allow the mixture to boil.*

Pass through a fine chinois or 2 layers of cheesecloth.

Cover loosely and quickly chill by placing the container in an ice-water bath or the freezer for 15 minutes.

Churn in an ice cream machine according to the manufacturer's instructions. Store for up to 12 hours.

Coconut Ice Cream

1 cup (180 g) Coconut, fresh, grated or
    chopped
2 Egg yolks
2 tablespoons (30 g) Sugar
1 cup (240 ml) Milk
3 tablespoons (45 ml) Heavy cream

. . . .

*To prepare fresh coconut, poke 3 spots in the top of 2
coconuts with a screwdriver or very sturdy, small
knife. Strain the coconut milk from the coconut
through a fine chinois or layer of cheesecloth. Reserve
it if you are making the coconut and macadamia
tart recipe (see p. 192). Crack the coconut on a very
hard surface, such as a brick floor, and pry the flesh
off the shell. Using a peeler, peel the brown skin off
the white coconut flesh. Grate the coconut flesh or
chop it in a food processor.*

. . . .

Place the coconut flesh in a sauté pan over
medium heat for 5 minutes, stirring occasionally to help release its natural milk and oil.

Whisk the yolks with the sugar. Set aside.

Add the milk and heavy cream to the coconut. Bring to a boil over medium heat.

Pour the boiling milk mixture into the
yolks, whisking continuously.

Return the mixture to the saucepan and
cook over medium heat, stirring constantly,
until it thickens just enough to coat a spatula.
Do not allow the mixture to boil.

Remove it from the heat and stir to
slightly cool. Pour into a blender, put the top
on, place a towel over the blender, and secure
it with your hand. Blend at a high speed for
30 seconds.

Pass through a fine chinois or 2 layers of
cheesecloth. Be sure to squeeze as much liquid
from the coconut pulp as possible.

Cover loosely and quickly chill by placing
the container in an ice-water bath or the freezer
for 15 minutes.

Churn in an ice cream machine according
to the manufacturer's instructions. Store for up
to 12 hours.

. . . .

*When blending a hot liquid, be very careful, as the
released steam can cause the top to come off.*

. . . .

Crème Fraîche–Black Pepper Ice Cream

2 Egg yolks
2 tablespoons (30 g) Sugar
1 cup (240 ml) Milk
4 ounces (115 g) Crème fraîche
1 teaspoon (1 g) Black pepper, ground

In a bowl, whisk together the yolks and sugar until smooth and the color of the yolks lightens.

Pour the milk into a medium-size saucepan and bring to a boil over medium heat.

Pour the boiling milk into the yolks, whisking continuously.

Return the mixture to the saucepan and whisk in the crème fraîche. Cook over medium heat, stirring constantly, until it thickens just enough to coat a spatula. *Do not allow the mixture to boil.*

Pass through a fine chinois or 2 layers of cheesecloth.

Whisk in the black pepper and cover loosely. Quickly chill by placing the container in an ice-water bath or the freezer for 15 minutes.

Churn in an ice cream machine according to the manufacturer's instructions. Store for up to 12 hours.

Espresso Ice Cream

2 Egg yolks
3 tablespoons (45 g) Sugar
1 cup (240 ml) Milk
2 tablespoons (30 ml) Cream
3 tablespoons (15 g) Espresso, ground

In a bowl, whisk together the yolks and sugar until smooth and the color of the yolks lightens.

In a medium-size saucepan, combine the milk, cream, and espresso and bring to a boil over medium heat.

Pour the boiling milk mixture into the yolks, whisking continuously.

Return the mixture to the saucepan and cook over medium heat, stirring constantly, until it thickens just enough to coat a spatula. *Do not allow the mixture to boil.*

Pass through a fine chinois or 2 layers of cheesecloth.

Cover loosely and quickly chill by placing the container in an ice-water bath or the freezer for 15 minutes.

Churn in an ice cream machine according to the manufacturer's instructions. Store for up to 12 hours.

Hazelnut Ice Cream

2 Egg yolks
2 tablespoons (30 g) Sugar
1 cup (240 ml) Milk
1 tablespoon (15 ml) Cream
2 teaspoons (10 ml) Hazelnut liqueur
½ cup (50 g) Hazelnuts, roasted, lightly
    chopped

In a bowl, whisk together the yolks and sugar until smooth and the color of the yolks lightens.

In a medium-size saucepan, combine the milk, cream, and liqueur. Bring to a boil over medium heat.

Pour the boiling milk mixture into the yolks, whisking continuously.

Return the mixture to the saucepan and cook over medium heat, stirring constantly, until it thickens just enough to coat a spatula. *Do not allow the mixture to boil.*

Pass through a fine chinois or 2 layers of cheesecloth. Stir in the hazelnuts.

Cover loosely and quickly chill by placing the container in an ice-water bath or the freezer for 15 minutes.

Churn in an ice cream machine according to the manufacturer's instructions. Store for up to 12 hours.

Nutmeg Ice Cream

2 Egg yolks
1 tablespoon + 1 teaspoon (20 g) Sugar
1 cup (240 ml) Milk
2 tablespoons (30 ml) Cream
1 teaspoon (1 g) Nutmeg, ground
Black pepper, a grind

In a bowl, whisk together the yolks and sugar until smooth and the color of the yolks lightens.

In a medium-size saucepan, combine the milk, cream, nutmeg, and pepper. Bring to a boil over medium heat.

Pour the boiling milk mixture into the yolks, whisking continuously.

Return the mixture to the saucepan and cook over medium heat, stirring constantly, until it thickens just enough to coat a spatula. *Do not allow the mixture to boil.*

Pass through a fine chinois or 2 layers of cheesecloth.

Cover loosely and quickly chill by placing the container in an ice-water bath or the freezer for 15 minutes.

Churn in an ice cream machine according to the manufacturer's instructions. Store for up to 12 hours.

Pistachio Ice Cream

2 Egg yolks

2 tablespoons (30 g) Sugar

1 cup (240 ml) Milk

2 tablespoons (30 ml) Cream

1/4 cup (25 g) Pistachios, raw, finely ground in a food processor

1/4 cup (25 g) Pistachios, roasted, roughly chopped

In a bowl, whisk together the yolks and sugar until smooth and the color of the yolks lightens.

In a medium-size saucepan, combine the milk, cream, and raw pistachios. Bring to a boil over medium heat.

Pour the boiling milk mixture into the yolks, whisking continuously.

Return the mixture to the saucepan and cook over medium heat, stirring constantly, until it thickens just enough to coat a spatula. *Do not allow the mixture to boil.*

Pass through a fine chinois or 2 layers of cheesecloth, squeezing as much liquid as possible from the strained nuts. The strained nuts can be rinsed and roasted for other uses if desired. Stir in the roasted pistachios.

Cover loosely and quickly chill by placing the container in an ice-water bath or the freezer for 15 minutes.

Churn in an ice cream machine according to the manufacturer's instructions. Store for up to 12 hours.

Red Wine Ice Cream

1 bottle (750 ml) Red wine, Cabernet Sauvignon or Merlot

3 Egg yolks

1/4 cup + 1 tablespoon (65 g) Sugar

1 cup (240 ml) Milk

2 tablespoons (30 ml) Cream

Salt, a dash

Black pepper, a grind

In a medium-size saucepan, cook the wine over high heat until it has reduced to 1/2 cup (115 ml).

In a bowl, whisk together the yolks and sugar until smooth and the color of the yolks lightens.

Add the milk, cream, salt, and pepper to the reduced wine. Bring to a boil over medium heat.

Pour the boiling mixture into the yolks, whisking continuously.

Return the mixture to the saucepan and cook over medium heat, stirring constantly, until it thickens just enough to coat a spatula. *Do not allow the mixture to boil.*

Pass through a fine chinois or 2 layers of cheesecloth.

Cover loosely and quickly chill by placing the container in an ice-water bath or the freezer for 15 minutes.

Churn in an ice cream machine according to the manufacturer's instructions. Store for up to 12 hours.

Spearmint Ice Cream

2 Egg yolks

2 tablespoons (30 g) Sugar

1 tablespoon (20 g) Glucose or corn syrup

1 cup (240 ml) Milk

1 tablespoon (15 ml) Cream

1 ounce (30 g) Spearmint leaves

Ice water, a bowl

In a bowl, whisk together the yolks, sugar, and glucose until smooth and the color of the yolks lightens.

Pour the milk and cream into a medium-size saucepan and bring to a boil over medium heat. Submerge the spearmint leaves in the boiling milk for 20 seconds, then retrieve them with a slotted spoon, and quickly dip them into a small bowl of ice water. Set aside.

Pour the boiling milk mixture into the yolks, whisking continuously.

Return the mixture to the saucepan and cook over medium heat, stirring constantly, until it thickens just enough to coat a spatula. *Do not allow the mixture to boil.*

Squeeze the excess water from the mint leaves by wringing them in a towel.

Pour the custard into a blender, add the mint leaves, put the top on, place a towel over the blender and secure it with your hand. Blend at high speed for 3 minutes.

Pass through a fine chinois or 2 layers of cheesecloth.

Cover loosely and quickly chill by placing the container in an ice-water bath or the freezer for 15 minutes.

Churn in an ice cream machine according to the manufacturer's instructions. Store for up to 12 hours.

. . . .

When blending a hot liquid, be very careful, as the released steam can cause the top to come off.

. . . .

Strawberry Ice Cream

11.5 ounces (340 g) Strawberries,
    approximately 2 cups, washed and hulled
1 teaspoon (5 g) Sugar
2 Egg yolks
2 tablespoons (30 g) Sugar
2 tablespoons (40 g) Glucose
1 cup (240 ml) Milk
1 tablespoon (15 ml) Cream

In a saucepan over medium heat, cook the strawberries and 1 teaspoon (5 g) of sugar. Stir occasionally until the fruit has cooked down considerably and begins to resemble preserves (about 10 to 12 minutes).

In a bowl, whisk together the yolks, 2 tablespoons (30 g) of sugar, and glucose until smooth and the color of the yolks lightens.

In a medium-size saucepan, combine the milk and cream. Bring to a boil over medium heat.

Pour the boiling milk mixture into the yolks, whisking continuously.

Return the mixture to the saucepan and cook over medium heat, stirring constantly, until it thickens just enough to coat a spatula. *Do not allow the mixture to boil.*

Pass through a fine chinois or 2 layers of cheesecloth. Stir in the cooked strawberries.

Cover loosely and quickly chill by placing the container in an ice-water bath or the freezer for 15 minutes.

Churn in an ice cream machine according to the manufacturer's instructions. Store for up to 12 hours.

Vanilla-Honey Ice Cream

2 Egg yolks
2 tablespoons (40 g) Honey
1 cup (240 ml) Milk
2 tablespoons (30 ml) Cream
1/2 Vanilla bean, scraped

In a bowl, whisk together the yolks and honey until smooth.

In a medium-size saucepan, combine the milk, cream, and vanilla bean. Bring to a boil over medium heat.

Pour the boiling milk mixture into the yolks, whisking continuously.

Return the mixture to the saucepan and cook over medium heat, stirring constantly, until it thickens just enough to coat a spatula. *Do not allow the mixture to boil.*

Pass through a fine chinois or 2 layers of cheesecloth.

Cover loosely and quickly chill by placing the container in an ice-water bath or the freezer for 15 minutes.

Churn in an ice cream machine according to the manufacturer's instructions. Store for up to 12 hours.

White Chocolate Ice Cream

3 ounces (85 g) White chocolate

3 tablespoons (45 ml) Cream

2 Egg yolks

1 tablespoon (15 g) Sugar

¾ cup (180 ml) Milk

Melt the chocolate in a small bowl over hot water. Stir the cream into the chocolate and set aside.

In another bowl, whisk together the yolks and sugar until smooth.

Pour the milk into a medium-size saucepan and bring to a boil over medium heat.

Pour the boiling milk mixture into the yolks, whisking continuously.

Return the mixture to the saucepan and cook over medium heat, stirring constantly, until it thickens just enough to coat a spatula. *Do not allow the mixture to boil.*

Thoroughly whisk in the white chocolate mixture. Pass through a fine chinois or 2 layers of cheesecloth.

Cover loosely and quickly chill by placing the container in an ice-water bath or the freezer for 15 minutes.

Churn in an ice cream machine according to the manufacturer's instructions. Store for up to 12 hours.

White Pepper Ice Cream

2 Egg yolks

2 tablespoons (30 g) Sugar

1 cup (240 ml) Milk

2 tablespoons (30 ml) Cream

½ teaspoon (.5 g) White pepper

In a bowl, whisk together the yolks and sugar until smooth.

In a medium-size saucepan, combine the milk, cream, and white pepper. Bring to a boil over medium heat.

Pour the boiling milk mixture into the yolks, whisking continuously.

Return the mixture to the saucepan and cook over medium heat, stirring constantly, until it thickens just enough to coat a spatula. *Do not allow the mixture to boil.*

Pass through a fine chinois or 2 layers of cheesecloth.

Cover loosely and quickly chill by placing the container in an ice-water bath or the freezer for 15 minutes.

Churn in an ice cream machine according to the manufacturer's instructions. Store for up to 12 hours.

Sorbets

Apricot Sorbet

6.5 ounces (180 g) Apricots, approximately 3,
    pitted
½ cup (120 ml) Water
2 tablespoons (30 ml) Muscat or Sauternes
    wine
¼ cup (50 g) Sugar

In a blender, puree all ingredients until the
sugar is completely dissolved. Pass through a
chinois or strainer.

    Churn in an ice cream machine according
to the manufacturer's instructions. Store in the
freezer for up to 8 hours.

Bing Cherry Sorbet

6 ounces (170 g) Bing cherries, pitted
1 cup (240 ml) Water
2 tablespoons (30 ml) Kirsch
½ cup (100 g) Sugar

In a blender, puree all ingredients until the
sugar is completely dissolved. Pass through a
fine chinois or 2 layers of cheesecloth.

    Churn in an ice cream machine according
to the manufacturer's instructions. Store in the
freezer for up to 8 hours.

Carrot Sorbet

Approximately 8 Carrots, medium-size
3 tablespoons (45 g) Sugar
1 tablespoon (20 g) Glucose or corn syrup

Wash the carrots well. Cut the ends off and process them through a juicing machine to obtain 1 cup (240 ml) of juice. Whisk together the juice, sugar, and glucose until completely dissolved.

Churn in an ice cream machine according to the manufacturer's instructions. Store in the freezer for up to 8 hours.

Chocolate Sorbet

½ cup + 2 tablespoons (130 g) Sugar
1⅔ cups (390 ml) Water, room temperature
1½ ounces (40 g) Chocolate, bittersweet, melted
½ cup (55 g) Cocoa powder
1 teaspoon (5 ml) Rum
Salt, a dash

Whisk the sugar into the water. Pour half the water into a separate bowl. Whisk in the chocolate, cocoa powder, rum, and salt. Add the remaining water. Quickly chill in an ice-water bath or the freezer for 15 minutes.

Churn in an ice cream machine according to the manufacturer's instructions. Store in the freezer for up to 8 hours.

Chestnut Sorbet

½ cup (120 ml) Water
2 tablespoons (40 g) Glucose or corn syrup
½ cup or ½ recipe (130 g) Chestnut Puree—see p. 47

Whisk together the water and glucose until it is dissolved. Stir the mixture into the chestnut puree until smooth.

Churn in an ice cream machine according to the manufacturer's instructions. Store in the freezer for up to 8 hours.

Earl Grey Tea Sorbet

1 cup (240 ml) Water
½ ounce (15 g) Earl Grey tea leaves
¼ cup (50 g) Sugar
1 tablespoon (20 g) Glucose or corn syrup
1 tablespoon (15 ml) Egg white

Bring the water to a boil and add the tea. Steep for 10 minutes. Strain, and squeeze the excess liquid from the tea. Whisk in the sugar and glucose until dissolved. Chill in an ice-water bath or the freezer for 15 minutes. Whisk in the egg white.

Churn in an ice cream machine according to the manufacturer's instructions. Store in the freezer for up to 8 hours.

Guava Sorbet

10 ounces (285 g) Guavas, approximately 3,
    peeled and quartered
1 cup (240 ml) Water
1/2 cup (100 g) Sugar
1/2 teaspoon (2 ml) Vanilla extract

In a medium-size saucepot, combine the cut
guavas with the water, sugar, and vanilla.
Bring to a boil over medium heat. Remove
from the heat and allow to cool for several
minutes.

Pour into a blender, put the top on, place
a towel over the blender and secure it with
your hand. Blend at high speed for 45 seconds.

Pass through a fine chinois or 2 layers of
cheesecloth. Be sure to squeeze as much liquid
from the guava pulp as possible.

Cover loosely and quickly chill by placing
the container in an ice-water bath or the freezer
for 15 minutes.

Churn in an ice cream machine according
to the manufacturer's instructions. Store in the
freezer for up to 8 hours.

. . . .

*When blending a hot liquid, be very careful, as the
released steam can cause the top to come off.*

. . . .

Honeydew Melon Sorbet

16 ounces (450 g) Honeydew melon,
    approximately 1/4, rind and seeds removed
2 tablespoons (30 g) Sugar

Process the melon through a juicing machine
to obtain 2 cups (480 ml) of juice. Set 1 cup
(240 ml) of the juice aside. Pour the remaining
juice into a saucepot. Cook over medium heat
to reduce it to 1/2 cup (120 ml).

Whisk the 2 juices with the sugar until
the sugar is dissolved.

Quickly chill the mixture in an ice-water
bath or the freezer for 15 minutes.

Churn in an ice cream machine according
to the manufacturer's instructions. Store in the
freezer for up to 8 hours.

Blender Method

Combine all the ingredients in a blender
and add 1/4 cup (60 ml) of water. Blend for 30
seconds.

Pass through a fine chinois or 2 layers of
cheesecloth, then proceed as for above, setting
half the puree aside and reducing the other.
Combine the 2, then chill and churn as above.

Lime Sorbet

Approximately 4 limes

1 cup (240 ml) Water

¼ cup + 2 tablespoons (80 g) Sugar

2 tablespoons (40 g) Glucose or corn syrup

Zest 1 of the limes. Chop the zest very fine. (See method for zesting, p. 54.) Juice all the limes to obtain 1 cup (240 ml). Set aside. Put the zest in a saucepot with the water, sugar, and glucose. Bring to a boil, and boil for 1 minute.

Allow to cool, then add the lime juice. Chill in an ice-water bath or the freezer for 15 minutes.

Churn in an ice cream machine according to the manufacturer's instructions. Store in the freezer for up to 8 hours.

. . . .

Depending on the juice content of the limes, the number needed will vary somewhat.

. . . .

McIntosh Apple Sorbet

2 McIntosh apples, large

¼ cup (50 g) Sugar

Cut the apples into quarters and process them through a juicing machine to obtain 1 cup (240 ml) of juice. Whisk together the juice and sugar until completely dissolved.

Churn in an ice cream machine according to the manufacturer's instructions. Store in the freezer for up to 8 hours.

Blender Method

2 McIntosh apples, large

¼ cup + 2 tablespoons (65 g) Sugar

¼ cup (60 ml) Water

Peel and core the apples and cut them into ½-inch pieces. In a blender, combine the apple, sugar, and water. Blend for 30 seconds.

Pass through a fine chinois or 2 layers of cheesecloth, then churn as above.

Red Apple Sorbet

For red apple sorbet, replace the McIntosh apples in the above recipe with Jonathan or Red Rome apples.

Mango Sorbet

10.5 ounces (300 g) Mango, approximately 1,
    ripe and peeled
³/₄ cup (180 ml) Water
2 tablespoons (30 g) Sugar

Cut the mango flesh from the pit with a knife.
In a blender, combine it with the water and
sugar. Process at high speed until the sugar is
completely dissolved.

Pass through a fine chinois or 2 layers of
cheesecloth.

Churn in an ice cream machine according
to the manufacturer's instructions. Store in the
freezer for up to 8 hours.

Passion Fruit Sorbet

5 ounces (140 g) Passion fruits, approximately
    7
³/₄ cup (180 ml) Water
¹/₂ cup (100 g) Sugar

Slice the passion fruits in half. Remove the
pulp and juice with a spoon. Puree the pulp in
a blender by pulsing several times in order to
loosen the seeds from the pulp and juice and
to strain it. Or, place the seeds and pulp in a
strainer and push the juice through, squeezing
to obtain as much of the juice as possible.

Whisk together the juice, water, and sugar
until completely dissolved.

Churn in an ice cream machine according
to the manufacturer's instructions. Store in the
freezer for up to 8 hours.

Nectarine Sorbet

12.5 ounces (350 g) Nectarines,
    approximately 4, pitted and quartered
³/₄ cup (180 ml) Water
¹/₄ cup + 2 tablespoons (80 g) Sugar

In a blender, puree all ingredients until the
sugar is completely dissolved. Pass through a
chinois or strainer.

Churn in an ice cream machine according
to the manufacturer's instructions. Store in the
freezer for up to 8 hours.

Plum Sorbet

10.5 to 12.5 ounces (300 g to 350 g) Plums,
    approximately 4, dark-skinned, pitted
³/₄ cup (180 ml) Water
¹/₄ cup + 2 tablespoons (80 g) Sugar

In a saucepot over medium heat, cook all the
ingredients. Boil for 6 minutes. Transfer to a
blender and puree for 30 seconds. Pass the liquid through a chinois or strainer.

Chill in an ice-water bath or in the freezer
for 15 minutes.

Churn in an ice cream machine according
to the manufacturer's instructions. Store in the
freezer for up to 8 hours.

Red Wine and Black Pepper Sorbet

1 bottle (750 ml) Merlot or Cabernet
　　Sauvignon wine
$\frac{1}{2}$ teaspoon (.50 g) Black pepper, cracked or
　　ground
$\frac{1}{4}$ cup (50 g) Sugar
2 tablespoons (60 g) Glucose
1 tablespoon (10 g) Egg White

In a saucepan over high heat, cook the wine and black pepper until the volume is reduced to 1$\frac{1}{2}$ cups (360 ml) (about 25 minutes). Add the sugar and glucose, stirring until dissolved.

Quickly chill in an ice-water bath or the freezer for 15 minutes. Whisk the egg white into the chilled wine mixture.

Churn in an ice cream machine according to the manufacturer's instructions. Store in the freezer for up to 8 hours.

Rum Raisin Sorbet

4 ounces (115 g) Raisins
1$\frac{1}{2}$ cups (360 ml) Water
1 tablespoon (15 g) Sugar
1 ounce (30 ml) Rum
Salt, a dash

In a saucepan over high heat, combine all the ingredients. Bring to a boil. Reduce the heat to low and simmer for 5 minutes. Remove the pan from the heat and allow to cool slightly.

Pour into a blender, put the top on, place a towel over the blender and secure it with your hand. Blend at high speed for 45 seconds.

Pass through a fine chinois or 2 layers of cheesecloth.

Cover loosely and quickly chill by placing the container in an ice-water bath or the freezer for 15 minutes.

Churn in an ice cream machine according to the manufacturer's instructions. Store in the freezer for up to 8 hours.

. . . .
When blending a hot liquid, be very careful, as the released steam can cause the top to come off.
. . . .

White Peach Sorbet

11 ounces (320 g) Babcock white peaches,
    approximately 3, ripe and pitted
3/4 cup (180 ml) Water
1/4 cup + 1 tablespoon (65 g) Sugar

Puree all the ingredients in a blender until the sugar is completely dissolved. Pass through a chinois or strainer.

Churn in an ice cream machine according to the manufacturer's instructions. Store in the freezer for up to 8 hours.

CHAPTER FOUR

Desserts of Spring and Summer

The desserts of spring and summer are distinguished by the wide array of available seasonal fruits. From the stone fruits, apricots, and plums of early spring to the strawberries of June and the peaches and blackberries of late summer, the delightful flavors of the season challenge the chef to find the best methods for presenting them in great desserts. Many desserts can be served chilled or at room temperature, and ice creams and sorbets are outstanding accompaniments to fruit compotes, fruit soups, and many other seasonally inspired dishes. Desserts that will complement the lighter meals of spring and summer need to have lighter flavors than the heavier ones of winter. For example, a summer dessert could be composed of a particular super-ripe fruit, enhanced by the subtle flavor of vanilla and the moderate use of nuts. Summer desserts rely less on foundation recipes, and more on fruits like apricots, strawberries, or peaches. Although some of the desserts in this chapter do call for basic pastry recipes, they are less prominent than in most of the winter desserts. The pastry components serve only to augment the fruit flavors, providing a vehicle for the fruit presentation or a complementary, divergent texture.

Spring and summer is truly the most wonderful time of year to closely follow the ever-changing array of fruits. I prefer to shop at a local farmers market every week, where area growers sell their own produce and I can find the most wonderful fruits. I once discovered a real gem—a variety of plum only known lo-cally. It was yellow with red pigments, very ripe, smaller than an apricot, and somewhat sweet, with an almost indescribable tropical flavor. The farmer explained that it was native to the area and had been growing on his farm before he had planted anything else. I quickly purchased the entire supply and created a unique dessert for that evening—native plum soup with native plum sorbet and tartlet. So, let the season be your inspiration and be guided by the continual tasting of your own creations.

Spring and Summer Fruits

Apricots are often available as early as February. These early-season apricots are generally imported from South America, and usually require a day or 2 of ripening at room temperature. The prime apricot season begins in early June and extends into July. This is when the fruit is most sweet and luscious, yet slightly acidic. Apricots contain significant amounts of pectin that gives them a soft, jamlike consistency when ripe. Some compatible flavors for apricots are honey, caramel, sesame, hazelnut, pistachio, ginger, vanilla, and other fruits such as cherries, plums, or nectarines.

Cherries are available in early to middle summer in many areas. The most commonly available variety is Bing, characterized when ripe by a deep ruby red to almost black color. They should be soft, juicy, and sweet. Avoid Bing cherries that are a mottled pink and red. Rainier cherries are yellow with a pink blush, and should also be soft, juicy, and sweet. Some compatible flavors for cherries are brandy, vanilla, chocolate, black pepper, caramel, nuts, and other fruits such as plums, apricots, nectarines, or peaches.

Strawberries, although available year-round, are often cultivated more for their appearance and size than for flavor. The best strawberries can usually be obtained locally in June when they are sweet and bursting with flavor. Compatible flavors should be used sparingly, so as not to overpower or compete with the delicate flavor of the strawberries. These include vanilla, nuts, citrus, rhubarb, caramel, red wine, pink peppercorn, cinnamon, champagne, and other mild fruits such as figs, bananas, and guavas.

Raspberries are best in mid-summer, while **blackberries** usually follow raspberries in mid- to late summer. They should always be slightly sweet and flavorful. Compatible flavors for these berries include citrus, vanilla, chocolate, black pepper, almonds, pistachios, and champagne.

Figs are available in early summer and in autumn. When ripe, they are soft to the touch, sweet, and juicy. Some compatible flavors are port or red wine, goat cheese, black pepper, nuts, vanilla, caramel, and other fruits such as strawberries and peaches.

Guavas are available in the summer months. They are about the size and color of limes, with an off-white or pink interior. Guavas must always be peeled to expose the flesh of the fruit. The flesh is seedy, tart, and fragrant. Guavas can be used to make wonderful sorbets or ice creams. Compatible flavors include vanilla and other tropical fruits like pineapple, banana, mango, and papaya.

Honeydew melons, cantaloupes, and *musk-melons* are all sweetest and most flavorful in the spring and summer. Their mild flavors are compatible with vanilla and various kinds of nuts. They make wonderful chilled soups, or can simply be cut up, warmed slightly, and served with 1 or more fruit sorbets.

Nectarines can be found from late June through August, while *peaches* are best in July, August, and early September. A ripe, sweet peach signals the peak of the summer fruit season. Some compatible flavors for nectarines and peaches are vanilla, caramel, champagne, ginger, cinnamon, black pepper, nuts, and other fruits such as figs, berries, or cherries.

Summertime *plums* are best from June to August, when the common dark-skinned varieties are sweetest. Plums often benefit from poaching or heating through with some spices, wine, and a small amount of sugar. Prune plums are smaller and more oval-shaped than the common plum. They are very rich in flavor when ripe, when they begin to appear wrinkled and shriveled. Some compatible flavors for plums are vanilla, ginger, cinnamon, Sauternes, Muscat, red wine, citrus, nuts, and other fruits such as apricots, nectarines, or cherries.

Rhubarb is available in early to mid-summer. It must be cooked with sugar and seasonings in order to balance its tartness. It is classically paired with strawberries, but can also be prepared alone as an excellent sorbet or sauce. Rhubarb is compatible with berries, black pepper, pink peppercorn, cinnamon, and citrus.

Fruit Processing Methods

To Peel Peaches, Plums, and Nectarines

3 cups (720 ml) Water

6 Peaches, plums, or nectarines (ripe)

Ice water

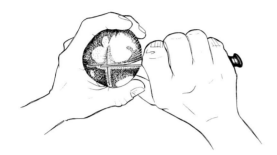

Place the water in a pot on high heat and bring to a rolling boil. Draw a paring knife across the surface of the fruit to just cut through the skin in an "X" pattern. Carefully plunge the fruit into the boiling water for 30 seconds. Remove them with a spoon and quickly plunge them into the ice water. If the fruit is properly ripened, the skin should easily pull off the flesh, or you may need to use a small paring knife.

To Remove the Stone from Plums or Apricots

Using a strawberry huller or the small end of a parisienne scoop, gently scoop out the plum or apricot flesh at the stem end. Push the huller into the fruit at the stem end, and loosen the stone on all sides where it is still attached to the fruit. Leaving the plum or apricot intact, pull the stone out of the fruit.

To Remove the Sections from Citrus Fruit

Slice the top and bottom off the citrus fruit to expose the sections on each end. Cut the skin from the sides of the fruit, removing all the white pith and outer membrane. Using a very sharp paring knife, remove each section of the fruit from between each membrane and place them in a small bowl. Squeeze the juice from the leftover membrane over the sections.

Warm Apricot and Honey Tartlet with Black Sesame Brittle Ice Cream

6 servings

One of the most versatile and flavorful fruits of spring and summer is the apricot. Here it is paired with honey and the unusual, savory influence of black sesame seeds.

Filling and Apricots

6 Apricots, washed, stones removed—see
    p. 81
½ cup (120 ml) Vanilla Pastry Cream—see
    p. 34
2 tablespoons (40 g) Honey
White pepper, a grind
Salt, a dash

Tart

1 recipe Three-Nut Linzer Dough, well chilled
    —see p. 22
½ sheet Puff Pastry—see p. 18
Egg wash

Sugar Cages

½ cup (100 g) Sugar
¼ cup + 1 tablespoon (70 ml) Water
1 tablespoon + 1 teaspoon (30 g) Glucose or
    corn syrup
Ice water
Vegetable oil

1 recipe Vanilla Sauce—see p. 48
1 recipe Black Sesame Brittle Ice Cream—see
    p. 59

Equipment Needs

Ice cream machine
Parisienne scoop or melon baller
6, 2½-inch Tart rings or tins
2-ounce Ladle
Set of round pastry cutters

Prepare the Filling

In a bowl, thoroughly combine the pastry cream with the honey, pepper, and salt. Set aside.

Make and Assemble the Tarts

Prepare 6, 2½-inch tart rings or fluted tart tins by brushing lightly with butter and dusting with flour. Roll the linzer dough on a floured work surface to ¼ inch thick and cut 6, 3½-inch circles. Carefully line the rings with the linzer circles so the insides of the rings are covered and the linzer is pressed into the corners.

Using a spoon or a pastry bag fitted with a
¼-inch plain tip, spread or pipe a ¼-inch-
thick layer of pastry cream into the bottoms of
the linzer tart shells. Spoon or pipe some of
the pastry cream mixture into each apricot
where the stone was removed and set each apricot, hole side up, into each tart. Spoon or pipe
the remaining pastry cream over the apricots.
Brush some egg wash on the top edge of the
linzer tarts.

Roll the puff pastry to ¹⁄₁₆ inch thick and
cut 6, 4½-inch circles. Place the puff pastry
circles over the apricots and press the circles'
edges against the linzer tart edge to seal them
closed. Egg wash the puff pastry tops and refrigerate the tarts until well chilled.

Make the Sugar Cages

. . . .

*This procedure will require some practice to master.
The key things to remember are to coat the back of
the ladle with the vegetable oil between cages in order
to keep the strands of sugar from sliding off and to
maintain the sugar at a temperature where it flows
in one continuous strand from the spoon and does not
drip.*

*The sugar cages are a decorative addition to this
dessert and may be omitted. If desired, proceed di-
rectly to the final assembly.*

. . . .

In a saucepot on high heat, combine the
sugar, water, and glucose. Cook the mixture
until it just begins to turn in color from crys-
tal clear to a very light amber (about 5 to 7
minutes). Dip the bottom of the pot in ice
water to stop the sugar from cooking.

Rub some vegetable oil on the back of a 2-
ounce ladle.

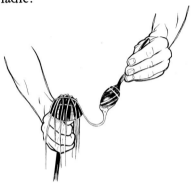

Dip the tip of a spoon into the sugar and
pull out a long strand that flows in a slow, fine
drizzle. Drape the sugar strand over the ladle
and then return the spoon over the ladle, draping another strand parallel to the first one. The
speed at which you need to drape the sugar
strand over the ladle depends on how fast the
sugar is flowing from the spoon.

Again dip the spoon into the sugar to
maintain the slow, fine drizzle. Cross the first
parallel lines at an angle and make several
more parallel lines that intersect the first lines.
Continue draping sugar strands over the ladle
until evenly spaced, parallel lines cover the
ladle in a crisscross pattern.

Pull a drizzle of the sugar around the edge
of the ladle; circle it 6 to 8 times. Gently break
any dangling strands of sugar. Remove the
cage from the ladle. You will need to reheat
the sugar several times during the cage-
making process.

Continue making the cages until you have
6. Reserve for the final assembly.

Assemble the Dessert

Preheat the oven to 400°F. Bake the tarts for 8 minutes, then lower the temperature to 350°F for an additional 7 minutes. Allow them to cool slightly, then remove from the tart rings. With a sharp, serrated knife, cut the tarts into thirds.

Place each cut tart onto a plate so the point of each third is facing outward and the round sides of the tart are back to back. Drizzle some vanilla sauce around the tarts. Place a scoop of ice cream on each center. Place a sugar cage over the ice cream. Serve at once.

Chef's Hint

You could easily replace the three-nut linzer dough with rich shortdough for the tarts' bottoms, and the black sesame brittle ice cream could be replaced with a good commercial, nut-flavored ice cream.

For easier preparation, this could be made whole in a large tart tin and cut into slices. First, line a 9-inch tart pan with the three-nut linzer dough or rich shortdough. Use all the pastry cream recipe and twice the amount of honey. Spread half of it into the bottom of the tart. Prepare about 12 to 14 apricots, depending on their size, and stand them hole side up, side by side in the tart bottom. Fill the apricots with the remaining pastry cream and cover the tart with a 10-inch circle of puff pastry, sealing it to the linzer or shortdough edges as above. Follow the baking temperatures for the individual tarts but double the baking time: 16 minutes at 400°F and 12 to 14 minutes at 350°F. Allow the baked tart to cool slightly; then slice and serve with some of the vanilla sauce and ice cream.

Bing Cherry and Pepper-
Custard-Spiced Timbale

9 servings

*Fruit baked in a custard is a classic sweet preparation, found in various
fruit tarts or molded puddings. Layers of cherries, spiced cake, and peppery
custard comprise this version.*

Timbales

1 recipe Spiced Génoise—see p. 26

12 ounces to 14 ounces (340 g to 390 g) Bing
    cherries, washed

Peppered Crème Brûlée Custard—see p. 38

1 recipe Cherry Coulis—see p. 52

Powdered sugar, for sprinkling

Equipment Needs

Scissors

6, 2¼-inch-tall Timbale molds

Set of round pastry cutters

Tongs

Blender

2-inch-high Baking pan

Make the Timbales

Preheat the oven to 325°F. Lightly brush
the inside of 6, 2¼-inch-tall timbale molds
with melted butter.

With a pair of scissors, cut 6 circles of
aluminum foil to fit into the bottom of each
timbale. Press the foil circles into the bottom
of each timbale and brush them with butter.

Using a set of round pastry cutters, cut the
spiced génoise as follows: 6 rounds to fit into
the bottoms of the timbales, 6 rounds the size
of the middle of the timbale, and 6 rounds to
fit into the top diameter of the timbales.

Cut the cherries in half and remove the
stone. Place the small rounds of génoise into
the bottoms of the timbales.

Press the cut side of the cherry halves
against the inside wall of the timbales in a

86

circle. Pour some of the custard into the timbales to the top of the cherry halves. Place the middle-size rounds of génoise over the custard and cherry halves, and press another circle of cherry halves around the inside wall of the timbales. Pour more of the custard to the top of the cherry halves. Top each timbale with the remaining large génoise circles.

Place the timbales in a 2-inch-high pan and pour in some warm water to come at least halfway up the sides of the timbales. (This is a water bath.) Bake at 325°F for about 40 minutes.

Check doneness by lifting up the génoise on 1 side of a timbale. If the custard is no longer liquid and somewhat firm, remove the timbales from the oven immediately. Place in the refrigerator for several hours to chill.

Assemble the Dessert

Unmold the timbales: dip them in some warm water for a few seconds and draw a paring knife around the custard. Invert the timbales into your hand and place them on a sheetpan. Generously sprinkle the tops with the sugar.

Over an open flame, heat the rolled edge of a small circular cutter until it is very hot. Pick it up with some tongs and press it into the sugar-covered timbale tops to make a caramelized circular line. Clean the cutter with a cloth and repeat the process to make a circle on the top of each timbale.

Place each timbale in the center of a plate and surround with a drizzle of cherry coulis. Top with a cherry. Serve at once.

Chef's Hint

Another option for presenting the same delicious flavors of these timbales in a simpler way is to tear the génoise into pieces and stir them into the custard with the pitted cherries. You can then bake the custard mixture in individual porcelain ramekins, crème brûlée dishes, or a single large porcelain casserole dish. Place the individual dishes or the large casserole dish on a larger pan that has edges and pour some water in this larger pan to create a water bath that will allow the delicate custard to bake gently.

To bake the individual dishes, follow the baking instructions for the timbales. Bake the large casserole dish at 325°F for approximately 1 hour, until it has "set up." To check to see whether the custard is firm, tap the edge of the dish. The resulting dessert is reminiscent of a trifle or rich flavorful bread pudding.

If baked whole, the custard can be scooped, still warm, into serving bowls or small dessert goblets, drizzled with the cherry coulis, and topped with a fresh cherry.

Warm Berry Compote with Pistachio Ice Cream

6 servings

This simple dessert consists of warmed seasonal berries topped with rich pistachio ice cream.

½ cup (120 ml) White wine, Muscat or Riesling

2 tablespoons (30 ml) Vanilla sugar—see discussion of vanilla, Chapter One, p. 9

Black pepper, a grind

24 ounces (680 g) Berries, such as strawberries (hulled, quartered), blackberries, raspberries, blueberries, or gooseberries, washed

1 recipe Pistachio Ice Cream—see p. 65

Equipment Needs

Ice cream machine

Sauté pan

In a sauté pan over high heat, combine the wine, sugar, and pepper and bring to a simmer. Add the berries and reduce the heat to low. Toss the berries in the wine until they are heated through.

Scoop a mound of the berries into each of 6 warm bowls. Divide any remaining juices in the pan over the berries. Place 2 scoops of pistachio ice cream atop each mound of berries. Serve at once.

Chef's Hint

The types of berries called for here could be replaced by any pleasing berry combination as the season may dictate.

Chocolate Soufflé with Oven-Roasted Fruits

7 servings

This is a chocolate dessert that is so light that I believe it deserves to be enjoyed in the heat of summer.

Fruit and Mango Puree

1 large or 2 small Mangos

21 Strawberries, washed, hulled

2 tablespoons (15 ml) Water

2 teaspoons (10 g) Sugar

Soufflé Mixture

5 Eggs, separated

1 teaspoon (5 ml) Lemon juice

3 tablespoons (45 g) Sugar

5 ounces (140 g) Chocolate, bittersweet, melted

2 tablespoons (30 ml) Espresso or strong coffee

1 teaspoon (5 ml) Vanilla extract

1 recipe Strawberry Coulis—see p. 53

Cocoa powder, for sprinkling

Powdered sugar, for sprinkling

Equipment Needs

Food processor or blender

Stickless sheetpan or parchment paper

6, 2½-inch-diameter Steel rings

Prepare the Fruit, Mango, and Mango Puree

Preheat the oven to 300°F.

Peel the mango and cut most of the flesh from each side of the pit, leaving some of the fruit still attached. Cut the fruit into 21 odd-size pieces, approximately 1½ inches by ¾ inches. Place the mango pieces 1 inch apart on a stickless pan or parchment-lined sheetpan brushed lightly with oil.

Stand the berries upright, also 1 inch apart on the sheetpan. Place in the oven for 35 to 40 minutes.

Peel them from the pan while still warm. Set aside for final assembly.

Trim the remaining mango from the pit; puree it in a food processor with the sugar and water.

Pass the puree through a fine strainer or layer of cheesecloth. Reserve for final assembly.

Make the Soufflé Mixture

Whip the egg whites and lemon juice to soft peaks. Continue to whip, sprinkling sugar into the whites. Whip to stiff peaks, set aside.

90

In a large bowl, whisk the espresso and vanilla into the chocolate. Whisk in the egg yolks. Gently fold in ⅓ of the egg whites. Continue to fold in the rest just until the mixture is combined. Be sure not to overfold, or the mixture could begin to lose volume. Place the soufflé mixture covered in the refrigerator. Final assembly should be begun no more than 1 hour after mixing.

Assemble the Dessert

Preheat the oven to 400°F.

Line the bottoms of 6, 2½-inch-diameter and 1½-inch-high steel rings with 5-inch-square pieces of aluminum foil. Wrap excess foil against the outside surface of the rings.

Brush the foil bottoms and sides with melted butter. Sprinkle them thoroughly with sugar, and place on a sheetpan. Fill the rings to the top with the soufflé mixture. Smooth the tops flat with a spatula. Create a water bath that comes ¼ inch up the sides of the rings.

Place in the oven and bake for 7 minutes. Reduce the oven temperature to 375°F; continue baking for 5 minutes.

While the soufflés are baking, arrange the fruit. For each plate, alternate 3 oven-roasted strawberries with 3 pieces of oven-roasted mango around a center area large enough for the soufflé.

With a spoon, drizzle some strawberry coulis over each strawberry and some mango puree over each piece of mango.

Delicately invert each soufflé into your hand, then turn it right side up onto the centers of each plate.

Sprinkle the tops with a little cocoa powder and a little powdered sugar. Serve at once.

Chef's Hint

I wanted to present this soufflé in a way that it could be eaten easily with the fruit and coulis. Nevertheless, it is perfectly acceptable to bake and serve this dessert in classic soufflé dishes and simply serve the fruit and coulis on the side.

For another dramatic option, bake the soufflé mixture in a single large soufflé dish or casserole dish. Bring it to the table hot from the oven, and use a large spoon to scoop it onto plates with the fruit and coulis.

Oven roasting the fruit serves to intensify its flavor, but the soufflé could also be served with fresh strawberries and mango.

Upside-Down Fig Tart with Frangipane and Red Wine Ice Cream

6 servings

In this dessert, figs are baked in almond frangipane and paired with the supporting flavor of red wine ice cream.

Tarts and Linzer Circles

12 Figs, ripe, washed

1 recipe Frangipane—see p. 28

1 recipe Three-Nut Linzer Dough—see
    p. 22

1 recipe Almond Sauce—see p. 51

1 recipe Red Wine Ice Cream—see p. 65

Equipment Needs

Ice cream machine

6, 3-inch-diameter Tart rings or tins

Pastry bag with ¼-inch plain tip

Prepare the Tarts and Linzer Circles

Preheat the oven to 350°F. Brush 6, 3-inch to 3¼-inch tart rings or tart tins with butter, dust them with flour, and set on a parchment-lined sheetpan.

Prepare the figs by cutting the stems and ½ inch of the tops off. Trim ¼ inch off the bottoms and cut them in half from top to bottom.

Place 4 halves, cut side facing outward, pressed against the inside of each tart ring (see diagram). Press gently downward with the palm of your hand to even them.

Fill a pastry bag fitted with a ¼-inch plain tip with the frangipane. Fill in the spaces be-

tween the 4 fig halves and the empty centers to within ½ inch of the tops of the fig halves.

On a well-floured work surface, roll the linzer dough to ¼ inch thick. Cut circles the size of the tart rings. Place the circles on a parchment-lined sheetpan and bake for 10 to 12 minutes. Reserve the tart rings and the linzer circles.

Assemble the Dessert
Preheat the oven to 375°F.

Bake the tarts for 16 to 18 minutes. Allow them to cool slightly. Draw a paring knife around the tarts to loosen them from the tart rings. Place a linzer circle on top of each tart. Turn the tarts upside down so that the linzer circle forms a base.

Place each tart in the center of 6 warm plates. Spoon almond sauce around each tart. Place 2 small quenelles (or scoops) of the ice cream, 1 on the tart and 1 next to the tart, on each dessert. Serve at once.

Chef's Hint

This fig tart can be prepared as a whole dessert in a 9-inch tart pan as follows. Line the tart pan with a ¼-inch-thick layer of three-nut linzer dough and bake at 350°F for 12 minutes. Cut the bottoms and tops off 14 to 16 figs (depending on their size) but do not cut them from top to bottom. Stand the figs up in the tart shell. Pipe frangipane into all the gaps between the figs and just around the inside edge of the tart's linzer dough rim. Bake the tart at 375°F for 18 to 20 minutes. Allow it to cool slightly before slicing. Serve with the almond sauce or other nut sauce and either the red wine ice cream or a rich vanilla ice cream.

Chilled Guava Soup with Sorbets

6 servings

Fruit soups—intense in flavor and loose in consistency, and served with assorted sorbets—make refreshing summer desserts. The soup truly offers a unique presentation for sorbets.

Guava Soup

5.5 ounces (160 g) Guavas, approximately
    2, ripe
4 cups (960 ml) Water
¼ cup (50 g) Sugar
½ Vanilla bean, scraped, or 2 teaspoons
    (10 ml) Vanilla extract

Sorbets

(choose one or more types from the list)
1 recipe Mango Sorbet—see p. 73
1 recipe Lime Sorbet—see p. 72
1 recipe Passion Fruit Sorbet—see p. 73
1 recipe Guava Sorbet—see p. 71
1 recipe Plum Sorbet—see p. 73

½ Mango, cut into ¼-inch cubes

Equipment Needs

Ice cream machine
Blender
Saucepot
Fine chinois or cheesecloth

Prepare the Soup

Peel the guavas. Place the peel in a saucepot and the guavas in a blender.

Pour 1½ cups (360 ml) of the water into the blender and the remaining water into the saucepot with the guava peel. Add the vanilla bean and scrapings or the extract and turn the heat to medium. Heat the mixture for about 30 to 35 minutes—until reduced to ¼ its volume.

Add the sugar to the blender. Puree for 45 seconds. Pass the puree through a fine chinois or three layers of cheesecloth.

Strain the guava peel water into the guava puree and discard the cooked peels.

Stir the soup, cover loosely, and refrigerate until well chilled. It may be kept refrigerated for 8 hours.

Assemble the Dessert

Place 5 scoops or quenelles of sorbet in a row or a circular pattern in the bottoms of 6 chilled bowls. (Preferably include 1 of each.) Divide the soup among the bowls and sprinkle the cubes of mango around the sorbets. Serve at once.

Chef's Hint

The number of sorbets could be limited to as few as 1 if desired. If you choose to serve 1 or 2 different sorbets instead of 5, make sure you increase the quantities of each accordingly so that you end up with the same amount.

Hazelnut Malt Bombe with Oven-Dried Banana and Banana Compote

6 servings

Frozen bombes are a striking way to present those favorite summer desserts of ice creams and fruits. Hazelnut, malt, and banana flavors are featured here.

1 recipe Hazelnut Ice Cream—see p. 64
1 recipe Malt Bombe Filling—see p. 38

Oven-Dried Banana Slices

2 Bananas, not too ripe, peeled
Powdered sugar, for sprinkling

Banana Compote

2 Bananas, not too ripe, peeled
2 tablespoons (30 g) Brown sugar
1 tablespoon (15 ml) Brandy
Cinnamon, a dash
1/2 cup (120 ml) Water

1 recipe Hazelnut Brittle—see p. 46

Equipment Needs

Ice cream machine
Small terrine mold or loaf pan or bombe mold
Stickless sheetpan or parchment paper
Oven broiler or propane torch
Sauté pan

Mold the Bombe

Line the bombe mold with plastic wrap and place in the freezer. Any type of half-cylinder mold or rectangular loaf pan approximately 8 inches long by 3 1/2 inches wide is ideal.

Line the inside of the bombe mold with a 1/2-inch- to 1-inch-thick layer of the hazelnut ice cream, using a rubber spatula and fingers to smooth the inside surface. Fill the bombe centers with the malt filling, cover the surface with plastic wrap, and freeze for at least 2 1/2 hours (or up to 24 hours) before serving.

Prepare the Banana Slices

....
These oven-dried banana slices add interesting texture to this dessert but they may be omitted if desired.
....

98

Preheat the oven to 300°F.

Using a very sharp knife, cut about 25 $\frac{1}{16}$-inch-thick slices, on a diagonal, so the slices are 1½ inches to 2½ inches long. Place on a stickless pan or parchment-lined sheetpan brushed lightly with oil.

Dry them in the oven for about 25 minutes. Check often, and peel the slices from the baking surface as they dry. Turn them over and continue to dry until the slices are still pliable but dry to the touch (not darkened and bitter).

When dry, remove them from the pan and line them up on the back side of a sheetpan. Sprinkle lightly with the powdered sugar. Using a propane torch in sweeping motions or a broiler, melt the sugar, watching very closely so as not to burn the banana slices. The sugar, which should melt and caramelize in spots, may give off a little smoke.

Make the Compote

Cut the bananas into thirds crossways, then cut each third lengthwise into 6 strips.

In a sauté pan on medium heat, cook the brown sugar and brandy. When very hot and beginning to caramelize, add the bananas and cinnamon. Toss the bananas in the pan, sautéing them for 30 seconds.

Add the water. Continue to cook for 1 minute. Remove from the heat and proceed to final assembly.

Assemble the Dessert

Slice the bombe into 12 equal pieces. Place 2, standing up, on the centers of each plate.

Spoon the warm banana compote around each side of the bombe and stick a few oven-dried banana slices among the cooked banana.

Sprinkle with some hazelnut brittle. Serve at once.

Chef's Hint

The bombe can be molded with a commercial nut-flavored ice cream and filled with the malt filling. The bombe could also be presented to a table or celebration in whole form, set on a platter and surrounded with the banana compote, and then cut and served on plates at the table.

Honeydew Melon and Pistachio Torte with Honeydew Sorbet and Pralines

6 servings

This torte, composed of layers of poached melon and pistachio sponge cake, is served with honeydew sorbet and honeydew juice.

Melon Preparation

1 cup (240 ml) Water
1 ounce (30 ml) Vodka
½ cup (100 g) Sugar
½ Honeydew melon

Sponge Cake

1 recipe Pistachio Sponge Cake—see p. 25

Praline Triangles

1 recipe Praline Batter (optional)—see p. 32

1 recipe Vanilla Pastry Cream—see p. 34
Powdered sugar, for sprinkling
1 recipe Honeydew Melon Sorbet—see p. 71
1 recipe Honeydew Melon Coulis—see p. 53

Equipment Needs

Ice cream machine
Blender
Stickless sheetpan or parchment paper
Pastry wheel
Serving fork or metal skewer
Saucepot

Prepare the Melon

In a saucepot on high heat, combine the water, vodka, and sugar. Bring to a boil, then reduce to low heat. Remove the seeds and cut the rind from the melon. Turn cut side down on the cutting board and cut melon crossways into ½-inch-thick slices. Add half the slices to the simmering liquid.

Poach the slices for 6 minutes. Remove them with a slotted spoon, then repeat the process with the remaining melon. Set them aside to cool. Reserve the melon and poaching liquid.

Prepare the Sponge Cake and Praline Triangles

Cut the cake into 18 triangles that are 3½ inches by 4 inches by 2 inches (see diagram). Set aside.

101

These praline triangles provide a textural twist to this dessert but may be omitted if desired.

. . . .

Preheat the oven to 350°F.

Drop 1-teaspoon (5-g) scoops of the praline batter 4 inches apart on a stickless or parchment-lined pan. Cover 1 of the scoops with a small piece of plastic wrap and with your fingers spread the cookie out very thin into the rough shape of a triangle. Pull the plastic off the cookie and proceed with the other scoops. Place in the oven. Bake for 7 to 8 minutes, or until the triangles are lightly browned. Remove from the oven and allow to cool slightly.

Carefully transfer a triangle to a cutting board. Using a pastry wheel, trim ¼ inch off the edges to make a straight-edge triangle. Continue transferring and cutting the remaining triangles, returning the tray to the oven as necessary to soften them. Continue this process to make 18 triangles.

Assemble the Dessert

Cut the melon into pieces roughly the same shape as the sponge cake triangles.

Using a pastry brush, soak the cake with the reserved poaching liquid. Use a spatula to spread the pastry cream onto 12 of the sponge cake triangles.

Generously sprinkle the 6 remaining sponge cake triangles with powdered sugar. Heat the prong of a serving fork or the end of a metal skewer over an open flame until it is red hot. Press the hot metal into the powdered sugar to make a caramelized line. Clean the fork or skewer and repeat the process to make 3 or 4 parallel lines on each triangle. Reserve them for the tops of the tortes.

Begin building the tortes by arranging the melon in the centers of 6 plates in a triangle-shaped base, cutting the melon if necessary to match the size of the sponge cake. Top this melon with a sponge cake triangle, then add another layer of melon. Add another sponge cake layer and the last layer of melon.

Place the sponge cake tops on each torte. Place 1 scoop of sorbet at the base of each side of the torte and stand a praline triangle between each sorbet scoop and the torte. Spoon the honeydew melon coulis around the tortes. Serve at once.

Chef's Hint

In order to make this dessert easier to assemble and more stable, the pistachio spongecake can be cut to equal-sided 3-inch triangles and the melon cut accordingly.
For another simple presentation of this dessert, cut larger equal-sided triangles of the spongecake (e.g., 4½-inch edges), spread them with the vanilla pastry cream, and serve the poached melon over them, with honeydew juice on one side and a good fruit sorbet on the other. The pralines can be replaced by pistachio brittle sprinkled over the sorbet.

Kirsch and Black Walnut Baba with Cherry Compote and Vanilla-Honey Ice Cream

6 servings

In classic French pastry, a baba is a leavened cake steeped in an alcohol syrup, usually rum, and decorated with candied fruit. In this version, a cherry compote and vanilla-honey ice cream surround a baba saturated with a light kirsch syrup.

The Babas
1 recipe Brioche Dough—see p. 17

Egg wash—see p. 55

4 ounces (115 g) Black walnuts, lightly
  chopped

Light Kirsch Syrup
1 cup (240 ml) Water

2 tablespoons (30 g) Sugar

2 ounces (60 ml) Kirsch

Cherry Compote
1 cup (240 ml) Water

¼ cup (50 g) Vanilla sugar

24 ounces (670 g) Bing or Rainier cherries,
  pitted

2 tablespoons (30 ml) Lemon juice

1 ounce (30 g) Candied Lemon Zest—see
  p. 54

2 Basil leaves, cut in chiffonnade—see
  Chapter One, p. 8

Black pepper, a grind

1 recipe Vanilla-Honey Ice Cream—see
  p. 67

Equipment Needs
Ice cream machine

Saucepot

Sauté pan

Parchment-lined sheetpan

Prepare the Babas
Measure out 6, 1-ounce pieces of brioche dough on a scale, or cut pieces roughly the same size as a whole walnut. Roll them into rounds in your hands, dip in egg wash, and roll in walnuts so that the nuts adhere to the dough.

Place the babas 2½ inches apart on a parchment-lined sheetpan. Cover with plastic wrap and allow to rise in a warm place for approximately 1½ hours. Preheat the oven to 375°F. Bake for 14 to 16 minutes, or until lightly browned.

Prepare the Kirsch Syrup

In a saucepot over medium heat, combine the water and sugar until the sugar is dissolved. Stir in the kirsch. Reserve the syrup for the final assembly.

Prepare the Compote

In a sauté pan over high heat, combine the water and sugar, heat to a simmer.

Add the cherries, lemon juice, and zest. Simmer for 6 minutes. Toss the compote with the basil and grind of pepper.

Assemble the Dessert

Heat the kirsch syrup to a simmer. Drop the babas into the syrup to completely saturate them, then remove them from the liquid and set them aside.

Spoon the cherries onto 6 warm plates, mounding them slightly in the plate centers. Place a warm, kirsch-syrup-soaked baba over the cherries in the center of each plate. Place 3 scoops of ice cream around each baba. Serve at once.

Chef's Hint

An alternative to making individual babas is to form a long loaf of brioche. Brush it with egg wash, roll it in nuts of your choice, and rise it or proof it as for the individual babas. Bake the brioche at 375°F for 18 to 20 minutes. Allow it to cool before slicing it. Soak the slices in the light kirsch syrup as directed above and serve each slice with cherry compote and vanilla ice cream or a quality commercial ice cream of your choice.

Lemon Tart with Blackberries and Peppered Blackberry Coulis

6 servings

The lemon tart, a perennial favorite, is always light and refreshing. In this version, tangy lemon custard is contrasted with succulent late-summer blackberries.

Lemon Tarts

1 recipe Rich Shortdough—see p. 20

1 recipe Lemon Custard—see p. 36

Tuile Tart Rings

4 Blackberries

1 teaspoon (5 ml) Water

1 recipe Tuile Batter (optional)—see p. 31

4 cups (600 g) Blackberries, washed

1 recipe Peppered Blackberry Coulis—see p. 53

1 recipe Candied Lemon Zest—see p. 54

6 Mint leaves, cut in chiffonnade—see Chapter One, p. 8

Equipment Needs

10-inch by 14-inch or 12-inch by 16-inch Sheetpan

3½-inch-diameter Pastry cutter

Blender or food processor

Pastry wheel

Prepare the Lemon Tarts

Preheat the oven to 350°F. Prepare a 10-inch by 14-inch pan by brushing with butter and dusting with flour.

Roll the shortdough to ³/₁₆ inch thick, cut it to 10 inches by 14 inches, and fit it into the bottom of the pan.

Place in the oven. Bake for 10 minutes.

Reduce temperature to 300°F. Pour the lemon custard over the shortdough and bake for 10 to 12 minutes.

Refrigerate the pan until cooled.

Place a 3½-inch-round pastry cutter in the corner of the pan and press it downward all the way through the custard and the shortdough. Turn the cutter slightly and pull the tart out of the pan.

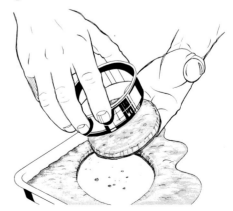

Gently slide the tart out of the cutter. Set aside. Cut 5 more tarts from the pan and reserve for final assembly.

Prepare the Tuile Tart Rings

. . . .

These tuile tart rings are an added visual and textural bonus for the dessert and may be omitted if desired.

. . . .

Preheat the oven to 375°F.

In a blender or food processor, puree the blackberries with the water. Strain to remove all seeds. Using a rubber spatula, take ¼ cup (50 g) of the tuile batter and mix it in a small bowl with the blackberry puree. Set it aside.

Spread the rest of the tuile approximately ¹⁄₁₆ inch thick in a 7-inch by 12-inch area onto a stickless sheetpan or parchment-lined pan brushed with butter.

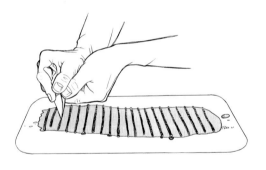

Put the blackberry tuile into a small pastry bag fitted with a very small plain tip and pipe consecutive 7-inch-long lines the width of the tuile, ½ inch apart.

Bake for 8 to 10 minutes, turning as necessary to attain even browning.

Starting at the corners, peel the tuile from the pan and quickly move it to a cutting board. Using a straight-edge pastry wheel, cut the tuile lengthwise into strips 1 inch wide by

12 inches long, returning the tuile to the oven as necessary to soften it for cutting.

Return the pieces 1 at a time to the oven for about 30 seconds, until they are softened.

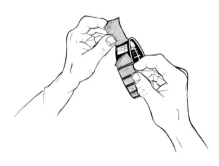

Take a strip and, using a 3½-inch-round pastry cutter as a form, wrap it around the pastry cutter, pressing at the point where the strip overlaps in order to make a 3½-inch-round ring (see diagram).

Remove the ring from the pastry cutter and repeat with the other tuile strips until you have 6 tuile tart rings with vertical, blackberry-colored stripes.

Assemble the Dessert

Cut 12 blackberries in half, lengthwise. Place 4 halves, with cut side down, approximately 1 inch apart, forming a circle in the center of each plate.

Place a lemon tart on top of the berries and place a tuile tart ring over each tart.

Stand a circle of blackberries around the edge of each tart, against the inside of each tuile tart ring. Drizzle the coulis around the tarts. Place a pinch of the zest in the centers of each tart and sprinkle the mint in the coulis.

Chef's Hint

You can omit the tuile tart rings and instead just place the blackberries or other desired, seasonal berries over the entire surface of each individual tart. This dessert can also be made as a whole 9-inch tart as follows: line a 9-inch tart pan with a 3/16-inch-thick layer of rich shortdough, then place a piece of tin foil over the shortdough. Fill the foil with an even weight, such as dried beans or rice, which will hold the shortdough in place and prevent bubbling and bake at 375°F for 12 minutes. Carefully remove the foil and dried beans from the tart, and using a pastry brush, coat the tart's interior with egg white and return it to the oven for 2$\frac{1}{2}$ to 3 minutes. This will seal the tart and keep the custard from making it soggy. Fill the pre-baked tart shell with the lemon custard and follow the same baking instructions as for the individual lemon tarts. Serve the tart well chilled. Two rows of blackberries around the inside edge of the tart are a striking touch and the peppered blackberry coulis will finish each plate nicely.

Chilled Muskmelon Soup
with Sorbets

6 servings

The mild melon flavor of this soup provides a perfect backdrop for an assortment of refreshing and flavorful sorbets.

Muskmelon Soup

2 pounds (910 g to 960 g) Muskmelon,
    approximately 1 large, peeled, seeded [or
    1½ pounds (650 g to 700 g) Cantaloupes,
    approximately 2, peeled, seeded]
3 tablespoons (45 g) Sugar
Salt, a dash

Sorbets

(choose one or more types from the list)
1 recipe Honeydew Melon Sorbet—see p. 71
1 recipe Passion Fruit Sorbet—see p. 73
1 recipe Apricot Sorbet—see p. 69
1 recipe White Peach Sorbet—see p. 75
1 recipe Plum Sorbet—see p. 73

Equipment Needs

Ice cream machine
Juicing machine (extractor) or blender

Prepare the Soup

Cut the melon into slices and process through a juicing machine to obtain approximately 6 cups (1,350 ml).

Reserve half the juice. In a saucepot over high heat, combine the other half with the sugar and salt. Reduce the liquid to ¼ of its volume (about 12 to 14 minutes).

Add the reduced juice to the reserved juice, stir, and refrigerate until well chilled.

Assemble the Dessert

Place a scoop or quenelle of each sorbet in a circular pattern in the bottoms of 6 chilled bowls. Divide the soup among the bowls. Serve at once.

. . . .
This soup may be refrigerated for 24 hours before serving.
. . . .

Chef's Hint

The number of sorbets can be limited to as few as 1 if desired. If you choose to serve 1 or 2 different sorbets rather than 5, the sorbet recipe amount will need to be doubled.

Napoleon of Vanilla Mascarpone and Peaches with White Pepper Ice Cream

6 servings

This napoleon pairs the classic flavors of peach and vanilla.

Vanilla Mascarpone

1 tablespoon (15 g) Vanilla sugar

2 teaspoons (10 ml) Water

1 teaspoon (5 ml) Vanilla extract

6 ounces (170 g) Mascarpone

Honey Wafers

1 recipe Honey Wafer Batter—see p. 31

6 Peaches, ripe, peeled

1 recipe Vanilla Sauce—see p. 48

Powdered sugar, for sprinkling

1 recipe White Pepper Ice Cream—see p. 68

Equipment Needs

Ice cream machine

Stickless sheetpan

Pastry bag with ¼-inch plain tip

Saucepot

Metal spatula

Prepare the Mascarpone

In a small saucepot over medium heat, combine the vanilla sugar, water, and extract until the sugar crystals are dissolved. Allow the syrup to cool.

In a mixing bowl, begin whipping the mascarpone on low speed. Gradually pour the vanilla syrup while watching closely. Increase the speed and whip to stiff peaks. Do not over-whip, or the mascarpone could separate.

Prepare the Honey Wafers

Preheat the oven to 400°F.

On a stickless sheetpan, with a metal spatula spread the batter thinly into 2½-inch circles about ½ inch apart. Bake for 2 to 3 minutes, watching closely, until they lightly brown.

Remove from the pan while still warm. Repeat until you have 30 wafers.

Prepare the Peaches

Slice the peaches in half, remove the pit. Cut the fruit into ¼-inch by ¼-inch strips. Reserve.

Assemble the Dessert

Fill a pastry bag fitted with a plain ¼-inch tip with the mascarpone.

In the centers of 6 plates, place 3 peach strips parallel to one another ¼ inch apart. Fill the spaces with some of the mascarpone and top with 6 honey wafers. Place 3 more peach strips on each wafer and fill the spaces with mascarpone. Continue building the napoleons until each has 5 peach/mascarpone layers and 5 wafer layers, ending with a wafer layer.

Drizzle the vanilla sauce around the napoleons.

Cut the remaining peach strips into a ¼-inch cube. Top each napoleon with a few peach cubes and sprinkle the remaining cubes in the sauce.

Sprinkle the tops lightly with some powdered sugar. Place 2 scoops of ice cream at the base of each napoleon. Serve at once.

Chef's Hint

This napoleon can be layered with baked phyllo layers instead of honey wafers. If this is desired, refer to the phyllo preparations in the chocolate crème brûlée and banana napoleon in Chapter Five (see p. 164).

Another idea is to spread the honey wafer batter in larger circles (e.g., 6-inch), bake them according to the instructions above, and while they are still hot from the oven, mold them into tulip shapes over the backs of small glasses or teacups. When they cool slightly, they will harden into this shape. The tulips could then be filled with some of the vanilla mascarpone, topped with peach strips, and served with vanilla sauce and a few scoops of white pepper ice cream or another desired flavor.

Napoleon of Vanilla Custard, Citrus, and Raspberries

6 servings

Vanilla provides a mild foundation for the bright flavors of orange, grapefruit, and raspberries

1 recipe Vanilla Custard—see p. 36

Phyllo Layers

2 sheets Phyllo—see p. 21

2 tablespoons (30 ml) Butter, melted

Powdered sugar, for sprinkling

Citrus Preparation

1 Grapefruit, peeled, sectioned

1 Orange, peeled, sectioned

8 ounces to 10 ounces (230 g to 280 g)
   Raspberries, approximately 1½ cups

1 recipe Orange Sauce—see p. 52

6 Mint leaves, cut in chiffonnade—see
   Chapter One, p. 8

Equipment Needs

7-inch by 7-inch or similar size small pan

Plastic wrap

Set of round pastry cutters

2 Sheetpans

Oven broiler or propane torch

Prepare the Custard

Line a 7-inch by 7-inch pan with plastic wrap. Pour a ½-inch-thick layer of custard into the pan. Chill in the refrigerator for about 25 minutes, or until it is set.

Using a 1-inch-round pastry cutter, cut 24 circles of the custard. Reserve on a chilled pan for the final assembly.

Prepare the Phyllo Layers

Preheat oven to 350°F.

Turn a sheetpan upside down and cover the back with parchment. Place 1 sheet of phyllo on a cutting board, brush with the butter, and sprinkle with powdered sugar. Top with the second sheet of phyllo and press the 2 layers firmly together.

Place a 2½-inch-round pastry cutter on 1 corner of the phyllo and press it firmly while turning to cut out a phyllo circle (or simply draw a paring knife around the pastry cutter). Continue cutting the circles in rows until you have 24. Transfer the circles to the parchment-covered sheetpan back. Place a second piece of parchment over the phyllo circles. Top with a second sheetpan, right side up.

Weight this sheetpan with either a cast-iron skillet or a foil-covered brick. Bake for approximately 12 to 15 minutes, or until the circles are evenly browned. Transfer the circles to a clean sheetpan and sprinkle them lightly with powdered sugar.

Use a propane torch in sweeping motions or a broiler to melt the sugar, watching very closely so as not to burn the circles. The sugar should melt and caramelize in spots, possibly sending off a little smoke. Set aside.

Assemble the Dessert

Place a custard circle in the center of each of 6 plates. Evenly space 3 raspberries around them so they touch the custards. Place 1 citrus piece between each raspberry, again touching the custards, and place a phyllo circle on top. Place a custard circle in the centers of each of the 6 phyllo circles. Place the raspberries and citrus pieces around each custard as before. Continue building the napoleons in this arrangement until each napoleon contains 4 custards and 4 phyllo circles.

Drizzle the orange sauce around each napoleon, sprinkle the sauce with some of the mint chiffonnade, and serve at once.

Chef's Hint

This is a good example of a dessert idea with several options for personal expression. Different fruits can be substituted for the citrus or raspberries, such as other berries, plums, or apricots, depending upon their availability. The phyllo layers can be substituted with honey wafers from the vanilla mascarpone and peach napoleon, or the phyllo can be cut into different shapes, such as triangles or rectangles, which would also eliminate the scraps. The citrus-raspberry-vanilla combination is a wonderful one but other fruit combinations can be substituted, such as wild strawberries (frais de bois) or larger strawberries cut into pieces and stacked with pieces of plum, or apricots stacked with black raspberries.

Nectarine and Orange Tartlet with Nectarine Puree and Sorbet

6 servings

This dessert of ripe nectarines paired with oranges is a lively combination suited to the bright days of summer.

Orange Tartlets

1 recipe Rich Shortdough—see p. 20

½ cup (40 g) Almonds, sliced or chopped, and roasted

1 recipe Orange Custard—see p. 37

Nectarine Puree

6 ounces (175 g) Nectarines, approximately 1 large or 2 small, pitted

½ cup (120 ml) Water

2 teaspoons (10 g) Sugar

1 teaspoon (5 ml) Lemon juice

1 Orange, peeled, sectioned—see p. 81

3 Nectarines, pitted, halved

Powdered sugar, for sprinkling

1 recipe Nectarine Sorbet—see p. 73

3 Basil leaves, cut in chiffonnade—see Chapter One, p. 8

Equipment Needs

Ice cream machine

2½-inch-diameter Steel rings

Set of round pastry cutters

Saucepot

Fine chinois or cheesecloth

Blender

Prepare the Tartlets

Preheat the oven to 350°F.

Put 8, 5-inch-square pieces of aluminum foil on a sheetpan. Place 1, 2½-inch-diameter, 1½-inch-tall steel ring (or use tart rings or tins) on top of each piece of foil and wrap the excess foil up around the outside surface of the rings. Brush the inside bottoms and sides of the rings lightly with melted butter and dust lightly with flour.

Roll the shortdough to ³/₁₆ inch thick. With a 2½-inch-round pastry cutter, cut 6 circles and fit them into the bottom of each ring. Place in the oven. Bake for 10 minutes, then remove.

Reduce the temperature to 300°F. Sprinkle the almonds over the shortdough circles. Pour the custard over the almonds, dividing the custard evenly among the rings, and bake for 10 to 12 minutes.

Remove the pan from the oven and allow to cool to room temperature. Refrigerate until chilled, then peel the foil from the sides of the rings, draw a paring knife carefully around the custard, and remove the rings and foil. Refrigerate the tartlets until final assembly.

Prepare the Puree

In a small saucepot on medium heat, sim-

mer all the ingredients for the puree for 8 minutes. Allow to cool.

Puree in a blender. Pass the puree through a fine chinois or 2 layers of cheesecloth. Reserve.

Assemble the Dessert

Cut the orange sections crossways into thirds. Set aside.

Place the nectarine halves, cut side down, on a cutting board. Using a sharp paring knife, slice them into $1/16$-inch slices. Feather about 6 to 8 of the slices evenly over the tops of the tartlets. Spoon the puree into the centers of 6 plates and spread it to 6-inch circles. Place the remaining nectarine slices on the puree, pointing out from each center, about $1/4$ inch apart, in a loose pinwheel pattern. Place a piece of orange segment between each nectarine slice. Lightly sprinkle the tartlets with some powdered sugar.

Using a propane torch in sweeping motions or a broiler, melt the sugar and lightly caramelize the thin nectarine slices covering the tartlets.

Place a tartlet in the center of each plate and surround with 2 scoops or quenelles of nectarine sorbet. Sprinkle the chiffonnade around the tartlets. Serve at once.

Chef's Hint

This dessert can be made as a whole 9-inch tart by simply doubling the orange custard recipe and following the whole 9-inch tart instructions in the chef's hint for the lemon tart, replacing the blackberries with nectarine slices spiraling from the center. The nectarine sorbet can be omitted if desired or replaced with a good commercial sorbet.

Tropical Fruit Compote with Lime and Passion Fruit Sorbets

6 servings

This is a light and refreshing dessert of barely poached ripe tropical fruits with Tahitian vanilla and intensely flavored sorbets.

Fruit

1 Papaya
¼ Pineapple
1 Mango
2 Kiwi

Sauternes Vanilla Syrup

1 cup (240 ml) Sauternes wine
½ cup (120 ml) Water
¼ cup (50 g) Vanilla sugar
1 Vanilla bean, split, scraped

1 recipe Passion Fruit Sorbet—see p. 73
1 recipe Lime Sorbet—see p. 72
1 recipe Roasted Coconut Shavings—see
     p. 47

Equipment Needs

Ice cream machine
Saucepot
Saucepan

Prepare the Fruit

Using a sharp knife, peel all the fruit. Cut the papaya in half lengthwise, scoop all the seeds out. Cut each half into 2½-inch-long by ¾-inch-thick slices. Set aside.

Remove the fibrous core from the center of the pineapple. Cut the ¼ pineapple lengthwise into ½-inch-thick strips. Cut the strips crossways into thirds. Set aside.

Cut the mango flesh from the pit. Cut it into 2½-inch-long by ½-inch-thick strips. Set aside.

Cut the kiwi lengthwise into ½-inch-thick wedges. Set aside.

Cover and refrigerate the fruit until final assembly.

Prepare the Syrup

In a saucepot over high heat, combine all ingredients. Bring to a simmer. Reserve.

Assemble the Dessert

. . . .
Depending on the ripeness of the fruits, cooking times will vary. If the fruit is very ripe, it only needs to be heated through in the syrup. Quite often, 1 fruit may not be as ripe as the others and may require more cooking time.
. . . .

In a saucepan on high heat, cook the syrup. When the syrup begins to boil, add the pineapple slices, and reduce heat to low. Add the mango, then the papaya, and finally the kiwi.

When the fruits are properly poached and warmed (in approximately 1 minute), spoon them and some of the syrup into 6 warm bowls. Place 1 scoop each of the sorbets in the centers of each compote, sprinkle with the shavings, and serve at once.

Chef's Hint

This simple dessert of poached fruits with sorbets can be personalized in many ways. Change the flavor or varieties of sorbet to your tastes or seasons. Add or subtract different fruits to correspond with or accentuate a particular season. Fruits such as melon, plums, peaches, or pears would be good alternatives. A wonderful serving idea is to present the warm, poached fruit in a large serving bowl with the sorbet(s) on the side, and spoon the servings into small bowls or dessert goblets at the table.

Peach Crème Brûlée Napoleon with Green Tea Sauce and Peach Coulis

6 servings

The flavors of peaches and vanilla are featured in this napoleon comprised of vanilla-infused crème brûlée, luscious ripe peach slices, and crisp, thin puff pastry layers.

Crisp Puff Pastry Layers

½ sheet (7½ inches by 12 inches) Puff Pastry
    —see p. 18
1 Egg white
Powdered sugar, for sprinkling

Crème Brûlée Squares

1 recipe Vanilla Crème Brûlée Custard—see
    p. 37
7¼ ounces (200 g) Peaches, approximately
    1½, peeled, cut into ¼-inch dice

Peach-Lemon Salad Garnish

¼ Peach
4 Mint leaves, cut in chiffonnade—see
    Chapter One, p. 8
1 recipe Candied Lemon Zest—see p. 54

2 Peaches
Sugar, for sprinkling
1 recipe Green Tea Sauce—see p. 51
1 recipe Peach Coulis—see p. 53

Equipment Needs

Pastry wheel
Parchment-lined sheetpan
10-inch by 14-inch or 12-inch by 16-inch
    Sheetpan
Metal spatula
Oven broiler or propane torch

Prepare the Pastry

Brush the top of the puff pastry with the egg white and sprinkle generously with powdered sugar. Beginning from the narrower edge, roll the puff pastry as tightly as possible.

Wrap the pastry roll in plastic wrap and place in the freezer for several hours, or until it is frozen solid.

123

Preheat the oven to 375°F. With a sharp knife, cut a ½-inch-thick crossways slice of the roll. Place it on a work surface dusted with powdered sugar.

With a rolling pin, roll the pastry extremely thin, dusting with powdered sugar as necessary to keep it from sticking.

With a pastry wheel, cut as many 2¼-inch- by 2¼-inch-square pieces as possible. Place them 2 inches apart on a parchment-lined sheetpan. Continue the process until you have 24 squares.

Bake for 4 to 6 minutes, or until lightly browned and crisp. Reserve.

Prepare the Crème Brûlée Squares

Reduce the oven heat to 300°F. Lightly brush the inside of a 10-inch by 12-inch baking pan with oil. Cut a piece of plastic food wrap exactly 10 inches by 12 inches and fit it into the bottom of the pan, smoothing the surface to remove all trapped air bubbles between the metal and plastic.

Pour the crème brûlée into the pan, being sure to cover the plastic entirely. Sprinkle the diced peaches onto the crème brûlée, distributing them evenly.

Place the pan in a larger, flat pan. Fill this pan with approximately ¼ inch of water, creating a water bath for the crème brûlée, so that it cooks gently. Bake until the custard is firm—approximately 25 minutes. When the pan is gently tapped on its side, the custard should not ripple, or have any liquid spots. Remove from the oven. When the cooked crème brûlée nears room temperature, place in the freezer until it is very firm but not solid (about 40 minutes).

Follow the method on p. 33 for removing crème brûlée from the pan.

Cut the custard into 24, 2-inch by 2-inch squares. Transfer the squares with a metal spatula, allowing at least ½ inch of space between them, onto the back of a metal sheetpan. Wrap the remaining custard with plastic and save it for extra desserts, if necessary.

Prepare the Garnish

Cut the ¼ peach into 1/16-inch matchstick-size strips. Place the peach, mint, and lemon zest in a bowl. Mix gently with a spoon. Reserve.

Assemble the Dessert

Slice the 2 peaches lengthwise into 1/8-inch-thick slices. Place 2 on top of each crème brûlée square. Sprinkle a liberal layer of sugar over the peaches. Carefully caramelize, using a propane torch in small sweeping motions, or under a broiler, turning as necessary.

Using a metal spatula, transfer 6 crème brûlée squares to the center of 6 plates. Top each with a puff pastry square. Repeat with another crème brûlée square and another puff pastry square until each napoleon has 4 layers, ending with pastry.

Top with a pinch of the garnish. Surround with a drizzle of the sauce and coulis. Serve at once.

Chef's Hint

Another option for presenting the same delicious flavors of these napoleons in a simpler way is to stir the peach slices into the custard and bake in individual porcelain ramekins or crème brûlée dishes or in a single large porcelain casserole dish. Place the individual dishes or the large casserole dish on a larger pan that has edges and pour some water in this larger pan to create a water bath that will allow the delicate custard to bake gently. To bake the individual dishes, reduce the baking time to approximately 15 minutes; for the large casserole dish, follow the baking instructions for the squares. To check doneness, tap the edge of the dish. Cooked custard will remain still, the top will not move.

If baked whole, the custard can be scooped, still warm, into serving bowls or small dessert goblets, and drizzled with the peach coulis and green tea sauce if desired.

Poached Plum Tart with Ginger Custard, Plum Sorbet, and Warm Plum Compote

6 servings

In this tart, the plum is poached whole, filled with a ginger-infused custard, and set atop plum-sorbet-layered hazelnut meringues.

1 recipe Hazelnut Meringue—see p. 30

Plums and Poaching Liquid
6 Plums, peeled, pitted, stones removed—see p. 81
1 cup (240 ml) Sauternes wine
1 Lime, zested, juiced—see p. 54
¼ cup (100 g) Sugar
1 cup (240 ml) Water
White pepper, a dash
1 Vanilla bean, split, scraped

Plum Compote
3 Plums
1 cup (240 ml) Poaching liquid

1 recipe Plum Sorbet—see p. 73
1 recipe Ginger Pastry Cream—see p. 35
Powdered sugar, for sprinkling

Equipment Needs
Ice cream machine
10-inch by 14-inch or 12-inch by 16-inch Sheetpan
3-inch-diameter Pastry cutter
Parisienne scoop or melon baller
Saucepan
Pastry bag with ¼-inch plain tip
Metal spatula

Prepare the Meringue
Preheat the oven to 350°F.

Line a sheetpan with parchment, generously brush with butter, dust with flour. (Be sure to adhere the parchment to the sheetpan

127

with some oil.) Spread the meringue batter on the sheetpan to an area of 10 inches by 14 inches and approximately $1/16$ inch thick. Bake for 12 minutes, turning as necessary to achieve even browning.

While the meringue is still hot, cut 12, 3-inch meringue circles with a round pastry cutter. Return the pan to the oven as necessary to reheat it to make the meringue pliable and prevent cracking. Reserve the circles for final assembly.

Poach the Plums

Set the 6 plums in a small saucepan. In a bowl, combine the wine, lime, sugar, water, white pepper, and vanilla bean. Pour this poaching liquid over the plums and place the pan on medium heat. Bring to a simmer, then turn the heat to low. Continue to simmer until the plums are slightly softened but still retain their shape (about 8 minutes). Reserve the plums and the poaching liquid.

Prepare the Compote

Halve the 3 plums, remove the stones, and slice each half into $1/4$-inch wedges. In a saucepan over medium heat, combine the wedges with the plum poaching liquid. Simmer for 6 to 8 minutes, or until the plum slices are softened. Reserve.

Assemble the Dessert

With a metal spatula, spread an even $1/2$-inch layer of plum sorbet onto 6 meringue circles, top them with the remaining 6 meringue circles, and place in the freezer. Fill a pastry bag fitted with a plain $1/4$-inch tip with the pastry cream and fill the poached plums.

Spoon the compote in the center of each plate to an area of about 5 inches. Center a meringue/sorbet circle on top of each compote. Dust lightly with powdered sugar. Top each circle with a filled plum, filling side down, and serve at once.

Chef's Hint

The meringue circles can be made a day ahead and stored in a sealed container, and the plum compote can be made a day ahead, refrigerated in a covered container and simply heated at the last moment.
A simpler version of this dessert with the same flavor combination can be made by replacing the hazelnut meringue circles with a sprinkle of hazelnut brittle (see p. 46) over the filled poached plum, plum compote, and two scoops of plum sorbet.

Prune Plum Soup with Black Sesame Brittle Ice Cream

6 servings

Prune plums, available in August and September, make a refreshing chilled soup. In this version, black sesame brittle ice cream provides an added richness and tasty surprise.

Black Sesame Tuile Strips (Optional)
1 recipe Tuile Batter—see p. 31
1 tablespoon (8 g) Black sesame seeds

Prune Plum Soup
16 Prune plums
5 cups (1200 ml) Water
1½ cups (360 ml) Cabernet Sauvignon wine
¾ cup (150 g) Sugar
2 Cinnamon sticks
3 Cloves, whole
1 teaspoon (5 g) Gingerroot, chopped
1 teaspoon (1 g) Coriander, ground
½ teaspoon (.5 g) Black pepper, ground
1 Vanilla bean, split, scraped

1 recipe Black Sesame Brittle Ice Cream—see p. 59

Equipment Needs
Ice cream machine
Stickless sheetpan
Pastry wheel
Blender

Prepare the Tuile Strips

. . . .
These black sesame tuile strips are an added textural bonus for this dessert and may be omitted if desired.
. . . .

Preheat the oven to 375°F.

On a stickless sheetpan, spread the tuile approximately ¹⁄₁₆ inch thick in a 4-inch by 6-inch area. Sprinkle the sesame seeds evenly over the tuile.

Bake for 8 to 10 minutes, turning as necessary to attain even browning.

Starting at the corners, peel the tuile from the pan, and quickly move it to a cutting board.

Using a straight-edge pastry wheel or a French knife, cut ¹⁄₁₆-inch- to ⅛-inch-wide by 4-inch-long strips, returning the tuile to the oven periodically as necessary to soften it for cutting. Reserve.

Prepare the Soup

Remove the stones from the plums. In a large saucepot on low heat, combine with the remaining ingredients. Simmer, stirring occasionally, for 1 hour.

Allow to cool slightly. Puree in a blender and strain through a fine chinois or 2 layers of cheesecloth. Cover loosely and refrigerate until well chilled. Or, surround the container with ice to make it very cold. The soup may be kept chilled for 24 hours before serving.

Assemble the Dessert

Divide the soup among 6 bowls and sprinkle some of the tuile strips in the centers. Float 2 quenelles or scoops of the ice cream on top of the tuile strips. Serve at once.

Chef's Hint

To make this soup with the more common, larger dark-skinned plums, simply reduce the number of plums in the recipe by half. The ice cream may be replaced with a commercial version of your choice. To make an ice cream quenelle, see p. 58.

Raspberry, Rhubarb, Gooseberry, and Pink Peppercorn Compote with a Crème Fraîche Ice Cream Cone

6 servings

This simple recipe pays tribute to a classic dessert favorite—berries with cream. The sugar and pink peppercorns serve to season the berries and bring out their best flavors.

Ice Cream Cones

Butter, melted, for brushing

2 ounces (60 g) Raspberries

1 recipe Tuile Batter (optional)—see p. 31

Compote

2 (240 g) Rhubarb stalks

½ cup (120 ml) Water

¼ cup (50 g) Sugar

2 teaspoons (2 g) Pink peppercorns, ground, roasted

Salt, a dash

10.5 ounces (300 g) Gooseberries, approximately 1½ cups

10.5 ounces (300 g) Raspberries, approximately 1½ cups

1 recipe Crème Fraîche and Black Pepper Ice Cream (eliminate the black pepper)—see p. 63

Equipment Needs

Ice cream machine

Metal pastry horn mold

Parchment paper

Pastry bag with very small plain tip

Prepare the Cones

. . . .

These ice cream cones are an added visual and textural bonus for this dessert and may be omitted or replaced with simple tuile cookies if desired (see p. 31).

. . . .

Preheat the oven to 375°F.

Wrap a piece of paper around a metal pastry horn. Mark it with a pencil to establish the size of an ice cream cone if it were laid out on a flat surface. Cut the rounded triangle shape from the paper with a pair of scissors. Place the shape onto a piece of parchment and,

132

with a pencil, trace around the shape. Continue tracing 5 more shapes, each at least 1 inch apart.

Turn the parchment over and place it onto a sheetpan. Lightly brush the parchment with the melted butter. Set aside.

In a blender or food processor, puree the raspberries. Strain through a fine chinois or sieve to remove all the seeds.

Using a rubber spatula, take ⅓ cup (50 g) of the tuile batter. In a small bowl, mix thoroughly with the raspberry puree. Put it in a small pastry bag fitted with a very small plain tip.

Using a metal spatula, thinly spread the plain tuile within the lines of the triangle shapes that show through the parchment (so the sheetpan surface is just barely visible through the batter).

Pipe the raspberry tuile in lines over the triangle shapes, ½ inch apart.

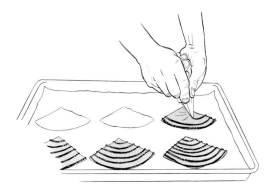

Bake for 8 to 10 minutes, turning as necessary to attain even browning.

Starting at the corners, peel a triangle shape from the parchment, and while it is still hot, quickly form it into a cone shape around the metal pastry horn. Return the shapes to the oven as necessary to soften them for molding.

Remove the cone from the pastry horn and repeat with the other triangle shapes until you have 6 cones.

Prepare the Compote/Assemble the Dessert

Slice the rhubarb lengthwise into ⅛-inch strips, then julienne into 1-inch-long pieces.

In a saucepan over medium heat, simmer the water, sugar, peppercorns, and salt. Add the rhubarb and simmer for about 1 minute, or until tender. Add the gooseberries, simmer for 30 seconds, and add the raspberries, lightly tossing them until they are just warmed through.

Spoon the mixture into 6 warm bowls and place a cone filled with ice cream on the top of each compote. Serve at once.

Chef's Hint

Substitutions for the berries can be made throughout the summer months, according to availability. For example, raspberries could be replaced by blackberries, or gooseberries by red currants.

Roasted Black Mission Figs with Chèvre Ice Cream and Warm Fig-Port Broth

6 servings

Some diners prefer a small amount of cheese, ripe fruit, and a glass of port after a meal to a sugary dessert. This example blends these classic ingredients in a delicious, not-too-sweet preparation.

The Figs

12 Black mission figs
1 tablespoon (15 ml) Olive oil
1 tablespoon (8 g) Powdered sugar

Fig-Port Broth

Reserved fig flesh and tops
1¼ cups (300 ml) Port
1 cup (240 ml) Water
2 teaspoons (10 g) Sugar
¼ teaspoon (.25 g) Cinnamon, ground
Black pepper, a grind
Salt, a dash

1 recipe Chèvre Ice Cream—see p. 61
1 recipe Almond Brittle—see p. 46

Equipment Needs

Ice cream machine
Parisienne scoop (melon baller)
Saucepot
Blender

Prepare the Figs

Place the figs and olive oil in a bowl and toss until the figs are coated. Place the figs under a broiler. Watch closely, turning the fruit occasionally from side to side for a few minutes until they darken and shrivel slightly.

. . . .

The figs could also be roasted on a wire baking rack in a 375°F oven for 12 to 14 minutes.

. . . .

Cut the tops off the figs to expose a ½-inch to 1-inch circle of flesh. Using a parisienne scoop, scoop some of the flesh out of the centers of the figs to make room for the ice cream. Reserve the tops and fig flesh for the broth. Dust the figs with the powdered sugar and set aside.

Prepare the Broth

In a saucepot over medium heat, combine all ingredients. Reduce the liquid by half (about 15 to 18 minutes). Remove from the heat and allow to cool slightly.

When blending a hot liquid, be very careful, as the released steam can cause the top to come off.

Pour the slightly cooled liquid into a blender, put the top on, place a towel over the blender, and secure with your hand. Blend at high speed for 20 seconds. Pass through a fine chinois or 2 layers of cheesecloth. Set aside.

Assemble the Dessert

Warm 6 bowls. Fill each fig with a scoop of ice cream and place 2 of them in each of the bowls. Pour the broth into the bowls and top the ice creams with the brittle. Serve at once.

Chef's Hint

The figs can be filled with goat cheese instead of chèvre ice cream, then topped with the almond or hazelnut brittle. A nut-flavored ice cream, such as hazelnut, would also be a fitting replacement for the chèvre (see p. 64).

Roasted Nectarines and Bing Cherries with Pine Nut Nougat and Bing Cherry Sorbet

6 servings

This dessert reminds me of the whole baked, spiced apples in the holidays of my childhood, though this summer fruit recipe is a bit more delicate. The process of oven roasting the nectarines and cherries in this dessert intensifies and enhances their flavors.

6 Nectarines, ripe
1 recipe Pine Nut Nougat—see p. 46
14 ounces (390 g) Bing cherries
Powdered sugar, for sprinkling
1 recipe Vanilla Sauce—see p. 48
1 recipe Bing Cherry Sorbet—see p. 69

Equipment Needs
Ice cream machine
2 Sheetpans
1-inch-diameter Pastry cutter

Fill the Nectarines

Press a 1-inch pastry cutter downward into the top of the nectarine until it meets the pit. Remove it, then press the cutter into the bottom until it meets the pit. Slide a paring knife into the round cut to free the nectarine pit and core and push the core out of the nectarine. Repeat the process for the 5 remaining nectarines.

Stand the nectarines on a sheetpan. Using a pastry bag or spoon, fill the cores with the nougat. At this point, refrigerate the nectar-

ines for up to 1 hour or proceed to final assembly.

Roast the Cherries

Preheat the oven to 400°F.

Pit the cherries and place them on a sheet-pan. Roast them in the oven for 14 minutes.

Assemble the Dessert

Place the pan with the nectarines in the oven and roast for 20 minutes.

Sprinkle the nectarines lightly with powdered sugar and place them in the centers of 6 warm plates. Place the cherries around each nectarine and drizzle the sauce over them. Place 2 scoops of the sorbet beside each nectarine. Serve at once.

Chef's Hint

Nougat is commonly made of egg whites, honey or sugar, and some type of nut, usually almonds or hazelnuts. It is baked in sheets and traditionally takes the form of a candy. For this recipe, I wanted to use pine nuts but the nougat filling can also be made with any nut of your choice.

Strawberry, Red Wine, and Caramel Compote with Strawberry Ice Cream

6 servings

In this dessert, ripe strawberries are seasoned with the flavors of red wine and caramel.

1 recipe Strawberry Ice Cream—see p. 67

Compote
½ cup (100 g) Sugar
1 cup (240 ml) Merlot or Pinot Noir wine
4 cups (800 g) Strawberries, washed, hulled, cut lengthwise into 6ths

Equipment Needs
Ice cream machine
Saucepan

Prepare the Compote
In a saucepan on high heat, melt the sugar. Watch closely as it begins to caramelize. When the sugar turns a dark amber and begins to smoke, carefully pour in the wine. Stir as the caramel dissolves and the mixture begins to simmer. Add the strawberries and simmer for 1 minute.

Assemble the Dessert
Spoon the strawberries into 6 bowls. Place 2 quenelles or scoops of ice cream in the centers of each compote. Serve at once.

Chef's Hint

Other soft fruits would take very well to the seasoning ideas of this utterly simple yet flavor-filled dessert: peaches, apricots, plums, nectarines, or even a combination of any of those. A different flavored ice cream such as a nut variety, vanilla-honey, black sesame brittle (p. 59), or a commercial one of your choice would complete the dessert. To make quenelles, see p. 58.

Strawberry Tart with a Warm Rhubarb Center

6 servings

Here's a version of the familiar summer pie: strawberry-rhubarb. These colorful tarts are a perfect ending for an open-air lunch or dinner.

1 recipe Rich Shortdough—see p. 20

Almond Brittle Tops and Coronets
¾ cup (150 g) Sugar
½ ounce (15 g) Almonds

Rhubarb Compote
2 (240 g) Rhubarb stalks
¼ cup (100 g) Sugar
¼ cup (60 ml) Water
½ teaspoon (.5 g) Pink peppercorns, roasted, ground
Salt, a dash

45 to 50 Strawberries, small to medium, washed, hulled
1 recipe Strawberry Coulis—see p. 53
6 Mint leaves, cut in chiffonnade—see Chapter One, p. 8

Equipment Needs
3½-inch-diameter Pastry cutter
Sheetpan
Food processor
Metal pastry horn mold
Saucepan

Prepare the Shortdough Circles
Preheat the oven to 350°F.

On a floured work surface, roll the shortdough to ⅛ inch thick. Using a round pastry cutter, make 6, 3½-inch circles.

Rest the circles in the refrigerator for 15 minutes, then place them on a parchment-lined sheetpan. Bake for 12 to 14 minutes, or until lightly browned. Set aside.

Prepare the Almond Brittle
In a saucepan over high heat, melt the sugar. When it begins to caramelize, stir with a spoon. When the sugar is light amber and completely melted, immediately remove from the heat and stir in the almonds. Pour the mixture out onto a lightly oiled sheetpan and allow to cool.

Pulverize the hardened mixture in a food processor until it is very fine. Lightly recoat the sheetpan with oil and transfer the pulverized nut mixture to a sifter. Shake the sifter over the oiled sheetpan to evenly cover its surface with about ¹/₁₆ inch of mixture.

With the oven still at 350°, bake the brittle for about 6 minutes, or until the caramelized sugar crystals melt and form a continuous, super-thin sheet and the nuts turn light brown.

Using the 3½-inch-round pastry cutter, cut 6 circles from the brittle. Return the pan to the oven as necessary to make the brittle pliable enough to cut without breaking the circles. It may be necessary to cut the circles from the melted brittle by drawing a paring knife around the pastry cutter.

Peel the circles from the sheetpan while they are still warm by lifting one side of the circle with a paring knife or a small spatula. Working quickly, peel the entire circle from the pan and lay it on a flat surface so that it hardens perfectly flat as it cools.

Using a metal pastry horn as a guide, cut a pattern from a piece of paper in the shape of a small coronet. Warm the remaining brittle in the oven; then using a paring knife, cut around the paper coronet pattern.

Working quickly, peel the brittle piece from the pan. Quickly shape the brittle around

the pointed end of the pastry horn, then remove it as soon as it cools slightly; it will retain its shape. Continue warming the brittle, cutting and reforming coronets, until you have 6. Using the tip of a knife heated on the stovetop, apply heat to the center of a brittle circle, then poke the point of a coronet through the circle, and hold it until it hardens. Continue this process with the remaining coronets and circles. Reserve.

Prepare the Compote
Cut the rhubarb lengthwise into ¼-inch-wide strips. Cut them crossways into ½-inch-long pieces. In a saucepan over medium heat, combine the pieces and the remaining ingredients. Simmer until the rhubarb is tender and slightly sweetened (about 10 minutes). Set aside.

Prepare the Strawberries
Trim ⅛ inch off the tops and ¼ inch off the tips of all the strawberries. Trim 18 of them to the exact same height and set aside.

Cut the remaining strawberries in half from top to bottom and reserve.

Assemble the Dessert

Stand 3 of the whole strawberries 2 inches apart, in a circle in the centers of each of 6 plates. Place a shortdough circle on top of the strawberries and line a row of the halved strawberries, cut side facing out, around the edge of each circle.

Fill the centers of the tarts with a few spoonfuls of the warmed compote and top each with a brittle circle. Surround each tart with 5 pieces of the remaining rhubarb and a drizzle of the coulis. Slice some wedges from the remaining strawberry halves, place them in the coronets on top of the tarts, and sprinkle with the mint. Serve at once.

Chef's Hint

The brittle circles could be omitted and the tart served with an open top. Simply don't trim the tips from the strawberries to be placed around the edge of the shortdough circles.

Strawberries and Honey in a Pistachio Popover with Champagne Semifreddo

6 servings

Strawberries and champagne fill this popover with flavors of early summer celebrations.

4 cups (500 g) Strawberries, washed, hulled

¼ cup (60 ml) Champagne

½ cup (160 g) Honey

White pepper, a dash

Popovers

1 recipe Pistachio Popover Batter—see p. 29

1 Egg white

2 tablespoons (20 g) Pistachios, lightly chopped

1 recipe Strawberry Coulis—see p. 53

1 recipe Champagne Semifreddo—see p. 40

1 recipe Pistachio Brittle—see p. 46

Equipment Needs

Muffin pan or 2¼-inch-tall timbale molds

Saucepan

Prepare the Strawberries

Quarter the strawberries. Place in a small bowl and set aside.

In a saucepan over medium heat, whisk together the champagne, honey, and pepper to a simmer.

Toss the strawberries with the warm champagne mixture and allow them to macerate at room temperature for 1 hour, stirring occasionally.

Prepare the Popovers

Preheat the oven to 400°F.

Fill 6 cavities of a stickless muffin pan, or a muffin pan that has been brushed with butter and dusted with flour, ⅔ of the way up with the batter.

. . . .

You can substitute ⅓- or ½-cup ceramic ramekins or 2¼-inch-tall timbale molds for the muffin pan.

. . . .

Bake for 15 minutes, then reduce temperature to 350°F. Continue baking for 12 minutes. Remove popovers from the pan, brush

tops with egg white, and sprinkle generously with the pistachios.

Return to the oven for 6 to 8 minutes to adhere the pistachios to the tops. Reserve.

Assemble the Dessert

Insert the tip of a paring knife into the top of the popovers and pull an approximately 2-inch piece up to expose the hollow center. Place each popover in the center of 6 plates and drop a spoonful of the semifreddo into each. Fill to the very top with the marinated strawberries and drizzle the coulis around each.

Drop 5 of the remaining strawberry quarters in the coulis around each popover and spoon 5 small quenelles or scoops of semifreddo next to each strawberry quarter. Sprinkle some brittle over the coulis and semifreddo quenelles and serve at once.

Chef's Hint

To simply this dessert and still retain the core flavors, omit the popovers themselves and serve the mascerated strawberries in small bowls or dessert goblets with the semifreddo and a sprinkle of the pistachio brittle (see p. 46). If you serve with the popovers, the number of semifreddo quenelles or scoops can be reduced to 2 or 3, or the semifreddo can be replaced with a quality commercial strawberry ice cream.

An Ensemble of Apricot: Tart, Strudel, Sorbet, and Ravioli

6 servings

In this dish, 4 different, small preparations of apricots celebrate the versatility and delightful flavor of this fruit.

Apricot Linzer Tart

1 recipe Three-Nut Linzer Dough—see
    p. 22
3 Apricots
Egg Wash
1/2 recipe Vanilla Pastry Cream—see p. 34

Strudel

3 1/2 ounces (100 g) Apricots, dried
1 ounce (30 g) Cherries, dried
1/2 cup (120 ml) Water
1 tablespoon (15 m) Brandy
Nutmeg, a dash
Salt, a dash
1 sheet Phyllo—see p. 21
Butter, melted, for brushing
Powdered sugar, for sprinkling

Ravioli

4 Apricots
1 tablespoon (15 ml) Water
2 teaspoons (10 g) Sugar
1 recipe Candied Ginger, chopped fine—see
    p. 55
1 recipe Vanilla Pasta—see p. 22

1 recipe Tuile Batter—see p. 31

Apricot Halves

3 Apricots (pitted)
Water
Powdered sugar, for sprinkling

Apricot Compote

3 Apricots
1/4 cup (60 ml) Water
1 tablespoon (15 g) Sugar
1/2 Vanilla bean, scraped

1 recipe Apricot Sorbet—see p. 69
1 recipe Apricot Coulis—see p. 52
Powdered sugar, for sprinkling

Equipment Needs

Ice cream machine
Food processor
Small pasta machine
Metal spatula
Pastry wheel
1 3/4-inch-diameter Fluted pastry cutter
Whisk
Serving fork or metal skewer

Prepare the Tart

Generously sprinkle the work surface with flour. Roll a piece of the linzer dough to 10 inches by 5 inches by ¼ inch thick. Using a French knife, cut the dough to 9 inches by 4 inches.

Transfer the rectangle to a parchment-lined sheetpan. Cut a ⅜-inch by 9-inch strip from the 2 sides of the rectangles. Brush the top of the tart with egg wash along each 9-inch edge. Place each ⅜-inch strip on top of the 9-inch edge of the linzer rectangle. Chill for several minutes.

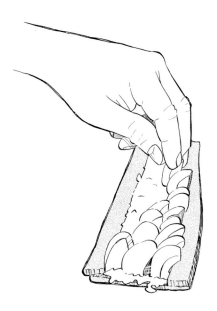

Cut the apricots in half, remove the stones, and cut the halves into ¼-inch wedges. Cut the wedges in half crossways. Spread the pastry cream between the edges of the linzer tart rectangle. Stand the apricot pieces, points up, in 3 parallel rows, the length of the tart. Refrigerate until final assembly.

Prepare the Strudel

Roughly chop the dried apricots into ½-inch pieces. In a saucepot on medium heat, combine the apricots with the next 5 ingredients. Simmer the fruit for 6 minutes, set aside to cool.

Spread out the sheet of phyllo, brush with butter, and sprinkle lightly with powdered sugar. Fold the sheet in half lengthwise by lifting the 2 top corners and aligning them atop the 2 bottom corners. Brush the top layer with butter. You should now have a 6-inch by 15-inch rectangle.

Spoon the cooled strudel filling in an even line along the edge of the 15-inch side and roll the strudel tightly, pressing out any trapped air along the way. Set the strudel on a sheetpan lined with parchment. Reserve.

Prepare the Ravioli

Cut the apricots in half and remove the stones. Set 1 apricot aside and roughly chop the remaining 3 into ½-inch pieces.

In a saucepot over medium heat, gently cook the chopped apricot, water, and sugar.

Stir occasionally, reducing the fruits' volume by 1/3 and making the mixture's consistency similar to that of jam or preserves. The water will evaporate and the fruit will begin to caramelize on the bottom of the pan.

Cut the remaining apricot into 1/4-inch cubes. Fold the cubes and candied ginger into the reduced apricot mixture.

Roll a sheet of pasta in a strip approximately 14 inches long to the thinnest width of your pasta machine. Egg wash 1/2 the length of pasta.

Using either a very small ice cream scoop or a spoon, scoop 6 mounds of filling measuring 1 inch in diameter onto the egg-washed end of the pasta, in 2 evenly spaced rows. Each mound should be approximately 1/2 inch apart (see diagram).

Fold the empty pasta half over the fillings. Carefully seal the top layer of pasta to the bottom around the fillings without disrupting their shape. With a 1 3/4-inch-diameter fluted pastry cutter, cut out each ravioli and pinch its edges well to seal in the filling. Set aside.

Prepare the Tuile Tubes

Preheat the oven to 375°F.

With a metal spatula, very thinly spread the tuile batter onto a stickless sheetpan in a 4-inch by 8-inch area so that the sheetpan surface is just visible through the batter. Bake for 7 to 9 minutes, turning as necessary to attain even browning.

Starting at the corners, peel the tuile from the pan and quickly move it to a cutting board. Using a straight-edge pastry wheel, cut the tuile in half to make 2, 4-inch by 4-inch squares. Cut each of these squares into 3, 1 1/4-inch-wide strips, returning the tuile to the oven as necessary to soften it. Return 1 strip to the oven on the pan for a few minutes until it is softened.

Take the strip and, using the handle of a whisk as a form (1 inch in diameter), wrap it around the handle, pressing at the point where it overlaps in order to make a tube (see diagram). Remove the tube from the handle and repeat with the other tuile strips until you have 6 tubes.

Prepare the Apricot Halves

Cut the apricots in half crossways. Trim the bottoms so they stand and do not roll when they are sitting cut side up on a flat surface.

Run the apricot halves under some water and roll them in powdered sugar. Place under a broiler or in a 400°F oven for 6 minutes to melt and caramelize the sugar onto the halves.

Sprinkle some more powdered sugar onto the cut side of the apricot halves. Heat to red hot the prong of a serving fork or the end of a metal skewer over an open flame and press it into the powdered sugar to make a caramelized line. Clean the fork. Repeat the process to make 3 or 4 parallel lines on top of each apricot. Reserve.

Prepare the Compote

Cut the apricots in half, remove the stones, and cut the halves into ¼-inch wedges. In a saucepan over medium heat, simmer the wedges, water, sugar, and vanilla bean for 3 minutes. Reserve.

Assemble the Dessert

Preheat the oven to 375°F and put a pot of water on to boil. Bake the tart and the strudel for 10 to 12 minutes.

Cut the tart crossways into 6 pieces. Trim 1 inch from each end of the strudel. Cut the strudel crossways into 3, 4-inch pieces. Diago-

nally cut each piece into 2 so that when the strudel pieces are stood on end, they are angled to a point. Drop the raviolis in the boiling water and boil for about 3 minutes.

Lay out 6 warm plates and place an apricot half in each plate center. To the right of the apricot halves, stand the tuile tubes, spoon some of the warm compote at the base of each, and top the tubes with the hot raviolis. Place the tarts in the front of the plates and the strudels at the top left of the plates. Top each apricot half with a scoop of the sorbet. Spoon the coulis around each tart and each strudel and dust the tart lightly with some powdered sugar. Serve at once.

Chef's Hint

To prepare this entire dessert, you will need to begin a few days ahead. Make the three-nut linzer dough, pastry cream, phyllo (unless purchased), tuile batter, vanilla pasta, and candied ginger in advance. You could then move on to the ravioli filling, tuile tubes, preparing the apricot tart, and so on.

Any single apricot element of this recipe could be presented with the sorbet and served as a complete and elegant dessert. You would only need to increase the serving size of the particular item. For example, the dried apricot and cherry strudel recipe amount could be doubled and, when finished, cut at an angle into 12 pieces and served warm with apricot coulis or vanilla sauce and a scoop of the sorbet. The apricot tart is wonderful with the apricot coulis or compote and a scoop of vanilla-honey ice cream or another purchased variety of your choice. It is useful to keep in mind that the study in apricot is many desserts in one and it involves several cooking and baking methods and techniques, but it can be broken down very easily if you decide to tackle one or two presentations and serve them with your own personal finishing ideas.

White Peach Soup with White Peach Sorbet

6 servings

*When the aromatic and luscious white peach is available, it is a treasure
to use as the featured ingredient in this dessert.*

White Peach Soup

4 White peaches, ripe

3 cups (720 ml) Water

1/4 cup (60 ml) Muscat or Riesling wine

2 tablespoons (30 g) Vanilla sugar

1 Cinnamon stick

White pepper, a dash

Salt, a dash

3 White peaches, peeled, halved, pitted—see
   p. 81

1 recipe White Peach Sorbet—see p. 75

4 Mint leaves, cut in chiffonnade—see
   Chapter One, p. 8

Equipment Needs

Ice cream machine

Saucepot

Blender

Prepare the Soup

Cut the peaches in half and remove the
stones. In a saucepot on low heat, combine
them with the remaining ingredients. Stirring
occasionally, simmer for 30 minutes.

. . . .

*When blending a hot liquid, be very careful, as the
released steam can cause the top to come off.*

. . . .

Allow to cool slightly, puree in a blender,
and strain it through a fine chinois or 2 layers
of cheesecloth.

Cover loosely and refrigerate until well
chilled. It may be kept chilled for 24 hours
before serving.

Assemble the Dessert

Slice the peach halves into 1/4-inch wedges.
Place in the bottom of 6 bowls in a pinwheel
pattern. In the center of each pinwheel, place
3 scoops of sorbet, then a final scoop of sorbet
atop the others, like a pyramid.

Pour the soup into bowls, sprinkle the
mint over the sorbets, and serve at once.

See p. 81 for preparation instructions for
peaches.

Chef's Hint

*High-quality, ripe yellow peaches will also work in the same proportions
in this recipe. Other milder-flavored fruit sorbets can be substituted for the
white peach sorbet, such as nectarine, apricot, or honeydew melon.*

CHAPTER FIVE

Desserts of Fall and Winter

The arrival of autumn marks an invigorating time of change signified by the first chills of the new season. With it come the appearance of local apples, pears, and pumpkins and the departure of the last peaches, prune plums, gooseberries, and blackberries. Many autumnal dishes, both savory and sweet, are heartier and warmer than the cool, light dishes of summer. Apples and pears, the most prominent autumn and winter fruits, have long been part of desserts, dating as far back as medieval times. The challenge of incorporating the flavors and ideas of autumn's harvest and winter's festive holidays in pastry calls for the use of a broad range of ingredients, including spices, coffee, citrus, chocolate, hazelnuts, chestnuts, and dried fruits. The desserts in this chapter illustrate some of the potential ways these components can be included. As summer's abundant fruits diminish in availability, the challenge is to find new combinations for the foodstuffs of winter. Inventive use of familiar pastry recipes and classic flavor combinations can make winter a most rewarding time of year in which to create desserts!

Fall and Winter Fruits

Apples are the staple autumn and winter fruit. McIntosh are thin-skinned, brightly flavored, and slightly sweet, whereas Granny Smiths are thick-skinned and tart. Other locally available varieties, such as Jonathan or Red Rome, are also suitable for baking. Compatible flavors for apples are caramel, various kinds of cheese, cinnamon, clove, nutmeg, black pepper, ginger, red wine, brandy, rum, madeira, walnut, hazelnut, almond, pistachio, and chestnut.

Pears are another autumn and winter staple fruit. They are ripe when soft to the touch, and often require 1 to 3 days of ripening at room temperature. The small varieties, such as Seckel and Forelli, are excellent for dessert-making, but you may also use the Bosc, d'Anjou, or Comice varieties. Compatible flavors are caramel, chocolate, red wine, bourbon, brandy, various kinds of cheese, cinnamon, clove, nutmeg, black pepper, ginger, and nuts.

Quince is an often neglected winter fruit that must be cooked to reduce its starch and tartness. Compatible flavors are the same as those for apples.

Clementines are small, seedless tangerines. They are usually available from late November through February. They should be sweet and juicy when ripe. Compatible flavors are chocolate, coffee, cinnamon, nutmeg, and ginger.

Blood oranges, which have a very short season, are available in February and March. The skin of the fruit is a deep orange color with a red blush. The flesh is colored a deep ruby red and should be very juicy. Compatible flavors are the same as those for clementines.

Kumquats are tiny, intensely flavored citrus fruits that benefit from cooking or candying to balance their bitterness. Compatible flavors are the same as those for clementines and blood oranges.

Coconuts are generally available year-round. Although the processing of fresh coconuts is somewhat labor-intensive, packaged or dried coconut is not nearly as flavorful. Coconut is excellent in custards, ice creams, and sorbets. Compatible flavors include chocolate; tropical nuts such as macadamia, cashew, or brazil nut; and tropical fruits such as pineapple, mango, banana, and papaya.

Pumpkins are available from September through November. They are classically prepared as a spiced custard for autumn and winter holidays. Compatible flavors are vanilla, cinnamon, nutmeg, clove, ginger, black pepper, brown sugar, caramel, and nuts.

Dates are commonly available year-round and are usually dried. They are a hardy flavor for winter desserts when combined with brandy, rum, vanilla, spices, and caramel.

Bananas are available year-round, but when combined with certain flavors make satisfying winter desserts. *Baby bananas,* usually available from January to early spring, have a more intense flavor than common bananas when ripe. Some compatible flavors are chocolate, brandy, rum, brown sugar, caramel, vanilla, malt, nuts, and other tropical fruits such as pineapple, mango, and papaya.

Mangos and *papayas* are available in late spring and also in the winter months. Quality ripe mangos should be soft to the touch, juicy, and not too stringy. Papayas should also be soft to the touch and their skins yellow in color. Quality *pineapples* are generally available year-round but may require ripening at room temperature for a few days. Each of these fruits is excellent when featured as the central flavor of a dessert or paired with one another. In addition, papaya pairs very well with lime.

Passion fruits are available in the winter months. Their skin should be colored either green or dark purple, and they are wrinkled when ripe. The interior of the fruit is a seedy, juicy pulp. Every drop of the pulp is precious and bursting with flavor, so great care should be taken in preparing and processing this fruit. Slice the fruits in half and use a spoon to scoop the pulp into a strainer and separate all the juice from the seeds. Passion fruits make unsurpassed sorbets and ice creams.

Mascarpone and Brown-Buttered Apple Cheesecake with Rum Raisin Sorbet

6 servings

In this cheesecake, the vanilla-flavored mascarpone harmonizes with slices of apple that have been seasoned with browned butter and cloves.

Phyllo

1 sheet Phyllo—see p. 21

Butter, melted, for brushing

Powdered sugar, for sprinkling

1 teaspoon (1 g) Bread crumbs, finely ground
—optional

Crust

½ cup (60 g) Almonds, lightly roasted

1 tablespoon (10 g) Powdered sugar

1 tablespoon (10 g) Flour

Brown-Buttered Apples

1 Granny Smith apple, peeled, cored, and cut
into ⅛-inch slices

1 tablespoon (15 g) Sugar

2 grinds Black pepper

½ teaspoon (.5 g) Cloves, ground

Salt, a dash

2 tablespoons (30 g) Butter

Cheesecake Filling

7 ounces (200 g) Mascarpone

⅓ cup (70 g) Vanilla sugar

2 Eggs, separated

½ cup (125 g) Crème fraîche or sour cream

1 teaspoon (5 ml) Vanilla extract

1 recipe Raisin Sauce—see p. 50

1 recipe Rum Raisin Sorbet—see p. 74

Equipment Needs

Ice cream machine

6, 2½-inch-diameter Steel rings

Pastry wheel

Blender

Parchment-lined sheetpan

Saucepan

Prepare the Phyllo

Preheat the oven to 375°F.

Brush the outside of 6, 2½-inch-diameter and 1½-inch-high steel rings with butter.

Cut the sheet of phyllo in half so that you have 2 pieces, each measuring approximately 7½ inches by 12 inches. Brush 1 sheet with butter. Sprinkle with the sugar and bread crumbs. Press the second sheet on top of the first.

Starting from the narrower edge, use a pastry wheel to cut 6, 12-inch-long strips of phyllo, each approximately 1¼ inches wide.

Wrap each of the strips around the outsides of the steel rings, loosely bunching it up in places. The bunching will allow room for the phyllo to contract while baking. Phyllo is delicate; if wrapped too tightly against the rings, it will crack while baking.

Place the rings on a parchment-lined sheetpan and bake 12 to 15 minutes, turning the pan, if necessary, to allow for even browning. Remove from the oven and allow to partially cool for a few minutes.

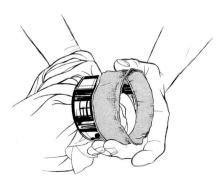

While they are still warm, remove the steel rings from the phyllo rings with both hands: wrap a towel around one hand and hold the very warm steel ring from the inside while gently easing the phyllo ring off with the other.

Prepare the Crust

Put 6, 5-inch-square pieces of aluminum foil on a sheetpan. Place 1 of the steel entrement rings on each piece and wrap the excess foil up around the outside surface of the rings. Brush the foil bottoms and inside of the rings with butter, dust lightly with flour, and place on the sheetpan.

In a food processor, pulverize the almonds with the sugar and flour. Divide the almond crust between the rings, pressing and flattening it into the bottoms. Set aside.

Prepare the Apples

Toss the apple slices in a bowl with the sugar, spices, and salt. In a saucepan on high heat, brown the butter. Watch it carefully. When it begins to smoke lightly and emits a nutty aroma (after about 45 seconds), add the apples carefully and sauté them until they are softened and cooked through (approximately 5 minutes).

Prepare the Cheesecake

Preheat the oven to 325°F.

Beat the mascarpone with the sugar, add the egg yolks, crème fraîche, and vanilla extract. Continue beating until smooth. Whip the egg whites to soft peaks and fold them into the mascarpone mixture.

Spoon enough of the cheesecake mixture into the bottom of the rings to fill just below halfway. Divide the apples among the rings and continue to fill the rings with the remaining cheesecake mixture, to approximately 1/4 inch below the tops of the rings.

. . . .

At this point, you could refrigerate the cheesecakes for later baking.

. . . .

Place the cakes in the oven and pour 1/4 inch of water in the bottom of the pan to allow for gentle baking. Bake for 25 to 30 minutes.

Remove from the oven and allow to cool for 12 to 14 minutes.

Assemble the Dessert

Pull the foil downward from the sides of the rings. Sauce 6 plates with a 4-inch circle of the raisin sauce. Slide a spatula under each cheesecake and steel ring and transfer to the centers of the plates. Draw a paring knife around the inside of each ring to release the cheesecake. Working quickly, pull each steel ring off and replace it with a phyllo ring.

Place 2 quenelles or scoops of sorbet on each plate, touching the side of the cheesecake. Serve at once.

Chef's Hint

You may make this cheesecake in one 8-inch or 9-inch springform pan as follows. First, omit the phyllo rings and double the amounts for the crust, brown-buttered apples, and cheesecake filling. Brush the inside of the springform pan with melted butter, dust with flour, and press the crust into the bottom and as far up the sides as possible. Follow the above instructions for final assembly for filling the crust with the brown-buttered apples and the cheesecake filling.

Wrap the bottom and part way up the outsides of the springform pan with foil and place the cheesecake on a larger pan with at least 1-inch-high edges. Pour 1/4 inch to 1/2 inch of water into the larger pan to make a water bath for gentle baking of the cheesecake and bake at 325°F for 1 hour. Cool the cheesecake slowly by leaving it in the oven with the door open for 1/2 hour; then it may be wrapped and refrigerated for the evening or the next day. Cut it into slices at room temperature or chilled from the refrigerator. Serve the slices warm with the raisin sauce, with or without the sorbet of your choice.

Banana and Chocolate Crème Brûlée Napoleon with Brazil Nut Brittle and Brazil Nut Sauce

6 servings

The rich chocolate crème brûlée and caramelized banana slices in this dessert are a classic flavor combination. Added contrast is provided by crispy layers of phyllo and the unique flavor of brazil nuts.

Phyllo

2 sheets Phyllo—see p. 21

Butter, melted, for brushing

Powdered sugar, for sprinkling

1 teaspoon (1 g) Bread crumbs, finely ground —optional

1 recipe Chocolate Crème Brûlée Custard—see p. 37

2 Bananas, ripe

Sugar, for sprinkling

Cocoa powder, for sprinkling

1 recipe Brazil Nut Sauce—see p. 51

1 recipe Brazil Nut Brittle—see p. 46

Equipment Needs

Parchment paper

Pastry wheel

Plastic wrap

9-inch by 9-inch Pan

Oven broiler or propane torch

2 Sheetpans

Prepare the Phyllo

Preheat oven to 350°F.

Cover the back of a sheetpan with parchment and place 1 sheet of phyllo on top of it. Brush the phyllo with the melted butter. Sprinkle with the sugar and bread crumbs. Top with the second sheet of phyllo and press the 2 layers firmly together.

Using a pastry wheel, cut the phyllo into 24 rectangles approximately 3 inches by 1½ inches. Place a second piece of parchment over the phyllo and top with a second sheetpan, right side up. Weight this sheetpan with either a cast-iron skillet or a foil-covered brick. Bake in the oven for approximately 12 to 15 minutes, or until evenly browned.

Prepare the Crème Brûlée Rectangles

Reduce the oven heat to 300°F. Lightly brush the inside of a 9-inch by 9-inch baking pan with oil. Cut a piece of plastic food wrap exactly the same size and fit it into the bottom of the pan, smoothing the surface to remove all trapped air bubbles between the metal and plastic.

Pour the crème brûlée into the pan, being sure that it covers the plastic entirely. Place on a larger flat pan. Fill the larger pan with approximately ¼ inch of water, creating a water bath for the crème brûlée so that it cooks gently. Bake just until firm, so that when the pan is tapped gently on its side, the custard does not ripple (approximately 20 minutes). Remove from the oven.

When the cooked crème brûlée nears room temperature, place it in the freezer until it is very firm but not solid (about 20 minutes). To remove the crème brûlée custard from the pan, follow method on p. 33.

Cut it into 24, 1¼-inch by 2¼-inch rectangles. Place the rectangles, allowing at least ½ inch of space in between them, on a metal sheetpan. Wrap the remaining custard with plastic and save it for extra desserts if necessary, or freeze for 1 week for use in other desserts.

Assemble the Dessert

Diagonally slice the bananas into ⅛-inch-thick pieces. Place 1 on top of each crème brûlée rectangle. Sprinkle a liberal layer of sugar over the bananas and carefully caramelize the sugar with a propane torch in small sweeping motions or under a broiler, turning as necessary.

Using a metal spatula, transfer a crème brûlée rectangle to each center of 6 individual plates. Top each with a phyllo rectangle. Repeat with another crème brûlée rectangle and another phyllo rectangle until there are 4 layers of each, ending with phyllo. Top with a sprinkle of cocoa powder. Spoon the sauce around each napoleon in an uneven fashion and sprinkle with the brittle.

Chef's Hint

Another way to serve the same rich flavors of these napoleons is to add the banana slices to the chocolate custard and bake the mixture in individual porcelain ramekins, crème brûlée dishes, or a single large porcelain casserole dish. Place the individual dishes or large casserole dish on a larger pan that has edges and pour some water in this larger pan to create a water bath. This will allow the delicate custard to bake gently.

To bake the individual dishes, reduce the baking time to approximately 15 minutes, and for the large casserole dish follow the above baking instructions for the rectangles. To check doneness, tap the edge of the dish to observe if the custard moves as a liquid or has "set up" and is still. If baked whole, the custard and bananas can be scooped, still warm, into serving bowls or small dessert goblets, sprinkled with the brazil nut brittle, and served. Simply the best chocolate pudding you've ever had!

Black-Bottom Chess Tart with Clementines

6 servings

This dessert is based on a traditional chess pie from the southern United States. The chess pie was a popular and inexpensive dessert during the Depression because most of the ingredients were inexpensive and readily available locally. I have added chocolate and citrus to revive the formula.

1 recipe Chocolate Shortdough—see p. 21

Tart Filling
3 Eggs, room temperature
½ cup (100 g) Vanilla sugar
½ cup (120 ml) Cream
2 tablespoons (30 ml) Milk
1 tablespoon (10 g) Flour
1 tablespoon (10 g) Semolina flour
¼ cup (60 ml) Butter, melted
½ teaspoon (3 ml) Vanilla extract
2 ounces (60 g) Chocolate, bittersweet, melted
1 tablespoon (10 g) Cocoa powder
2 teaspoons (10 ml) Bourbon
1 Nutmeg, whole

Clementines
8 Clementines
2 teaspoons (10 g) Sugar
2 teaspoons (10 ml) Orange liqueur (Grand Marnier)
White pepper, a grind

1 Nutmeg, whole
1 recipe Nutmeg Ice Cream—see p. 64

Equipment Needs
Ice cream machine
2½-inch-diameter Steel rings
Round pastry cutters
Fine grater

Prepare the Steel Rings and Shortdough Bottoms
Preheat the oven to 400°F.

Line the bottoms of 6, 2½-inch-diameter and 1½-inch-high steel rings with 5-inch square pieces of aluminum foil, wrapping the excess foil against the outside surface of the rings. Brush the foil bottoms with butter and dust lightly with flour. Place on a sheetpan lined with parchment.

Sprinkle the shortdough and work surface with flour and roll the dough to an even ⅛-inch thickness. Cut out 6, 2½-inch circles. Press each circle into the bottom of a ring,

using your fingers to seal the dough to the inside bottom steel edge. Bake for 10 minutes, remove from the oven, and reduce temperature to 325°F.

Prepare the Filling

Whisk the eggs with the vanilla sugar until the sugar begins to dissolve and the eggs lighten in color. Whisk in the cream, milk, flours, melted butter, and vanilla extract until all the ingredients are thoroughly combined. Transfer 1 cup (230 ml) of the mixture to a separate bowl.

While whisking continuously, pour the melted chocolate into this custard until the chocolate is dissolved. Sprinkle in the cocoa powder and add the rum. Whisk briskly to dissolve any lumps. If any lumps remain, place the bowl over some simmering water and stir until the mixture is smooth.

Brush the inside of the rings lightly with melted butter. Divide the chocolate mixture among the 6 rings, pouring evenly over the shortdough. Bake at 325°F until the custard is just barely set (about 12 to 14 minutes).

Grate some of the nutmeg into the remaining plain filling, whisk briefly, and divide it among the rings, pouring it evenly over the partially cooked chocolate layer. Return the tarts to the oven until just set—an inserted knife will come out clean (or another 16 to 18 minutes).

Prepare the Clementines

Peel 4 clementines and break into sections, removing as much of the bitter white pith as possible. Juice the 4 remaining clementines. Reduce the juice with the sugar and liqueur over medium heat until approximately 2 tablespoons (15 ml) of liquid remain. Add the clementine sections and white pepper. Cook in the hot juice until they are heated through (about 20 seconds). Remove from heat.

Assemble the Dessert

Run a paring knife between the warm custards and the steel rings, pressing against the inside edge of the rings. Place each tart in the center of a warm plate. Surround with the clementines and juice. Grate some nutmeg over the top of each tart. Top with a scoop of ice cream. Serve immediately.

Chef's Hint

You can use standard fluted or straight-sided 2¹/₂-inch-diameter tart tins lined with shortdough; or use a whole 8-inch to 9-inch tart pan and follow the instuctions for "blind" baking a tart shell in the chef's hint for the lemon tart with blackberries and peppered blackberry coulis (see p. 110).

Rather than layering the custards, pour them into the tart shell simultaneously to bake all at once. This creates a marbled effect. You can also purchase a quality ice cream of your choice and replace the clementines with orange segments.

Blood Orange Gratin and Chocolate Bread Pudding with Chocolate Sorbet

8 servings

This dessert of citrus and chocolate celebrates the flavorful and strikingly colorful blood orange, usually available only in the depths of winter—especially during the month of February.

Chocolate Bread Pudding Rings

1 recipe Chocolate Génoise—see p. 26

3 Eggs

¼ cup (60 g) Sugar

½ cup (120 ml) Milk

½ cup (120 ml) Cream

½ teaspoon (.5 g) Cloves, ground

1 ounce (30 ml) Brandy

1 recipe Chocolate Mousse—see p. 43

1 recipe Vanilla Pastry Cream—see p. 34

1 recipe Sabayon—see p. 48

1 recipe Blood Orange Sauce—see p. 52

1 recipe Chocolate Sorbet—see p. 70

Mint leaves, cut into small squares

Equipment Needs

Ice cream machine

6, 2½-inch-diameter Steel rings

1½-inch-diameter Pastry cutter

Oven broiler or propane torch

Prepare the Bread Pudding Rings

Preheat the oven to 350°F.

Put 8, 5-inch-square pieces of aluminum foil on a sheetpan. Place 1, 2½-inch-diameter, 1½-inch-tall steel ring on top of each piece of foil. Wrap the excess foil up around the outside surface of the rings. Brush the foil bottoms and inside of the rings with butter and dust lightly with flour.

Break the génoise into uneven 1-inch pieces and fill the rings to within ½ inch of the top, pressing them lightly into each. Whisk together the eggs, sugar, milk, cream, clove, and brandy. Pour over the génoise. Press the génoise down, where necessary, to be certain it is saturated with the custard.

Pour ¼ inch of water into the pan in order to create a water bath.

Bake for 17 to 20 minutes, or until a knife inserted into the pudding comes out clean. Allow to cool.

Using a 1½-inch-diameter pastry cutter, cut the centers out of each pudding. Loosen

the puddings from the edges of the rings with a paring knife and remove the steel rings. Save the bread pudding rings and centers for the final assembly.

Prepare Blood Oranges

Use 4 blood oranges, with the zest of 1 candied (see p. 54). All should be peeled and sectioned (see p. 81).

Assemble the Dessert

Warm the rings and centers in the oven and mix the zest into the pastry cream. Slice each pudding center crossways into 3 circles.

Place each ring in the centers of 8 warm plates. Place a spoonful of the mousse and a spoonful of pastry cream into the center of each bread pudding ring. Place the orange segments in a pinwheel fashion on top of the pudding rings and spoon some sabayon over them.

Place each plate under a broiler, watching carefully. Turn the plates to lightly brown the sabayon or use a propane torch in sweeping motions.

Surround each ring with 3 slices of pudding centers, evenly spaced. Spoon some pastry cream onto each of the 3 slices and top each with a blood orange segment and a small scoop of the sorbet. Drizzle the sauce around each pudding center slice. Finish with a sprinkle of the mint. Serve at once.

Chef's Hint

Other high-quality oranges can be substituted for the blood oranges in this recipe. In addition, the chocolate mousse and pastry cream can be omitted.

Rather than individual steel rings, the chocolate bread pudding can be baked in a 9-inch by 9-inch by 2-inch pan and cut into 3-inch by 3-inch servings. The orange segments can simply be served over the bread pudding squares with the sabayon and blood orange sauce. The chocolate sorbet can also be replaced with a quality, store-bought sorbet or ice cream.

Bourbon-Poached Pear in Brioche with Hazelnut Praline and Burnt-Honey Ice Cream

6 servings

The warmth of the bourbon-infused pears, with the flavors of the hazelnuts and honey, makes this an ideal dessert for a cold, wintery evening.

Pears

2 cups (480 ml) Bourbon whiskey

2½ cups (600 ml) Water

¾ cup (150 g) Sugar

½ Vanilla bean, split, scraped

2 Cinnamon sticks

White pepper, a grind

Salt, a dash

8 Forelli pears, or other smaller pears just beginning to ripen (d'Anjou, Comice, or Bosc pears can also be used)

1 recipe Hazelnut Praline Cream—see p. 35

1 recipe Brioche, chilled—see p. 17

Egg wash

Egg wash—see p. 55

Sugar, for sprinkling

1 recipe Hazelnut Sauce—see p. 52

1 recipe Burnt-Honey Ice Cream—see p. 60

Equipment Needs

Ice cream machine

Food processor

Peeler

Apple corer

Poach the Pears

Heat the bourbon, water, sugar, vanilla bean, and seasonings to a simmer. Peel and core the pears and add them to the pot. Depending on the ripeness of the pears, the cooking time will vary (approximately 20 minutes). The pears will be done when they can be easily pierced with a paring knife. Remove from the poaching liquid and set on a tray to cool.

. . . .

Take special care not to overcook the pears when poaching or they will lose their structure and begin to break apart. (The poaching process can be done up to 2 days in advance, if desired. Simply leave the pears in the liquid, wrap well, and refrigerate. The longer the pears soak in the mixture, the more bourbon flavor they will acquire.)

. . . .

Assemble the Pears

Stand 6 of the pears upright. Fill a pastry bag fitted with a plain tip with the cream. Fill the core of each pear with the cream.

Dust the brioche and work surface with flour. Using a rolling pin, roll the brioche into an imperfect rectangle, ⅛ inch thick. With a paring knife, cut the brioche into 6 pieces.

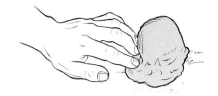

Stand each pear on top of a piece of brioche near its edge and pull the opposite edge over the pear, stretching the dough slightly and pinching it to seal it around the bottom of each pear. Draw a paring knife around the bottom of each pear to remove the excess dough. Continue to pinch the seams together while turning each pear in your hand to assure that the brioche thickness is evenly distributed over them.

Assemble the Dessert

Preheat the oven to 400°F.

Brush the entire surface of the brioche-covered pears with the egg wash and sprinkle with some sugar. Place on a pan lined with parchment, a few inches apart. Bake for 12 to 15 minutes, or until brioche is browned on top.

Slice the 2 remaining poached pears lengthwise into equal wedges (you will need at least 18), and on 6 very warm plates, arrange 3 each so they point out from the center. Slice each brioche-covered pear in half crossways and arrange the halves in the centers of the plates. Spoon some sauce over the halves and drizzle unevenly onto the plates. Finish with quenelles of the ice cream. Serve at once.

Chef's Hint

For a simpler and somewhat lighter version of this dessert that still achieves the same flavor goals, the brioche, hazelnut praline cream, and sauce may by omitted by serving the bourbon-poached pears sliced, in bowls with the burnt-honey ice cream or a quality commercial nut ice cream and a sprinkling of roasted hazelnuts or hazelnut brittle (see p. 46).

Caramelized Apple and Chèvre in Phyllo with Red Wine and Black Pepper Sorbet

6 servings

This dessert draws influences from the classic tarte tatin or an apple pie. Apple and cheese are a classic flavor combination, as are cheese and red wine. The small hint of goat cheese and chilly red wine in this dessert carries the apple to new heights.

Chèvre Mousse
2 ounces (60 g) Goat's cheese
1 Egg white
1 tablespoon (15 g) Sugar

Dried Apple Chips
1 McIntosh apple
Powdered sugar, for sprinkling

Caramelized Apples
3 Granny Smith apples
2 tablespoons (30 g) Butter
½ cup (100 g) Sugar

Red Wine and Caramel Sauce
Caramel, reserved from caramelized apples
½ cup (120 ml) Red wine
Sugar to taste

Apple Packages
3 sheets Phyllo—see p. 21
Powdered sugar, for sprinkling

¼ cup (60 ml) Butter, melted
Bread crumbs, finely ground—optional
1 recipe Hazelnut Génoise—see p. 27
1 recipe Red Wine and Black Pepper Sorbet—
see p. 74

Equipment Needs
Ice cream machine
Peeler
Apple corer
Oven broiler or propane torch
Stickless sheetpan or parchment paper
Saucepan

Prepare the Mousse
In a bowl with a rubber spatula, cream the goat's cheese. With a mixer, whisk the egg white at high speed to soft peaks. Sprinkle in the sugar and whip for another 30 seconds. Fold ⅓ whipped white into the goat's cheese until smooth, then fold in the remaining egg white.

Prepare the Apple Chips

. . . .

These dried apple chips are an added textural and flavor accent to this dessert and may be omitted if desired.

. . . .

Preheat oven to 300°F. Peel and core the apple. Slice it crossways into 1/16-inch-thick circles. Place 1/8 inch apart on a stickless or parchment-lined pan lightly coated with oil. Dry chips in the oven for approximately 25 minutes. Check frequently, turning them over from time to time, until they are lightly browned and dried.

Remove from the pan while still warm and line them up on top of an upside-down baking pan. Sprinkle with powdered sugar. Carefully melt the sugar with a propane torch in a sweeping motion or under a hot broiler, watching very closely.

Prepare the Apples

Peel and core the apples. Cut in half crossways, so the hole is in the center of each half. Be sure to remove any of the remaining fibrous seed pod, with a paring knife, if necessary.

On low heat, melt the butter in a 10-inch thick-bottomed saucepan. Pour the sugar evenly into the pan and turn the heat to high. When the sugar begins to melt, stir gently with a spoon and turn the heat down to medium.

When the sugar turns amber and lightly smokes, carefully place the apple halves in the pan. Turn with a spatula from side to side until they are saturated with the caramel but still somewhat firm (about 8 to 10 minutes). Place on a pan to cool. Set aside with the caramel.

Prepare the Sauce

Over medium heat, warm the leftover caramel in the pan. Watch closely as the caramel melts and darkens. When it begins to lightly smoke, carefully add the wine. Stir until the caramel is dissolved. Remove from the heat and adjust sweetness with additional sugar, if necessary.

Assemble the Apple Packages

Brush a sheet of phyllo with the melted butter. Sprinkle with sugar and bread crumbs. Press the second sheet of phyllo on top and repeat the process, then cover with the last sheet. Using a ruler or straight edge, cut the phyllo into 6 equal squares (each measuring approximately 5 inches by 6 inches).

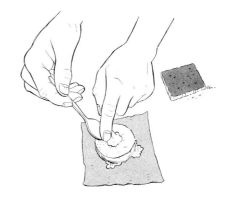

Place 1 apple half, flat side down, in the center of each square. Using a small spoon, fill the empty centers with the mousse.

Cut the génoise into 6, 2-inch squares. Brush well with some of the sauce. Place a square on top of each apple half. Pull each corner of phyllo to the top of the génoise, wrapping it like a package, and turn it over. The phyllo may not entirely wrap the package of apple and génoise, but as long as the corners are tucked underneath when it is turned over,

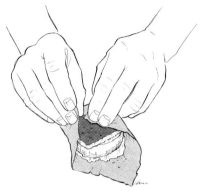

the package will remain intact in the oven. Refrigerate until ready to use.

The remaining génoise can be wrapped well and frozen for 2 weeks. At a later time, it could be used to make a small cake filled with a recipe of chocolate mousse and a coating of ganache.

Assemble the Dessert

Preheat oven to 400°F.

Bake the apple packages for about 13 to 15 minutes, or until the phyllo is golden brown and crisp.

Ladle some sauce onto 6 warm plates and place a package on each. Top with a dried apple chip and a scoop of the sorbet. Finish with another dried apple chip sticking out of the sorbet. Serve immediately.

Chef's Hint

This dessert can also be assembled as a whole instead of as individual packages. Line an 8-inch or 9-inch round cake pan or springform pan with foil. Make the chèvre mousse and caramelize the apples as instructed above. Layer the 3 sheets of phyllo as above, but instead of cutting it into pieces, lay it over the round pan and press it gently into the corners, leaving excess dough draped over the edges of the pan.

Fit the prepared apple halves in a circle in the phyllo-lined pan, then fill the cores with the chèvre mousse as above. Cut an 8-inch- to 9-inch-diameter circle of génoise to fit on top of the apples, soak it with some of the red wine caramel sauce, and then fold the excess phyllo over the génoise. Place a sheetpan over the round pan, and while pressing together the two (one with each hand), flip them over so that the round pan is now upside down on the sheetpan. Remove the round pan and foil and bake the large apple package at 400°F for 15 to 18 minutes. Allow it to cool slightly before cutting it into slices with a serrated knife. Serve each slice with some of the reserved sauce and sorbet of your choice.

Chèvre Cheesecake with Pear Gratin

6 servings

*Varieties of cheese, paired with fruits such as pears and apples, have been
served as dessert for centuries. This dessert is a playful interpretation of the
classic combination and features the unique flavor of goat's cheese.*

Pears

2 d'Anjou or Comice pears

2 cups (480 ml) Port wine

1 recipe Sabayon—see p. 48

¼ cup (60 g) Sugar

Black pepper, a grind

Salt, a dash

Chèvre Cheesecake Mixture

4 ounces (110 g) Goat's cheese

2 tablespoons (30 g) Sugar

1 tablespoon (15 ml) Cream

1 Egg

Equipment Needs

Peeler

Apple corer

6 Small timbale molds

Small sheetpan

Food processor

Poach the Pears

Peel and core the pears. Slice them lengthwise into ¼-inch wedges. Put in a saucepan with the wine, sugar, pepper, and salt. Turn the heat to medium and bring to a simmer. Depending on the ripeness of the pears, their cooking time will vary. (They will be done when they can be easily pierced with a paring knife.) Reserve the pears and poaching liquid.

Prepare the Cheesecake

Prepare 6, 1-ounce timbale molds by brushing them lightly with butter and coating them with sugar.

Cream together the cheese and sugar. Add the cream and beat until smooth. Beat the egg with a fork, then whisk it into the cheese mixture until smooth. Fill the timbale molds up to ⅛ inch from the top. Place on a sheetpan.

Assemble the Dessert

Preheat the oven to 325°F.

Pour ½ of the water onto the sheetpan with the timbales to assure gentle cooking. Bake for approximately 25 minutes.

On 6 plates, arrange the pear wedges in a row or pinwheel fashion, spoon some poaching

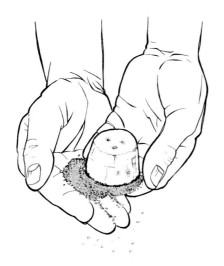

liquid onto them, and drizzle the sabayon over them. Place each plate under a broiler, watching carefully, and turning the plates to lightly brown the sabayon, or use a propane torch in sweeping motions.

Cut around each cheesecake with a paring knife, unmold each, and press some of the finely ground brittle around their bottom edges (the thicker end). Place them on the plates adjacent to the pear gratin, as desired. Sprinkle the remaining brittle over the gratin. Serve at once.

Chef's Hint

A simple alternative for this dessert is to bake the chèvre cheesecake mixture whole in a small terrine, bread loaf pan, or small springform pan. Unmold, slice, and serve with poached pear slices, or the pear gratin as described above.

Chocolate, Kumquat, and Espresso Torte

6 servings

The strong flavors in this dessert make it a fitting choice for the holidays or for cozy winter celebrations.

Crème Brûlée Triangles
1 recipe Espresso Crème Brûlée Custard—see
  p. 38

Chocolate Triangles
6 ounces (170 g) Chocolate, bittersweet,
  melted

Candy Kumquats
16 Kumquats, medium-size
2 cups (480 ml) Water, for blanching
1 cup (200 g) Sugar
1 ounce (30 ml) Orange liqueur (Grand
  Marnier)

1 recipe Bittersweet Chocolate Sauce—see
  p. 49

Equipment Needs
10-inch by 14-inch or 12-inch by 16-inch
  Sheetpan
Plastic wrap

Prepare the Crème Brûlée Triangles
Preheat the oven to 300°F.

Lightly brush the bottom of a 10-inch by 14-inch pan with oil. Cut a piece of plastic food wrap the same size and place it in the bottom of the pan, smoothing the surface to eliminate any air bubbles trapped between the plastic and the metal.

Pour the custard into the pan, making sure it covers entirely the surface of the plastic, and place on a larger flat pan. Fill this larger pan with ¼ inch of water, creating a water bath so that the custard cooks gently. Bake just until firm—when the pan is gently tapped on its side, the custard does not ripple (about 20 minutes).

Allow to cool to room temperature, then place in the freezer for about 20 minutes, or until very firm but not solid. To remove the crème brûlée custard from the pan, follow the method on p. 33.

Cut the custard into 24, 2-inch equal-side triangles. Wrap the remaining custard with plastic and save for extra desserts, if necessary. Refrigerate.

Prepare the Chocolate Triangles

Place a piece of parchment on the back of a large sheetpan. Using a metal spatula, very thinly spread the chocolate approximately $1/16$ inch thick throughout an area 12 inches by 16 inches. Refrigerate until the chocolate begins to set but has not quite hardened.

Using a paring knife, cut the chocolate into 24, $2\frac{1}{4}$-inch equal-side triangles. If the chocolate is too hard to cut, heat the knife with a few sweeps over a flame and wipe it with a towel between each cut. Return the triangles to the refrigerator until they can be peeled from the parchment, then peel them off with a metal spatula. Reserve.

Candy the Kumquats

Boil the kumquats in water for 15 minutes. Drain, discarding the water. Return the kumquats to the pot with the sugar, liqueur, and 2 cups of fresh water. Turn the heat to high until it boils, then reduce heat to low. Simmer until the kumquats are somewhat translucent and intense in flavor, but no longer bitter (about 30 minutes).

When they are cooled, slice them in half and remove the seeds. Set 6 halves aside for the garnish. Roughly chop the remaining kumquats to $1/4$ inch in size.

Prepare the Kumquat Garnish

Using a small spoon, make 6 small quenelles or scoops from the excess custard. Fit them into each kumquat half. Dip halfway into the bittersweet chocolate sauce. Save for final assembly.

Assemble the Dessert

Using a spatula, place a crème brûlée triangle in the center of 6 room-temperature plates. Scatter a spoonful of chopped kumquats onto each triangle. Top with a chocolate triangle.

Continue layering in this order until you place the last chocolate triangle on top. Finish with a drizzle of sauce. Sprinkle the remaining chopped kumquats around the dessert. Place the kumquat garnish on top. Serve at once.

Chef's Hint

If desired, the chocolate and custard layers can be cut into different shapes, such as rectangles or squares, to make the desserts a different shape. Alternatively, the espresso crème brûlée can be poured into a small porcelain casserole dish or individual porcelain ramekins, brushed with butter, placed on a pan in $1/4$ to $1/2$ inch of water to allow the custard to bake gently, and baked as above. Draw a paring knife around the edge of the custards before unmolding them on plates and serve with the candied kumquat pieces or orange segments and chocolate sauce.

Chocolate Rainforest Torte

8 servings

This dessert was created as a way to incorporate rainforest nuts and newly available chocolate made from South Pacific cocoa beans.

1 Mango, ripe

Torte

1 recipe Rainforest Meringue—see p. 30

1 recipe Chocolate Génoise—see p. 26

1 recipe Chocolate Mousse (made with
   Valrhona Manjari)—see p. 43

1 recipe White Wine Simple Syrup—see
   p. 54

1 recipe Roasted Coconut Shavings—see
   p. 47

1 recipe White Chocolate Mousse—see p. 44

Tuile Decorations

1 recipe Tuile Batter—see p. 31

1 recipe Chocolate Ganache (made with
   Valrhona Manjari)—see p. 42

1 recipe Mango-Vanilla Sauce—see p. 52

Powdered sugar, for sprinkling

Cocoa powder, for sprinkling

Equipment Needs

Metal spatula

Pastry bag with small plain tip

Stickless sheetpan or parchment paper

Prepare the Mango

Peel the mango and cut the flesh from the pit, discarding any that is fibrous. Cut the flesh into ¼-inch-thick slices. Set aside.

Assemble the Torte

Using a serrated knife, cut the meringue to a roughly 9-inch by 5-inch piece. Cut the génoise into 2 pieces measuring 9 inches by 5 inches.

With a metal spatula, spread a ½-inch-thick layer of the chocolate mousse over the meringue, and place the first génoise layer on top. Sprinkle the entire surface with some syrup. Lay the mango slices over the génoise. Sprinkle the coconut over the mangos; spread a ½-inch layer of the white chocolate mousse over the coconut. Place the second génoise

layer on top. Soak the entire surface with some more syrup. Refrigerate until well chilled (about 1 hour).

Prepare the Tuile Decorations

Preheat the oven to 375°F.

Put the tuile into a small pastry bag fitted with a 1/16-inch tip. On a stickless pan or a sheetpan lined with parchment and brushed with butter, pipe the tuile into long strips, spirals, or other desired shapes. Bake for about 6 minutes, or until lightly browned.

Removing 1 tuile shape from the oven at a time, wrap them rapidly in spirals around a whisk handle or into other desired shapes.

Assemble the Dessert

Adjust the temperature of the ganache so that it is of spreadable consistency and very smooth. Spread a generous layer, about 1/4 inch thick, over the torte. Smooth the top with 1 motion, so the final layer of ganache is 1/8 inch thick.

Warm a serrated knife over a flame (in a few waves), and trim the uneven sides of the torte, cutting 1/2 inch from each edge. Clean and dry the knife between each of the cuts. Using the same method, cut the torte in half lengthwise, then cut it into 8, 2-inch squares. Allow the tortes to come to room temperature.

Place each torte on a plate and spoon sauce generously around them. Stick the tuile pieces on the tops. Sprinkle lightly with powdered sugar and cocoa powder. Serve at once.

Chef's Hint

Start preparing the "in advance" items a day ahead: rainforest meringue, chocolate génoise, mousses, and ganache. To simplify the torte, the assembly can be modified to omit different layers. For example, from the bottom: rainforest meringue, chocolate mousse, chocolate génoise, chocolate ganache. The mango slices can also be served beside each torte, perhaps in the form of a compote, warmed in a sauté pan with a little water and a sprinkle of sugar.

Chocolate Universe

6 servings

*This whimsical and futuristic dessert evolved as a way of presenting
different chocolate preparations on 1 plate. Its various components showcase
several ways of preparing chocolate in a variety of forms and textures, from
the crunchy brittle and the praline moon to the warm richness of chocolate-espresso cake.*

Universe Spirals and Tuile Tubes

1 recipe Tuile Batter—see p. 31

2 teaspoons (3 g) Cocoa powder

1 teaspoon (5 ml) Water

Phyllo Rectangles

½ sheet Phyllo—see p. 21

Butter, melted, for brushing

Powdered sugar, for sprinkling

Génoise

1 ounce (30 ml) Brandy

1 ounce (30 ml) Water

1 tablespoon (15 g) Sugar

1 recipe Chocolate Génoise—see p. 26

1 recipe Bittersweet Chocolate Sauce—see
p. 49

Chocolate Mousse Orbs

1 recipe Chocolate Mousse—see p. 43

6 Hazelnuts, roasted

Chocolate-Espresso Cake Mixture

Butter, melted, for brushing

Sugar, for sprinkling

2 ounces (60 g) Chocolate, bittersweet, melted

1 tablespoon (15 ml) Espresso, hot, or strong
coffee

1 teaspoon (3 g) Espresso, ground, or coffee,
ground

2 Eggs, separated

1 tablespoon (15 g) Butter, melted

2 teaspoons (10 g) Sugar

Praline Moons

1 recipe Praline Chocolate—see p. 45

1 recipe Chocolate Marquise, cut into 1-inch
squares—see p. 44

1 recipe White Chocolate Mousse—see p. 44

1 recipe Mango-Vanilla Sauce—see p. 52

1 recipe Mango Sorbet—see p. 73

1 recipe Chocolate Sorbet—see p. 70

Equipment Needs

Ice cream machine

Stickless sheetpan or parchment paper

Pastry bag with small plain tip, larger plain
tip

2 Sheetpans

Pastry wheel

Set of round pastry cutters

1½- and 1-inch-diameter Ice cream scoop

Small timbale molds

2½-inch Round pastry cutter

Prepare Spirals and Tuile Tubes

. . . .

These spirals and tubes are added textural and decorative elements and can be omitted without changing the main flavors of the dessert.

. . . .

Preheat the oven to 375°F.

Using a rubber spatula, take ¼ of the tuile batter. Mix in a small bowl with the cocoa powder and water until very smooth. Put the chocolate tuile into a small pastry bag fitted with a very small plain tip. Pipe 6 spirals about 4½ inches in diameter (see diagram) onto a stickless sheetpan or a parchment-lined pan that has been brushed with butter. (Be sure to secure the parchment to the pan with a dab of tuile in each corner.) Bake the spirals for 5 to 6 minutes.

Carefully remove from the pan with a metal spatula, 1 by 1, while they are still hot. Peel them off and lay them flat on a table or countertop, reheating if necessary to make them flat. On the stickless sheetpan, spread some of the remaining plain tuile a little less than ¹⁄₁₆ inch thick in a 4-inch by 9-inch area, so that the sheetpan surface is just barely visible through the tuile. Bake for 8 to 10 minutes, turning as necessary to attain even browning.

Starting at the corners, peel the tuile from the pan. Quickly move it to a cutting board. Using a straight-edge pastry wheel, cut the tuile crossways into 1½-inch-wide by 4-inch-long strips, returning the tuile to the oven as necessary to soften it. Return the strips, 1 or 2 at a time, to the oven for about 1 minute, until softened.

Using the handle of a whisk as a form *(approximately 1 inch in diameter)*, wrap the tuile around the handle, pressing at the point where it overlaps in order to make a tube (see diagram). Remove the tube from the handle. Repeat with the other tuile strips until you have 6 tubes.

Prepare the Phyllo Rectangles

Reduce the oven temperature to 350°F. Place the phyllo sheet on a cutting board. Brush half of the 12-inch length of phyllo with melted butter and sprinkle with powdered

sugar. Fold the other half of dough over the butter and sugar. Press firmly together. The phyllo sheet now measures 7½ inches by 6 inches.

Cut the phyllo into 18 pieces as follows: 6, 1-inch by 3-inch rectangles; 6, 1-inch by 2-inch rectangles; and 6, 1-inch by 1-inch squares (see diagram). Turn a sheetpan upside down and line it with a piece of parchment. Transfer the phyllo pieces to the back of the sheetpan. Top with another piece of parchment and then a second sheetpan, right side up. Weight the top sheetpan with a foil-covered brick or other heavy, oven-proof item. Bake for 12 to 15 minutes, or until evenly browned. Reserve.

. . . .

When baking the phyllo rectangles, you may remove the weight and top sheetpan for the final few minutes of baking to observe the phyllo as it approaches an even golden brown color.

. . . .

Prepare the Génoise

Heat the brandy, water, and sugar to a simmer over medium heat, then remove from heat and allow to cool. Using a 1-inch-diameter pastry cutter, cut 12 circles from the génoise. Dip 1 circle into the chocolate sauce and glue it to a second circle. Repeat this process to make 6 stacks of the double-layered génoise circles. Using a pastry brush, soak them generously with the brandy liquid.

With a serrated knife, dice the remaining génoise into ¼-inch cubes. Reserve the cubes for the orbs and the rest of the chocolate sauce for the final assembly.

Prepare the Chocolate Mousse Orbs

Using a 1½-inch-diameter ice cream scoop, scoop a half-sphere of the mousse and push a hazelnut into its center. Drop the orb into the génoise cubes. Roll the orbs about to press the cubes into the entire surface of the mousse. Rinse the scoop in warm water and repeat the process to make 6 orbs.

Set the orbs on a tray, cover with plastic, and refrigerate. Set aside the leftover génoise cubes and remaining mousse for final assembly.

Prepare the Chocolate-Espresso Cake Mixture

Prepare 6, 1½-inch-diameter timbale molds by brushing with some melted butter and sprinkling liberally with sugar.

Whisk together the chocolate, hot espresso, ground espresso, egg yolks, and butter. Whip the egg whites until stiff, then add the sugar. Continue whipping until the sugar crystals are dissolved. Fold the egg whites into the chocolate mixture until combined.

Fill the timbale molds with the mixture, leaving at least a ¼-inch space at the top.

Prepare the Praline Moons

Lightly coat with oil the back of a perfectly clean, flat sheetpan. Pour the praline chocolate onto the oiled surface. Cover with a large piece of plastic wrap. Spread the chocolate first with your hands, pressing it outward from the center, then with a rolling pin to an even ³/16 inch thick.

Allow the chocolate to cool and harden by placing the pan in the refrigerator for a few minutes; then peel the plastic wrap from its surface.

Starting at 1 edge, press a 2½-inch pastry cutter through the chocolate. Pull the cutter toward you. Set the uneven chocolate piece aside. Place the cutter overlapping the round edge of the first cut to make a half-circle moon shape ½ inch thick at the widest point. Press the cutter through the chocolate and pull the cutter toward you. Continue cutting moons until you have 6.

Assemble the Dessert

Preheat the oven to 375°F. Bake the chocolate-espresso cakes for 8 to 10 minutes.

Using a ladle or spoon, sauce 6 room-temperature plates as follows: 2-inch circle of chocolate sauce in the plate centers, 2-inch circle of chocolate sauce to the right of centers, 1-inch circle of the mango-vanilla sauce above the centers.

Place the stacks of génoise in the center sauce.

Place the marquise in the 1-inch circle of mango-vanilla sauce and push a praline moon into each marquise so that it stands up.

Moving clockwise to the right of the center sauce, place the tuile tubes on end. Fill a pastry bag fitted with a plain tip with the chocolate mousse. Fill each tube to the top. Cap with the orbs.

To the left of the empty 2-inch circle of chocolate sauce, place 4 or 5 of the génoise cubes, which will serve as anchors to keep the chocolate sorbet from sliding.

Between the génoise cubes and the praline moon and marquise, place the 3-inch-tall phyllo rectangle. Hold it upright and pipe some white chocolate mousse from the plate 2 inches up the side of the rectangle. Press the 2-inch-tall phyllo piece against the white chocolate mousse and pipe more mousse at the base of it. Press the 1-inch-tall piece of phyllo against this mousse. The white chocolate mousse should sufficiently anchor the upright phyllo pieces so they stand alone.

Loosen the chocolate-espresso cakes from the molds by drawing a paring knife around, then tapping them out into your hand. Place them in the empty 2-inch sauce circles to the right of the génoise cubes.

Place a 1½-inch scoop of mango sorbet on top of the génoise stacks in the centers and 1-inch scoop of chocolate sorbet onto the génoise cubes. Carefully set the center of a universe spiral on the mango sorbet, and serve at once.

Chef's Hint

This dessert must be made over a period of several days. The tuile and phyllo preparations should be made first and sealed in a plastic container. The marquise, praline moons, mousses, and génoise can also be prepared up to 2 days ahead of time. A smaller version of the final presentation can also be made, perhaps with the orbs and moons surrounding the mango "sun." Use any of the parts of this universe recipe to create your own interpretation of a chocolate galaxy.

Coconut and Macadamia Nut Tart with Coconut Ice Cream

6 servings

The paired flavors of coconut and chocolate may be most memorable from popular childhood candy bars or some European-style chocolates. Although labor-intensive, freshly grated coconut is well worth the trouble.

Tart Shells

1 recipe Chocolate Shortdough—see p. 21
1 Egg white, slightly beaten with a fork

Chocolate "Coconut Shells"

1 recipe Tuile Batter—see p. 31
2 ounces (60 g) Chocolate, bittersweet, melted

Coconut Milk Sauce

¼ cup (60 ml) Coconut Ice Cream—see p. 62
¼ cup (60 ml) Coconut milk, reserved from the coconut ice cream recipe

Tart Filling

½ cup (50 g) Coconut, freshly grated, lightly roasted
½ cup (60 g) Macadamia nuts, lightly roasted
1 tablespoon + 2 teaspoons (25 g) Vanilla sugar
1 Egg
⅔ cup (160 ml) Milk

Equipment Needs

Ice cream machine
6, 2½-inch-diameter Tart tins
4-ounce Ladle
3½-inch-diameter Round pastry cutter

Prepare the Tart Shells

Preheat the oven to 400°F.

Butter and dust with flour 6, 2½-inch-diameter tart tins. Place on a sheetpan.

Sprinkle the shortdough and your work surface with flour, and roll the dough approximately ³⁄₁₆ inch thick. Cut 6, 3½-inch circles. Carefully press them into the tart tins, making sure the dough does not crack in the corners. Fit the inside of each tart with a small piece of foil. Fill with some dried beans or other weight to prevent the shortdough from bubbling while baking. Chill in the freezer for 15 minutes, then bake for 8 minutes.

Remove the weighted tin foil from the tarts. Allow to cool for a few minutes.

With a pastry brush, coat the inside of the tarts with the egg white, in order to seal them, and return to the hot oven for 4 to 5 minutes. Reserve.

Prepare the Chocolate "Coconut Shells"

Reduce the oven temperature to 375°F. Using a metal cake spatula, spread 6, 5-inch-diameter circles of tuile, approximately 1/16 inch thick, onto a stickless pan, or a pan lined with parchment and brushed generously with butter. Bake for approximately 8 to 10 minutes, turning the pan as necessary to evenly brown the tuile.

Lightly coat the outside of a 4-ounce ladle with vegetable oil. While they're still hot from the oven, rapidly press each tuile over the back of the ladle to create a half-sphere shape (see diagram). Use a clean cloth towel to protect your hand from the heat of the tuile. Peel the towel from each shaped tuile before proceeding to the next. It may be necessary to reheat the tuiles several times during this process in order to make each 1 malleable enough to conform to the shape of the ladle without breaking.

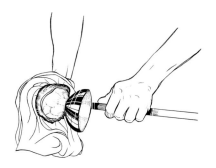

Using a pastry brush, coat the top of each tuile with the melted chocolate, allowing the pattern in the chocolate left by the brush bristles to simulate the rough exterior of a coconut shell. Allow to cool for 10 minutes.

Poke a paring knife through the "shell" at connected angular intervals from the top of each shell to the bottom edge, creating a jaggedlike pattern that resembles a cracked coconut shell (see diagram). The tuile should be softened enough by the chocolate coating so that it does not shatter. If it breaks in unexpected places, it can still be used in the finished dessert to represent the imperfect nature of a shattered coconut shell.

Prepare the Sauce

In a saucepan on low heat, combine the ice cream and coconut milk. Stir until the ice cream is melted and thoroughly mixed with the milk. Reserve.

Prepare the Tart Filling

Preheat the oven to 350°F.

Divide the grated coconut and nuts evenly between the 6 tarts. Whisk the sugar into the egg, then whisk in the milk. Pour this custard into the tarts over the coconut and macada-

Return 1 of the pieces to the oven until it has softened again, remove from the oven, and cut into 4, 1½-inch strips (measure 1½-inch intervals across the 6-inch side).

Repeat this process with the 2 remaining pieces of tuile, returning any portion to the oven to resoften as necessary to complete the cutting. You should end up with 12 strips 1½ inches by 3 inches.

Prepare the Pineapple

Preheat the oven to 300°F.

Peel the pineapple and remove the core. Using a very sharp knife, cut 12 slices of pineapple lengthwise, approximately ⅛ inch thick. Place on a stickless pan or parchment-lined sheetpan lightly brushed with oil. Set the remaining pineapple aside.

Dry the pineapple slices in the oven for about 30 minutes, checking them occasionally. Peel the slices off the baking surface, turn them over, and continue drying until the slices are still pliable but dry to the touch.

Remove from the pan and line them up on the back side of a sheetpan. Sprinkle generously with powdered sugar. Melt the sugar with a propane torch in sweeping motions or under a broiler, watching very closely so as not to burn the pineapple. The sugar should melt and caramelize in spots and send off a little smoke.

Prepare the Fruit

Cut the starfruit in half and remove the seeds that run on both sides of its center. Cut the fruit into ¼-inch-wide strips.

Peel the mango and slice the main part of the fruit from each side of its large, flat pit. Trim off any remaining pieces. Slice the halves lengthwise into ½-inch-thick pieces.

Cut 6 pieces of the reserved fresh pineapple lengthwise, approximately ⅛ inch thick.

Bring the water, rum, sugar, and vanilla bean seeds and pod to a boil. Add the cut fruit to the pot. Reduce heat to low, poaching the fruit gently to release more of its flavors. Remove the fruit from the poaching liquid, basing the length of cooking time on your own judgment of the fruits' ripeness (probably about 2 minutes). Reserve the poaching liquid.

Assemble the Dessert

Using a pastry bag fitted with a plain tip, or a spoon, place approximately 1 ounce of pastry cream in a rectangular shape in the centers of 6 individual plates. Build the napoleons in the following order: macadamia tuile, then a piece each of poached pineapple, then oven-dried pineapple, pastry cream, strips of starfruit, another tuile, more pastry cream, and pieces of mango. Top with a final slice of oven-dried pineapple.

The structure can be "settled" slightly by applying some even pressure with your fingers from the top. Surround each napoleon with a random drizzle of the mango-vanilla sauce. Serve immediately.

Chef's Hint

Any combination of tropical fruit, such as papaya and kiwi, can be used to structure a similar napoleon. You could also omit the tuile layers, replacing them with crispy pineapple layers, or vice versa.

Warm Date Pithiviers with Cardamom Ice Cream

6 servings

In this dessert, the classic French pithiviers (from the town of the same name in the Orléans region of France) has been reduced in size to an individual serving. Its traditional almond cream filling has been replaced with a date filling.

Date Filling

16 (120 g) Dates, pitted

2 ounces (60 ml) Scotch whiskey

½ cup (120 ml) Water

½ teaspoon (.5 g) Cardamom, ground

3 grinds Black pepper

Salt, a pinch

½ recipe (150 g) Vanilla Pastry Cream—see p. 34

2 tablespoons (30 g) Butter, softened

2 tablespoons (15 g) Flour

Pithiviers

1 sheet Puff Pastry—see p. 18

Egg wash

Powdered sugar, for sprinkling

1 recipe Caramel Sauce—see p. 49

2 Dates, sliced into matchstick-size strips

1 recipe Cardamom Ice Crem—see p. 61

Equipment Needs

Ice cream machine

Set of round pastry cutters

Prepare the Filling

In a saucepan, cover the dates with the scotch and water. Add the spices and salt, place on medium heat, and simmer until the dates become very soft, and most of the liquid has evaporated (approximately 7 to 9 minutes). Allow to cool in the refrigerator.

In a food processor, puree the mixture. Add the pastry cream, butter, and flour. Puree until smooth. Spread on a sheetpan and refrigerate until well chilled.

Assemble the Pithiviers

Using round pastry cutters, cut 12 circles of puff pastry (6 bottoms and 6 tops): ⅛-inch-thick, 3½-inch-diameter bottoms and ⅛-inch-thick, 4-inch-diameter tops. Place the tops and bottoms on a pan lined with parchment. Rest in the refrigerator for 30 minutes.

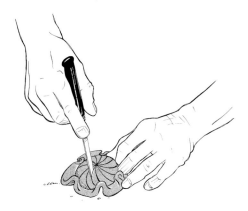

Scoop half-sphere mounds (approximately 2 inches in diameter) of the filling onto the center of each bottom. With a pastry brush, egg wash the ½-inch edge of puff pastry that surrounds each filling. Top each filling with the 4-inch circles. Gently seal by pressing the top edge to the egg-washed bottom edge without disrupting the shape of the filling. Gently slide a 2½-inch-round pastry cutter, turned upside down, over the pastry-covered mound of filling. Press slightly to assure a stong seal.

Scallop the edge at 6 evenly spaced points by pressing the dull side of a paring knife at the edge of the pastry and drawing it inward toward the inverted pastry cutter. Repeat this process for each pithivier. Generously egg wash the pithiviers. Place in the freezer for 20 minutes.

Remove from the freezer. Use a sharp paring knife to score the pithiviers in ¼-inch increments by holding the knife loosely in your hand and drawing it from the top center of the filling mounds to their base in a semicircular motion (see diagram). Be extremely careful to cut only through the egg-washed surface, not all the way through to expose the filling.

Assemble the Dessert

Preheat the oven to 420°F.

Bake the pithiviers for 6 minutes. Reduce the temperature to 375°F for an additional 8 minutes, or until pastry is evenly browned. At this point, you could sift a fine layer of powdered sugar over the pithiviers and melt it with a propane torch in sweeping motions or carefully under a broiler, to provide extra shine.

Drizzle the sauce in an uneven fashion onto 6 warm plates. Place a pithivier on each. Sprinkle the sliced dates to 1 side of the pithiviers, and place 2 quenelles or round scoops of ice cream on top of them, touching the side of the pithivier. Serve at once.

Chef's Hint

A simpler version of this pithivier can be made in a single whole as follows. Cut an 8-inch-diameter circle bottom and 10-inch-diameter circle top of prepared puff pastry and place the 8-inch bottom on a parchment- or foil-lined sheetpan. Mound the filling in the center of the circle, smoothing it to within 1 inch of the circle's edge. Brush the 1-inch edge with egg wash and drape the 10-inch top circle over the filling.

Seal the two circles as for the individual pithiviers above, without disrupting the shape of the filling, and decoratively scallop the edge if desired. Brush the surface of the pithivier with egg wash, place it in the freezer for 20 minutes, remove from the freezer, and score the surface of the pithivier as above or according to your own desired pattern before baking. Any mildly flavored ice cream, such as vanilla, almond, or rum raisin, may be substituted for the cardamom.

Gingered Apple Tart with Hazelnut Ice Cream and Caramelized Cider

6 servings

In this tart, the pastry and apples are prepared separately and brought together at the last minute. This retains the pastry's crispness and allows the apples to saturate with flavor.

Puff Pastry Rounds

1 sheet Puff Pastry—see p. 18

Powdered sugar, for sprinkling

1 recipe Ginger Pastry Cream—see p. 35

2 Granny Smith apples

1 tablespoon (15 g) Butter

½ cup (100 g) Sugar

1 cup (240 ml) Apple cider

Black pepper, a grind

Salt, a dash

1 recipe Hazelnut Ice Cream—see p. 64

Equipment Needs

Ice cream machine

3¼-inch-diameter Pastry cutter

2 Sheetpans

Oven broiler or propane torch

Pastry bag with ¼-inch plain tip

Saucepan

Prepare the Puff Pastry Rounds

Preheat the oven to 400°F.

Cut 6, 3¼-inch circles from the pastry. Rest them in the freezer for 15 minutes. Place the circles on a sheetpan lined with parchment, away from the corners. In each of the corners, stack some inverted tart tins or other oven-proof items that measure approximately 1 inch in height.

Lightly oil the back of another sheetpan of the same size and press a piece of parchment onto it. Place this sheetpan, paper side down, on top of the inverted tart tins. Place a weighted object, such as a cast-iron pan or a foil-covered brick, atop the sheetpan.

You have now created a space of 1 inch in which the puff pastry can rise while baking. This will also force the pastry to have perfectly flat sides. Bake for 12 to 14 minutes, or until the pastry is a deep golden brown color. Allow to cool.

Place the puff pastry rounds on the back of a sheetpan and sprinkle generously with the powdered sugar. Melt the sugar with a propane torch in sweeping motions or under a broiler, turning as necessary to distribute the heat evenly. Repeat with the other side of the rounds.

Assemble the Dessert

Set the oven to 350°F. Fill a pastry bag fitted with a ¼-inch plain tip with the pastry

cream. Poke a hole with the tip through the tops of the pastry rounds and inject each with the cream. (You may need to poke 2 holes in the rounds in order to adequately fill them.) Place them on a sheetpan lined with parchment and warm in the oven.

Peel and core the apples. Cut in half lengthwise and slice lengthwise into ¼-inch slices.

On medium heat, melt the butter in a thick-bottom saucepan. Pour the sugar evenly into the pan and turn the heat to high. Stir gently as the sugar melts. Turn the heat to medium.

When the sugar turns a dark amber and begins to lightly smoke, carefully and slowly pour in the cider. Add the apples, salt, and pepper. Cook, stirring occasionally, until they are softened and translucent (about 4 to 5 minutes). Reserve the caramelized cider in the pan.

Place the puff pastry rounds on 6 very warm plates and overlap slices of the apples on each round. Pour the caramelized cider around each tart. Top each with a scoop or quenelle of ice cream. Serve at once.

Chef's Hint

Prepare a whole version of this apple tart as follows. Cut an 8-inch to 10-inch circle from prepared puff pastry and bake approximately 1 inch high as instructed above. Fill the baked puff pastry round with the ginger pastry cream or simply spread a ¼-inch-thick layer over the top. Cook the apples as instructed above and spiral them or arrange as desired over the prepared puff pastry round. Slice the tart with a serrated knife and serve with the reserved caramelized cider sauce and ice cream of your choice.

Liquid-Center Chocolate Cake with 3 Ice Creams

8 servings

Lovers of chocolate will be stirred when their forks pierce this animated dessert and they discover its warm, rich center of melted chocolate!

Chocolate Cake Mixture

2 Egg yolks, room temperature

1 Egg, room temperature

¼ cup (60 g) Sugar

2 tablespoons (30 ml) Coffee, strong

2 tablespoons (15 g) Flour

8 ounces (225 g) Chocolate, bittersweet, melted, very warm

4 Egg whites

1 recipe Chocolate Ganache—see p. 42

1 recipe Chocolate Génoise—see p. 26

1 ounce (30 ml) Brandy

Butter, melted, for brushing

Cocoa powder, for sprinkling

1 recipe Spearmint Ice Cream—see p. 66

1 recipe Espresso Ice Cream—see p. 63

1 recipe White Chocolate Ice Cream—see p. 68

1 recipe Bittersweet Chocolate Sauce—see p. 49

Equipment Needs

Ice cream machine

2½-inch-diameter Pastry cutter

8, 2½-inch-diameter Steel rings

Metal spatula

Prepare the Cake Mixture

In a mixer equipped with a whip, whip the egg yolks, whole egg, and sugar on high speed until light in color and doubled in volume. Reduce the speed and add the coffee, mixing until combined. Sift the flour over the mixture. Whisk until combined and smooth.

Transfer to a large bowl. Slowly pour in the melted chocolate, folding continuously with a rubber spatula. Whip the egg whites to soft peaks, then carefully and gently fold them with the rubber spatula into the chocolate mixture, so as to maintain the volume they bring to the mixture. Place mixture in the refrigerator.

Prepare the Ganache and Génoise

Adjust the temperature of the ganache so that it has a consistency that can be scooped

205

with an ice cream scoop and still retain its shape.

Cut 8, 2½-inch-diameter circles from the génoise. If the génoise is at least ½ inch thick, you can cut 4 circles and carefully slice each 1 in half with a serrated knife. Drizzle each circle with some brandy.

Assemble the Cake

Preheat oven to 400°F.

Place 8, 2½-inch-diameter, 1½-inch-tall steel rings on a parchment-lined sheetpan. Put a génoise circle in the bottom of each. Lightly brush the inside of each ring with some melted butter.

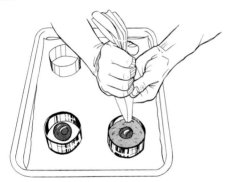

Scoop a ball of ganache no larger than 1 inch in diameter into each ring, in the center of the génoise circles. Using a pastry bag or a spoon, fill the chilled chocolate cake mixture around each ganache and against the inside of the ring up to ¼ inch from the top. The ganache scoop should be covered and the surface of the cake should be reasonably level.

. . . .

At this point, the cakes can be held, covered, and refrigerated for a few hours. However, the best results will be obtained by proceeding with the final assembly.

. . . .

Assemble the Dessert

Bake the cakes for approximately 9 to 11 minutes. When done, remove the cakes from the oven and allow to cool slightly (about 30 seconds). Use a paring knife to cut around their edges and carefully pull the rings off. If there is some resistance, the cakes may not be fully baked. Simply return them to the oven for a few more mintues, and try again. Sprinkle lightly with some cocoa powder.

Sauce 8 plates with an uneven drizzle of the sauce. Use a spatula to plate each cake. With a spoon, quenelle the ice creams onto the plates, touching the sides of the cakes to keep them from sliding. Serve at once.

Chef's Hint

This cake can be baked whole in a loaf pan that has been brushed with butter and sprinkled with sugar. Half the cake mixture should be spread into the bottom of the pan; then the ganache can be piped from a pastry bag or spooned down the center, and the remaining cake mixture spread over the top. It will need to be baked slightly longer than the individual cakes, approximately 15 to 17 minutes. Cool slightly, then unmold, slice, and serve with 1 or more ice creams.

Warm McIntosh Soup with Crispy Apple Dumpling and McIntosh Sorbet

6 servings

This refreshingly warm but light dessert is a wonderful way to use newly harvested apples in autumn. The bright flavors of the McIntosh apple contrast in 3 different ways—with the spiced warmth of the soup, the concentrated and cool flavor of the sorbet, and the crispy apple package.

McIntosh Soup

1½ cups (360 ml) Water

½ cup (120 ml) Apple cider

2½ tablespoons (35 g) Vanilla sugar

1 teaspoon (5 ml) Lemon juice

2 McIntosh apples

1 Cinnamon stick

Crispy Apple Dumpling Filling

1 McIntosh apple

1 tablespoon (10 g) Currants or apricots, dried, or dried fruit of your choice

¼ teaspoon (1 g) Nutmeg, grated

Black pepper, a grind

¼ cup (40 g) Hazelnuts, roasted

1 tablespoon (7 g) Powdered sugar

1 tablespoon (15 ml) Hazelnut liqueur or rum

Dumpling Shell

2 sheets Phyllo—see p. 21

Powdered sugar, for sprinkling

1 teaspoon (3 g) Bread crumbs, finely ground —optional

⅓ McIntosh apple, in matchstick-size strips

1 recipe McIntosh Apple Sorbet—see p. 72

Equipment Needs

Saucepot

Peeler

Apple corer

Ice cream machine

Blender

Food processor

6, 1½-inch-tall Timbale molds

Prepare the Soup

In a saucepot over high heat, bring the water, cider, sugar, and lemon juice to a boil. Peel, core, and quarter the apples. Add the apples and the cinnamon stick to the boiling mixture, reduce the heat to medium, and cover. Simmer until the mixture is reduced by ⅓ (about 15 minutes).

Remove from the heat. Puree in a blender. Strain through a fine chinois or cheesecloth.

207

Prepare the Filling

Peel and core the apple. Dice into ¼-inch pieces. Dice the dried fruit into similar-size pieces. Combine the apple, fruit, nutmeg, and pepper in a bowl. Set aside.

In a food processor, pulverize the hazelnuts with the sugar; add liqueur and continue to process until the mixture becomes somewhat smooth. Add this mixture to the apple mixture. Mix by hand, using a spoon, until all ingredients are completely incorporated.

Assemble the Dumplings

Prepare 6, 1½-inch-tall timbale molds by brushing them lightly with melted butter. Brush a sheet of phyllo with the melted butter and sprinkle with powdered sugar and bread crumbs. Top with the second sheet of phyllo. Press the 2 layers firmly together. Cut the phyllo into 6, 4-inch squares.

Working quickly so the phyllo does not dry out and become too brittle, carefully line each timbale mold with a phyllo square by bending it at the center and pressing the folds against the inside of the mold. Fill each timbale with the filling and bend the corners of the phyllo over to enclose.

Assemble the Dessert

Preheat the oven to 400°F.

In a saucepan over medium heat, warm the soup. Place the timbales with the dumplings on a sheetpan. Bake for approximately 12 minutes.

Sprinkle the apple strips onto the bottom centers of 6 warm bowls. Remove the dumplings from the oven. Tap the timbales to remove the dumplings from them. If they stick, run a paring knife around the edges and tap them again. Place the dumplings on top of the apple strips. Surround each with 3 scoops of the sorbet. Pour the very warm soup into the bowls and serve immediately.

Chef's Hint

This soup can be made a day ahead, tightly covered and refrigerated, and then warmed in a saucepot before being served. Either the sorbet or dumplings can be omitted if desired without greatly reducing the intensity of the apple flavors.

Malt and Bitter Chocolate Terrine
with Malt Sauce

8 servings

In this dessert, the mild flavor of malt is contrasted with dark chocolate.

Terrine

2 sheets or 2 teaspoons powdered (7 g) Gelatin

2 cups (480 ml) Crème Anglaise—see p. 34

6 tablespoons (55 g) Barley malt powder

1 teaspoon (5 ml) Brandy

¼ cup (30 g) Cocoa powder

1 ounce (30 g) Chocolate, bittersweet, melted

2 tablespoons (30 ml) Water, warm

¾ cup (180 ml) Heavy cream, whipped

Tuile Support Squares

1 recipe Tuile Batter—see p. 31

¾ ounce (25 g) Almonds, lightly chopped

1 recipe Hazelnut Brittle—see p. 46

1 recipe Chocolate Génoise—see p. 26

1 ounce (30 ml) Brandy

1 recipe Chocolate Ganache—see p. 42

1 recipe Malt Sauce—see p. 50

Equipment Needs

Small terrine mold or loaf pan

Plastic wrap

Pastry wheel

Prepare the Terrine

Cover the sheets of gelatin in cold water to soften them (or bloom the powdered gelatin in 1 tablespoon of cold water). Place a medium-size pot, half filled with water, on low heat.

Divide the crème anglaise into 2 bowls. Whisk the malt powder, a little at a time, into 1 of the bowls, then add the brandy and set aside. In the other bowl, whisk in the cocoa powder and set it aside. In a separate, smaller bowl, whisk together the chocolate and warm water until smooth, then whisk this into the cocoa powder anglaise.

Heat each bowl separately over the pot of simmering water, stirring constantly to dissolve any remaining lumps of malt or cocoa, until the anglaise is very warm to the touch. Whisk 1 of the softened sheets of gelatin into each bowl (or half the powdered, bloomed gelatin into each), until completely dissolved.

Place both bowls of anglaise in the refrigerator. Chill until they begin to thicken and set. Whisk half of the whipped cream into each anglaise, until thoroughly combined.

Lightly brush with oil a 2¼-inch-wide by 2¼-inch-high by 6-inch-long terrine mold or similar-size loaf pan. Line with a piece of plastic wrap that has enough excess to cover the

210

top when the mold is full. Spread a ½-inch layer of the malt cream into the bottom of the mold. Smooth the top with the end of a small rubber spatula. Chill in the freezer until set (about 10 minutes).

Spread a ½-inch layer of the chocolate cream over the first layer, smooth the top, and return to the freezer. Continue with 2 more layers, alternating the flavors, chilling each. Wrap the plastic over the top and chill for 1 hour (the terrine also can be refrigerated for 24 hours).

Prepare the Support Squares
Preheat the oven to 375°F.

On a stickless pan or a pan lined with parchment and generously brushed with but-ter, spread the tuile batter to an area slightly larger than 6 inches square and approximately ¹⁄₁₆ inch thick, so that the sheetpan surface is just barely visible. Sprinkle the almonds evenly over the tuile. Place in the oven, turn-ing the pan as necessary to allow for even browning (about 10 minutes).

Starting from 2 corners of the tuile, peel it from the baking surface and lay it on a large cutting board. Using a straight-edge pastry wheel or a large French knife, rapidly cut the tuile into 3, 2-inch by 6-inch pieces. Cut each of these into 3 pieces, 2 inches by 2 inches. Reheat the tuile as necessary to soften it for cutting.

Assemble the Dessert
Unwrap the terrine and roll it in the brit-tle. Slice into 8, ¾-inch slices. Place each on a tuile support square. Cut the génoise into 8, 2-inch squares, sprinkle the brandy over them, and spread the tops with a ⅛-inch layer of ganache.

Place the squares in the centers of 8 room-temperature plates, set a tuile-supported ter-rine slice on each, and drizzle the sauce around them. Allow to come to room temperature for about 5 minutes, then serve.

Chef's Hint

Instead of layering the 2 creams, they can be swirled together in a torte version of this dessert as follows. Omit the tuile batter from the "in advance" items since tuile support squares are unnecessary for this method, and cut the génoise to fit into the bottom of a 6-inch to 9-inch springform pan and sprinkle it with brandy.

Immediately after folding the whipped cream into the 2 anglaises, pour them simultaneously into the springform pan. Swirl together the 2 a few times with the handle end of a spoon. Place the pan in the refrigerator until set, about 1 hour. Draw a knife around the inside edge of the pan to release the torte and press some hazelnut brittle around the outer edge. Cut it into slices with a slightly warm knife and serve with malt sauce.

Port-Poached Pear in Brioche with Chestnut Sorbet and Dried Black Mission Figs

6 servings

In this dessert, the poached pear—a staple of many winter dessert menus —is enhanced by the richness of chestnuts and deep flavors of the dried figs.

Poached Pears

1 bottle (750 ml) Port wine

1 teaspoon (1 g) Black peppercorns, crushed

6 Cloves, whole

6 Forelli pears (or other smaller-size pears just beginning to ripen)

Figs

6 Black Mission figs, dried

1 recipe Chestnut Puree—see p. 47 (half will be used for the sorbet, the remaining half to fill the poached pears)

1 recipe Brioche—see p. 17

Egg wash—see p. 55

Sugar, for sprinkling

1 recipe Chestnut Sorbet—see p. 70

Equipment Needs

Ice cream machine

Apple corer

Food processor

Pastry bag with ¼-inch to ½-inch plain tip

Prepare the Pears

In a medium-size saucepan, heat the port to a simmer; then add the peppercorns and cloves. Peel and core the pears, leaving them whole, and add to the port. Cook the pears for about 20 minutes. Remove the pears from the port and set on a tray to cool.

. . . .

The cooking time of the pears will depend on their ripeness. The pears will be done when they can be easily pierced with a knife. Take special care not to overcook them, or they will lose their firm structure and begin to break apart. Poaching the pears can be done up to 2 days in advance, if desired. Simply leave the pears in the port mixture, wrap well, and refrigerate. The longer the pears soak in the mixture, the more they will soak up the flavor of the port.

. . . .

Prepare the Figs

Remove and discard the hard stem from the tops of the figs. Slice them into approximately ¹⁄₁₆-inch-thick pieces. Add the slices to the simmering port. Cook long enough so that they soften and the amount of port wine reduces to half. This will be used as the sauce for

213

the dessert. As it reduces and thickens, it draws sweetness from the dried fruit.

Assemble the Pears

Fill a pastry bag fitted with a plain tip with the chestnut puree. Stand the pears upright. Using the pastry bag, fill the core of each with the puree.

Lightly dust the chilled brioche and your work surface with flour. Using a rolling pin, roll the brioche into an imperfect rectangle approximately ⅛ inch thick. With a paring knife, cut the brioche into 6 pieces.

Stand each pear on top of a piece of brioche near its edge. Pull the opposite edge over the pear, stretching the dough slightly and pinching around the bottom of the pear to seal it.

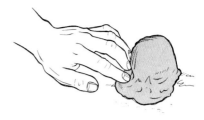

Draw the paring knife around the bottom of each pear to remove excess dough. Continue to pinch the seams together while turning each pear in your hand to assure that the brioche thickness is evenly distributed over them.

Assemble the Dessert

Preheat oven to 400°F.

Brush the egg wash over the entire surface of the brioche-covered pears. Sprinkle with sugar and place on a pan lined with parchment. Bake for 12 to 15 minutes, or until the brioche is uniformly brown.

Warm the sauce and figs. Spoon the figs on 6 warm plates, off center. Slice each pear in half crossways and arrange both halves in the center of each plate. Spoon some port sauce over the halves. Finish each of the plates with 2 scoops of sorbet. Serve at once.

Chef's Hint

You may omit the chestnut puree and brioche and simply serve slices of poached pear with the warmed figs and port sauce. You may also replace the chestnut sorbet with a store-bought, mild-flavored nut ice cream.

Pear and Orange French-Toast Tart with Red Wine Ice Cream

6 servings

In this dessert, the familiar idea of French toast served with fruit is refined with seasoned pear and orange segments and tangy red wine ice cream.

Brioche

½ recipe Brioche—see p. 17

1 teaspoon (1 g) Cardamom, ground

½ cup (80 g) Papaya, dried, diced

Fruit

2 Pears, ripe

2 Oranges, peeled and sectioned

1 ounce (30 ml) Brandy

White pepper, a grind

Cinnamon, a dash

French Toast Mixture

1½ cups (360 ml) Milk

1 ounce (30 ml) Orange liqueur (Grand Marnier)

1 Cinnamon stick

½ Vanilla bean, scraped

¼ cup (80 g) Honey

1 Egg

1 recipe Pear Coulis—see p. 53

1 recipe Vanilla Pastry Cream—see p. 34

1 recipe Red Wine Ice Cream—see p. 65

Powdered sugar, for sprinkling

Equipment Needs

Ice cream machine

Cylindrical baking mold (optional)

Sauté pan

Prepare the Brioche

Preheat oven to 400°F.

Using your hands, mix the cardamom and papaya into the brioche dough. Butter the surfaces of a cylindrical mold no more than 3 inches in diameter (you can use a soup can that has both ends removed), or the brioche can be rolled into 3 equal-weight round loaves.

Generously dust the work surface with flour. Roll the brioche as you would a loaf of bread, for the cylindrical mold, or into the 3 round loaves. Place the loaves on the pan or stand the cylindrical mold on end on a parch-

ment-lined pan. Proof the brioche in a warm (70°F to 80°F) place for approximately 1 hour, or until the brioche does not spring back when poked. Bake for about 20 minutes.

Allow to cool, remove from the mold, and cut crossways to make 6 circles, each approximately ¾ inch thick. Or cut the 3 loaves from the sides to get 6 rounds of roughly the same size.

Prepare the Fruit

Peel and core the pears. Slice into wedges. Pour the orange juice from the sectioning process into a sauté pan and add the brandy and spices. Over high heat, bring the mixture to a boil. Add the pear wedges and orange segments, then immediately turn off the heat.

Prepare the French Toast Mixture

Heat the milk, liqueur, cinnamon stick, vanilla bean, and honey to a simmer in a small pot. Remove from the heat and allow the mixture to cool for several minutes, stirring occasionally. Whisk in the egg.

Assemble the Dessert

Melt some butter in a stickless sauté pan with the heat set to medium or medium low. Soak the brioche rounds in the French toast mixture. Sauté each slice until golden brown on each side.

Spoon some coulis onto 6 warm plates and spread it in uneven circles. Using a spatula, spread the pastry cream evenly over 1 side of each brioche toast. Place a toast in each coulis, with the pastry cream facing up. On top of each toast, alternate the orange and pear slices to complete a circle. Sprinkle with some powdered sugar and finish off with a quenelle of ice cream. Serve at once.

Chef's Hint

This dessert can be made using a high-quality commercially made bread, like a sourdough, instead of the brioche and a quality commercially made ice cream of your choice.

Pumpkin Ravioli with Candied Ginger and Roasted, Caramelized Pumpkin Broth

6 servings

Vanilla pasta is used in this dessert as a way to present the pumpkin and to texturally complement the pumpkin puree and rich pumpkin broth.

Pumpkin Filling

1 Pumpkin, small

1 tablespoon (20 g) Molasses

1 teaspoon (5 ml) Brandy

½ teaspoon (.5 g) Cinnamon

½ teaspoon (.5 g) Cocoa powder

Salt, a dash

Pepper, a grind

1 Egg white

1 tablespoon (15 g) Vanilla sugar

¼ cup (60 ml) Heavy cream, whipped

Caramelized Pumpkin Broth

2 quarts (1.89 l) Water

¼ cup (60 g) Sugar

Ravioli

1 recipe Vanilla Pasta—see p. 22

Egg wash

1 recipe Candied Ginger—see p. 55

1 recipe Macadamia Nut Brittle—see p. 46

Equipment Needs

Skillet or saucepot

Food processor

Small pasta machine

2¼-inch-diameter Fluted pastry cutter

Prepare the Pumpkin

Preheat oven to 400°F.

Cut the pumpkin into quarters, remove the seeds, and place the quarters on a foil- or parchment-lined pan. Bake for about 35 minutes, or until a knife slides easily through the pumpkin. Remove from the oven and allow to cool slightly. Reserve any pumpkin juices that remain in the pan.

Skin the pumpkin and place into a thick-bottom skillet or pot on medium heat. Cook for about 15 minutes, stirring occasionally and allowing some of it to stick to the pot while reducing the volume. (You will use the pumpkin that sticks to the pot in the caramelized pumpkin broth, so don't wash it out!) Spread ¾ of the reduced pumpkin onto a sheetpan. Chill in the refrigerator. Leave ¼ of the reduced pumpkin in the pot. (While the pumpkin cools, you can make the pumpkin broth.)

219

Prepare the Pumpkin Broth

Fill the pot that you used for cooking the pumpkin half full with water. Place on high heat. Add any juices reserved from the baking pan. Reduce the liquid to ¼ of its original amount. The flavors from the pumpkin bits in the pan and the reduced pumpkin have now been infused into the water. The reduced liquid should appear very rich and dark.

In a separate saucepan of similar size, cook the sugar over medium heat. As the sugar melts and begins to brown, stir occasionally with a spoon. When it turns deep amber and begins to smoke, reduce the heat to low.

Slowly and carefully pour ¼ of the pumpkin broth into the caramel. It should bubble and rise up as it cools and dissolves. Pour the remaining broth into the caramel. Stir gently over the heat to dissolve any remaining caramel. Sweeten with additional sugar to taste. Pass through a cheesecloth or fine chinois.

Prepare the Filling

In a food processor, combine the chilled, reduced pumpkin, molasses, brandy, cinnamon, cocoa powder, salt, and pepper. Puree until smooth. Whip the egg white to stiff peaks and add the vanilla sugar. Continue to whip until dissolved. Fold the egg white and whipped cream into the pumpkin mixture. Return it to the refrigerator until well chilled.

Prepare the Ravioli

Roll a sheet of pasta in a strip approximately 18 inches long to the thinnest width of

your pasta machine. Egg wash half of the length of pasta.

Using either a 1½-inch-diameter ice cream scoop or a spoon, scoop 6 mounds of filling onto the egg-washed pasta end in 2 evenly spaced rows, with each mound approximately ½ inch apart. Fold the empty half of pasta over the fillings. Carefully seal the top layer to the bottom around the fillings, without disrupting their shape. With a 2¼-inch-diameter fluted pastry cutter, cut out each ravioli. Pinch edges well to seal in the filling.

Assemble the Dessert

Cook the raviolis in boiling water for approximately 2 minutes. Meanwhile, reheat the pumpkin broth.

Place a few strips of candied ginger in the centers of each of 6 warm bowls. Place the cooked raviolis on top of them. Place a few more strips of candied ginger on top of the raviolis. Sprinkle the brittle around the raviolis. At the very last moment before serving, pour enough pumpkin broth over the raviolis to cover the bottom of each bowl. Serve immediately.

Chef's Hint

In lieu of making raviolis, this delicious pumpkin filling could replace the date filling in the date pithivier recipe (see p. 199). Serve the pumpkin pithivier with the macadamia brittle and pumpkin broth described above or, alternatively, with a caramelized orange sauce (see p. 49).

Quince and Dried-Fruits Terrine with Mincemeat Strudel and Madeira Sauce

8 servings

When choosing winter fruits, one often overlooks the quince. This dessert, which pairs quince with dried apricots, cherries, and prunes, is perfect fare for the holiday season.

Quince

1 quince

¼ cup (60 g) Sugar

2 cups (480 ml) Madeira

3 Cinnamon sticks

5 Cloves, whole

Black pepper, a grind

Salt, a dash

1 recipe Frangipane—see p. 28

Strudel

1 Granny Smith apple, peeled, cored, diced

½ Orange, pith removed, diced

½ cup (70 g) Raisins, chopped

½ Lemon, juiced, zest finely chopped

1 ounce (30 ml) Brandy

1 tablespoon (15 g) Sugar

¼ cup (60 ml) Water

½ teaspoon (.5 g) Cinnamon, ground

½ teaspoon (.5 g) Allspice, ground

Black pepper, a grind

Salt, a dash

2 sheets Phyllo—see p. 21

Butter, melted, for brushing

Powdered sugar, for sprinkling

½ cup (100 g) Fruits, dried

Vanilla pastry cream—reserved from frangipane

4 Crêpes—see p. 28

Equipment Needs

Saucepan

Food processor

Peeler

Apple corer

Small terrine mold or loaf pan

Plastic wrap

Prepare the Quince

Peel and core the quince, slice lengthwise into ¼-inch slices, toss with the sugar. Heat a large saucepan over high heat and add the quince slices. Toss and turn them until they begin to caramelize and soften (about 10 minutes). Add the madeira, spices, and seasonings. Simmer until cooked through (about 15 minutes). Remove the quince.

Continue to reduce the madeira to about ⅓ cup (80 ml). Reserve for use as the sauce.

Bake the Frangipane

Preheat the oven to 375°F.

Line a small sheetpan with parchment; brush lightly with butter and dust with flour. Spread the frangipane to an area 7 inches by 10 inches by ⅜ inch thick. Bake for 12 to 14 minutes. Reserve for constructing the terrine.

Prepare the Strudel

Mix the apple, orange, raisins, lemon juice and zest, brandy, sugar, water, spices, and seasonings in a saucepan. Cook over medium heat, stirring occasionally, until it is reduced in volume by ¼ (about 14 to 16 minutes). Allow to cool.

Spread out the 2 sheets of phyllo, end to end. Brush with the butter and sprinkle lightly with powdered sugar. Fold each sheet in half lengthwise by lifting the 2 top corners and aligning them atop the 2 bottom corners. Brush the top layer with butter. You should now have 2 rectangles, 6 inches by 15 inches.

Spoon the filling in even lines along the edge of each 15-inch side. Roll the strudels tightly, pressing out any trapped air along the way. Set on a parchment-lined sheetpan. Save for final assembly.

Construct the Terrine

Lightly brush with oil a 2¼-inch-wide by 2¼-inch-high by 6-inch-long terrine mold or similar-size loaf pan. Line with a piece of plastic wrap that has enough excess to cover the top when the mold is full.

Cut the frangipane layer into 4, 6-inch by 2¼-inch pieces. Spread them with a ⅛-inch layer of the pastry cream. Place 1 frangipane layer, pastry cream side up, in the bottom of the mold. Layer some quince slices, end to end, overlapping in places. Sprinkle some softened dried fruits over the quince, then add another layer of frangipane. Continue layering the terrine in this order until the 4th layer of frangipane is placed on top.

Cover the top with the extra plastic wrap and apply firm, downward pressure to the terrine to remove any air pockets. Place in the freezer for 20 minutes.

Remove the terrine from the mold and unwrap it. Use a metal spatula to spread a thin layer of pastry cream over the tops, sides, and bottom.

Spread out the 4 crêpes, overlapping each other, to cover an area of at least 6 inches by 9 inches. Place the terrine on the 6-inch length of the crêpes. Roll the terrine over to wrap the crêpes around the terrine. Trim the overhang-

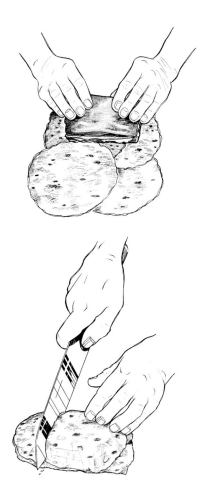

Assemble the Dessert

Preheat the oven to 400°F.

Bake the strudels until browned and crisp (about 12 to 14 minutes).

With the plastic wrap still on it, cut the terrine into 8, ³/₄-inch-thick slices with a sharp serrated knife. Place each slice flat on a sheet-pan lined with parchment. Remove the plastic wrap surrounding them.

Trim ¹/₂ inch off the ends of the strudels. Cut them crossways into 6, 2¹/₄-inch lengths. Cut each length in half at an angle so that when the strudel pieces are stood on end, they are angled to a point. Warm the strudel and terrines in the oven.

ing excess crêpe from the ends. (Any spots where the crêpes are not sticking to the terrine can be secured by smearing a little pastry cream underneath to hold it down.) Wrap well in plastic and refrigerate until final assembly.

In the center of 8 warm plates, place a terrine and surround each with 3 pieces of strudel. Sauce each plate by drizzling some around each strudel and a little over the top of the terrine. Serve at once.

Chef's Hint

After cooking the quince in the madeira, it could be served with the softened, dried fruits in a compote style, perhaps accompanied by some vanilla ice cream. The strudel could also be served alone with the madeira sauce and an ice cream.

Baby Banana Split with Chocolate Sorbet

6 servings

This dessert is my version of the familiar dime-store banana split, using intensely flavored baby bananas, bittersweet chocolate, and macadamia nuts.

Bread Pudding

1 recipe Chocolate Génoise—see p. 26
2 Eggs
1 tablespoon (15 g) Vanilla sugar
²⁄₃ cup (160 ml) Milk
¼ teaspoon (.25 g) Nutmeg, grated
1 ounce (30 ml) Brandy

¼ cup (60 ml) Heavy cream
2 teaspoons (10 g) Vanilla sugar
1 tablespoon (15 g) Butter
1 tablespoon (12 g) Brown sugar
6 Baby bananas, peeled
Cinnamon, a dash
Pepper, white or black, a grind
1 ounce (30 ml) Brandy

1 recipe Vanilla Sauce—see p. 48
1 recipe Macadamia Nut Brittle—see p. 46
1 recipe Chocolate Sorbet—see p. 70
1 recipe Roasted Coconut Shavings—see
   p. 47
6 Cherries, sour, dried

Equipment Needs

Ice cream machine
Small terrine mold or loaf pan
Saucepan

Prepare the Pudding

Preheat the oven to 350°F.

Line a 7¼-inch by 3¼-inch loaf pan with foil. Brush lightly with oil.

Break enough of the génoise into uneven 1-inch pieces. Lightly place them into the pan, in order to fill it 1¼ inches high.

Whisk together the eggs, sugar, milk, nutmeg, and brandy. Pour over the génoise. Press the génoise down, where necessary, to ensure that the custard saturates it. Bake for 14 to 16 minutes, or until a knife inserted into the pudding comes out clean. Allow to cool.

Cut around the edge of the pudding. Remove the foil and pudding from the pan and cut the pudding into 6, 1¼-inch-wide strips.

Assemble the Dessert

Whip the cream with the sugar to stiff peaks. Set aside. Place the strips of bread pudding in the oven to heat.

In a saucepan over high heat, melt the butter; add the brown sugar and stir to heat the sugar. When the pan is very hot, add the bananas, cinnamon, and pepper. Sauté the bananas, turning and carefully flipping them in the brown sugar mixture for several minutes. Add the brandy. Remove the bananas from the pan.

. . . .

When adding brandy, be extremely careful. Pour it into the pan in 1 motion and stand back as the pan flames and the alcohol burns out.

. . . .

Place the bread pudding strips in the centers of 6 warm plates, surround them with drizzle of the vanilla sauce and a sprinkle of the brittle.

With the side of a paring knife, press an indentation into the top length of the bread pudding strip so the split banana will sit securely without rolling off. Make a slice in the inward curved side of the bananas, being sure not to cut all the way through them. Set each banana, split side up, into the bread pudding indentation. Pull the splits open.

Put 2 scoops of sorbet into each banana and top with a small scoop of the whipped cream, some coconut shavings, and a dried cherry. Serve at once.

Chef's Hint

The bread pudding can be omitted and the sautéed bananas served in a small serving bowl or dessert goblet with a commercial chocolate ice cream, the vanilla sauce, and nut brittle. The dried cherries and coconut are also optional.

Banana Tart with Walnut Raviolis and Chocolate Mousse

6 servings

In this dessert, spiraling slices of caramelized bananas are supported by chocolate mousse and complemented by flavorful raviolis.

Puff Pastry Rounds

½ sheet Puff Pastry—see p. 18

Powdered sugar, for sprinkling

Ravioli

1 recipe Vanilla Pasta—see p. 22

1 recipe Walnut Paste—see p. 45

Egg wash

1 recipe Bittersweet Chocolate Sauce—see p. 49

1 recipe Chocolate Mousse—see p. 43

2 Bananas, ripe

Sugar, for sprinkling

Equipment Needs

3-inch-diameter Pastry cutter

Oven broiler or propane torch

Food processor

Small pasta machine

1¼-inch-diameter Fluted pastry cutter

Prepare the Pastry Rounds

Preheat the oven to 400°F.

Cut 6, 3-inch-diameter circles from the pastry. Place them on a pan in the freeze to rest for 15 minutes. Place the circles towards the center of a parchment-lined sheetpan. In each of the corners of the sheetpan, stack some inverted tart tins, or other oven-proof items, that measure approximately 1 inch high.

Lightly oil the back of another sheetpan of the same size. Press a piece of parchment onto it. Place this sheetpan, paper side down, on top of the inverted tart tins. Place a weighted object, such as a cast-iron pan or a foil-covered brick, atop the sheetpan.

You have now created a space of 1 inch in which the puff pastry can rise while baking. This will also force the pastry to have perfectly flat sides. Bake for 12 to 14 minutes, or until the pastry is a deep golden brown color. Allow to cool.

Place the rounds on the back of a sheetpan and sprinkle generously with powdered sugar. Melt the sugar with a propane torch in sweeping motions or under a broiler, turning as necessary to distribute the heat evenly. Repeat this process with the other side of the pastry rounds.

Assemble the Ravioli

Roll a sheet of pasta into a strip approximately 24 inches long to the thinnest width of your pasta machine. Egg wash half the length of pasta.

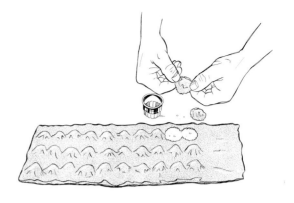

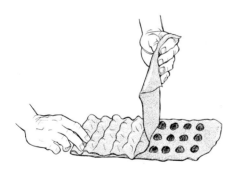

Using the smaller end of a melon baller, scoop 10 mounds of walnut paste onto the egg-washed end of the pasta in evenly spaced rows of 3 each for a total of 30. Each mound should be approximately 1 inch apart (see diagram). Fold the empty pasta half over the fillings. Carefully seal the top layer to the bottom around the fillings, without disrupting their shape. With a 1¼-inch-diameter fluted pastry cutter, cut out each ravioli. Pinch its edges well to seal in the filling.

Assemble the Dessert

Put a pot of water over high heat to boil. Spread a 5-inch-diameter circle of sauce on 6 warm plates. Slice the bananas diagonally, ⅛ inch thick and 2½ inch long.

Using a paring knife, cut a circle in the tops of the pastry rounds, ¼ inch in from their edge, and press it down gently. Fill in the centers of the pastry rounds with a mound of mousse. Stand the banana slices against the mousse, overlapping all the way around the tart. Sprinkle with sugar. Melt the sugar with a propane torch in sweeping motions, or under a broiler, turning as necessary to distribute the heat evenly. Lightly caramelize the bananas without burning the pastry. Place each tart in the center of each sauce.

Cook the raviolis in the boiling water for about 1 minute. Drain and place 5 raviolis around each tart. Serve at once.

Chef's Hint

You may prepare a whole version of the banana tart as follows. Cut an 8-inch to 10-inch circle from prepared puff pastry and bake it 1 inch high as instructed above. Pipe a $^{1}/_{2}$-inch layer of chocolate mousse from a pastry bag over the baked puff pastry round or simply spread the mousse over the top of the puff pastry with a metal spatula. Slice the bananas as instructed above and spiral or arrange them as desired over the chocolate mousse. Sprinkle the bananas lightly with sugar and melt the sugar as described above. Slice the tart with a serrated knife and serve with the chocolate sauce and any desired number of walnut raviolis or a simple sprinkle of walnut brittle (see p. 46).

Thai Rice Pudding with Candied Thai Pepper, Dried Apricots, and Carrot Sorbet

6 servings

This dessert involves the pleasantly surprising use of vegetables, which add intriguing flavors to the rice pudding.

Candied Thai Pepper

2 Thai peppers, preferably 1 red, 1 green
Water, for blanching
¼ cup (60 ml) Water
¼ cup (60 g) Sugar

Crispy Carrot Slices

1 Carrot, large, peeled
½ cup (120 ml) Water
½ cup (100 g) Sugar
1 cup (230 g) Vegetable oil, preferably peanut
    or grapeseed

Rice Pudding

½ cup (90 g) Thai or Jasmine rice
1 cup (240 ml) Milk
1 cup (240 ml) Water
1 Egg
2 tablespoons (30 g) Sugar
½ cup (120 ml) Cream
¼ cup (60 ml) Milk
½ teaspoon (.5 g) Coriander, ground
Salt, a dash

Dried Fruit

12 (90 g) Apricots, dried
¼ cup (40 g) Blueberries, dried
1 ounce (30 ml) Brandy
½ cup (120 ml) Water

1 recipe Vanilla Sauce—see p. 48
1 recipe Carrot Sorbet—see p. 70
1 recipe Pistachio Brittle—see p. 46

Equipment Needs

Ice cream machine
Wire rack
6, 2¼-inch-tall Timbale molds

Prepare the Candied Peppers

Remove the tops and seeds from the peppers. Slice the peppers lengthwise into very thin slivers, about ¹⁄₁₆ inch thick. Put the slices in the blanching water. Turn the heat to high, bring to a boil, then reduce and simmer for 2 minutes. Strain the slices, then return them to

the pot with ¼ cup of fresh water and the sugar. Bring to a boil. Reduce the heat and simmer for 5 minutes. Allow the slivers to cool in the syrup.

Prepare the Carrot Slices

. . . .

These crispy carrot slices are an added textural and visual bonus for this dessert and may be omitted if desired.

. . . .

Using a carrot peeler or mandolin, make 14 very thin slices the length of the carrot. Bring the water and sugar to a boil. Reduce to a simmer, add the carrot slices, and simmer for 8 minutes.

. . . .

Use extreme caution while working with hot oil. After a few minutes, test its temperature by dropping a small piece of carrot in the oil. It should bubble and rise to the top.

. . . .

In a separate pot, heat the oil over medium heat. Carefully drop the carrot slices into the hot oil. After about 2½ minutes, or when the carrots' bubbling has subsided considerably,

use a slotted spoon to strain them from the oil. Place on a wire rack to drain.

Working quickly while they are still hot and before they harden, stretch the slices out so that they do not touch one another. They should harden as they cool. If they remain limp or very flexible, return them to the oil for a little longer. Allow to cool and reserve.

Prepare the Rice Pudding

Preheat the oven to 325°F.

Rinse the rice well under running water. In a pot over medium heat, combine the rice with the cup of milk and the water. When it comes to a boil, lower the heat and simmer until the liquid is evaporated and the rice is cooked through.

Whisk the egg with the sugar, then add the cream, ¼ cup of milk, coriander, salt, and candied pepper. Add the cooked rice and pour the mixture into 6, 2¼-inch-high timbale molds or ramekins that have been brushed lightly with melted butter and sprinkled with sugar. Place the molds on a pan filled with water so they bake gently. Bake for about 23 to 25 minutes, or until the custard is firm and an inserted knife comes out clean. Reserve.

Prepare the Dried Fruits

Slice the apricots into ¼-inch-thick slices. Place in a pot with the blueberries, brandy, and water. Bring to a boil. Strain the fruit and save for final assembly.

Assemble the Dessert

On 6 very warm plates, arrange the dried apricots, pointing outward from the center of the plate. Sprinkle the blueberries over them. Cut around the warm rice puddings with a paring knife and unmold them onto the plates next to the dried fruit. Drizzle some sauce in circles around the pudding and lean 2 or more carrot slices against the pudding. Place 2 small scoops of the sorbet at their base and sprinkle some brittle closely around the dessert. Serve at once.

Chef's Hint

The carrot slices could be omitted. The pudding could be baked whole in a small bread pan and cut into portions. The carrot sorbet could also be replaced with a mild-flavored commercially made sorbet.

Valentine Roulade of Red Fruits with Pistachio Ice Cream

8 servings

Valentine's Day is the 1 day in winter when splurging with unseasonal berries and plums is appropriate.

Red Fruit Filling

2 sheets or 2 teaspoons powdered (7 g) Gelatin

7 ounces (200 g) Strawberries, approximately 1 cup, quartered

7 ounces (200 g) Raspberries, approximately 1 cup

7 ounces (200 g) Plums, approximately 3, pitted, sliced

1 cup (240 ml) White wine

3 tablespoons (45 g) Sugar

¾ cup (180 ml) Heavy cream, whipped

Roulade

1 recipe Chocolate Roulade Sponge Cake—see p. 25

1 recipe Chocolate Ganache—see p. 42

1 recipe Pistachio Ice Cream—see p. 65

Equipment Needs

Ice cream machine

Saucepan

Metal spatula

Prepare the Fruit Filling

Soften the gelatin sheet in enough cold water to cover it for 10 minutes, or bloom the powdered gelatin in 1 tablespoon (15 ml) of cold water for 10 minutes.

In a saucepan over medium heat, place the fruits, wine, and sugar. Bring the wine to a simmer. Toss until fruits are warmed through.

Strain the fruits from the wine. Reserve half the wine for use as the sauce. Dissolve the bloomed gelatin in the other half. Mix this back into the fruits. Place the fruit mixture in the refrigerator to cool. When it is just beginning to thicken and set, fold the cream into the mixture. Reserve.

Assemble the Roulade

Cut the sponge cake into 2 pieces, each measuring 12 inches by 15 inches. Using a serrated knife, slice off the top 1/16 inch from each piece in order to even them out. Place the sponge pieces lengthwise, side by side, with a few inches between them, on a sheetpan lined with parchment.

Mound the fruit filling evenly down the center of each piece. Pick up the parchment

237

warm metal spatula. Gently and quickly press the 2 halves together, making sure they have sealed and become 1 piece. Return to the refrigerator for several minutes. If necessary, shape a little more by using your hands to apply pressure in spots to make it a perfect heart shape.

Using a spatula, smooth the ganache over the surface, completing half the roulade. Chill it. Turn it over and complete the other half with ganache and chill.

from the long side. Roll the edge of the sponge over the fruits to touch down on the parchment to make a half-pipe shape with the flat side down. Gently push on the length of 1 edge with your thumbs to tuck it under slightly and to form the shape of a half-heart. Repeat this process with the other sponge piece. Refrigerate the 2 halves for about 20 minutes.

Peel the halves from the parchment and heat the fruit filling surface, using a few sweeping motions with a propane torch or a

Assemble the Dessert

Using a warm, clean serrated knife for each cut, slice the roulade into 8, 1½-inch-thick pieces. Place them in the centers of 8 plates. Pour the reserved wine sauce around each and place 3 scoops of the ice cream around the roulade. Serve at once.

Chef's Hint

Instead of making a roulade, you could cut 16 heart shapes from the sponge cake spread with ganache. Serve them next to a red fruit and white wine compote and a quality, commercially made nut ice cream.

Warm Caramelized Apple and Black Walnut Torte with Golden Raisins and Red Apple Sorbet

6 servings

Apples seasoned with caramel and flavorful black walnuts, along with the festive presentation, make this an ideal dessert for midwinter or New Year's Eve.

Caramel Sticks and Caramelized Apples

2 teaspoons (10 ml) Water

³/₄ cup (150 g) Sugar

6 Gala or Jonathan apples

1 tablespoon (15 g) Butter

Génoise

1 tablespoon (15 g) Sugar

1 tablespoon (15 ml) Brandy

1 tablespoon (15 ml) Water

1 recipe Black Walnut Génoise—see p. 27

1 recipe Black Walnut Paste—see p. 45

1 recipe Golden Raisin Sauce—see p. 50

36 Golden raisins, plumped in hot water for 10 minutes

1 recipe Red Apple Sorbet—see p. 72

Powdered sugar, for sprinkling

Equipment Needs

Ice cream machine

Peeler

Apple corer

Sheetpan

Saucepan

Metal spatula

2³/₄-inch-diameter Pastry cutter

Prepare the Caramel Sticks and Apples

. . . .

These caramel sticks are an added textural and visual bonus and may be omitted if desired.

. . . .

Peel, core, and halve the apples crossways so that the hole is in the center of each. Set aside.

Lightly coat a sheetpan with oil and keep it nearby.

. . . .

Be extremely careful, as melted sugar is very hot.

. . . .

In a thick-bottom saucepan, pour the water, then pour the sugar over the water evenly. Turn the heat to medium high. When the sugar begins to melt, stir gently with a spoon. Turn the heat down to medium. When the sugar crystals are melted and light amber, turn off the heat and dip the bottom of the pot in some cold water to stop the sugar from cooking.

Place the sheetpan next to the saucepan with the caramel so that they are touching, dip a spoon into the caramel, pull a string to the opposite end of the sheetpan, and return the spoon to the caramel in 1 motion. The caramel should remain in 1 continuous, long string. You can adjust the speed of this motion to get a very fine caramel stick. You will need to reheat the caramel from time to time. When you have made 22 or more very thin sticks of the caramel, break them apart where they connect and set aside until final assembly.

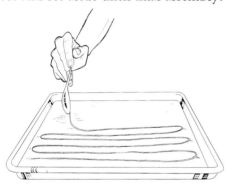

Place the pan of caramel back on medium heat and add the butter. When the caramel darkens and lightly smokes, carefully place 3 or 4 of the apple halves in the pan. Turn them from side to side with a spatula until they are saturated with the caramel, but still firm enough to hold together (about 8 minutes). Place them on a sheetpan to cool. Continue the cooking process with the remaining apple halves.

Prepare the Génoise

Heat the sugar, water, and brandy until the sugar dissolves. Cut 12, 2¾-inch circles from the génoise and soak them with the brandy liquid. Using a metal spatula, spread half of the paste over each of the circles. Set the remaining paste aside for the final assembly.

Assemble the Dessert

Heat the apple halves in the oven.

Spread the raisin sauce in 4-inch circles on 6 warm plates. Sprinkle the raisins around the edge of the sauce. Place an apple half in each sauce. Using a pastry bag or small spoon, fill the centers of each with the nut paste. Top with the génoise circles, then with the last apple halves. Fill the centers with more nut paste. Place the final génoise circle on top. Sprinkle lightly with powdered sugar.

Finish with a scoop of the sorbet on top. Lean 3 caramel sticks against each sorbet from 3 separate points on the plate, like a tepee. Serve at once.

Chef's Hint

You could omit the nut paste, génoise, and caramel sticks, instead serving the caramelized apple with a commercially made nut ice cream, the raisin sauce, and a sprinkle of black walnut brittle (see p. 46).

CHAPTER SIX

Petit Fours and Chocolates

Petit fours should not be dismissed as trivial—they are an important part of the dining experience. As a last offering to the guest, they are the finishing touch, the enduring final impression of the meal. The diner may have experienced an array of flavors and indulgences throughout the meal; a few additional delicious morsels are an appropriate accompaniment to espresso or coffee, dessert wine, or a glass of port.

A good petit four exhibits the same characteristics as a good dessert—just in miniature form. A petit four should be inspired by the best of current dessert practices, just as the petit fours created by the great pastry cooks of earlier generations were tiny, bite-size replicas of the favorite cakes and pastries of the day. Nuts, fruits, and chocolate continue to provide the basic flavors for the recipes in this chapter. Although chocolate making, an elaborate subject deserving its own cookbook, could never be entirely covered here, I have included a few unique representative chocolate recipes. Many petit fours can be prepared well in advance. However, if they are chilled, it is best to bring them to room temperature before serving, to allow the flavors to fully develop. Making these scaled-down creations requires patience and attention to detail. You may find, however, that they spark your imagination to create more miniature, inventive combinations of pastry and foods offering seasonal flavors.

Black Walnut Tortes

25 to 30 petit fours

1 recipe Dobos Sponge Cake—see p. 24
1 recipe Black Walnut Paste—see p. 45
1 recipe Chocolate Ganache—see p. 42
1 recipe White Chocolate Ganache—see
   p. 43

Equipment Needs
Food processor
Plastic wrap
Metal spatula
Plastic pastry comb

Cut one of the Dobos sponge layers into equal quarters. Allow the paste to come to room temperature, if necessary. Spread an even $3/16$-inch layer of the paste over the surface of one of the Dobos quarters, then layer a second Dobos piece over the filling. Spread another even $3/16$-inch layer of the paste over the second Dobos layer and top it with a third Dobos layer.

Cover with plastic wrap and refrigerate for at least 15 minutes. Reserve the remaining Dobos for future tortes.

Meanwhile, stretch a piece of plastic wrap tightly over the back of a small sheetpan. Work the 2 ganaches separately by heating them over hot water or chilling them in the refrigerator as necessary to bring them to a smooth, spreadable consistency.

Spread an even $1/16$-inch of the chocolate ganache onto the plastic in an area somewhat larger than the torte (about 6 inches by 8 inches). Draw a flexible plastic pastry comb through the ganache, leaving evenly spaced lines. Chill the pan for 10 minutes.

Spread the white chocolate ganache over and between the dark chocolate ganache lines. Press the rectangular torte firmly upside down onto the ganache stripes. At this point, return the torte to chill for $1/2$ hour.

With a very sharp knife, trim the uneven edges of the torte, cutting through the plastic to the surface of the sheetpan. Turn the torte over. Starting at 1 corner, peel the plastic wrap off the top.

Cut the torte into ³/₄-inch to 1-inch squares or desired shapes.

The tortes may be refrigerated in an airtight container for 3 days.

. . . .

An effective pastry comb can be made by using a pair of scissors to cut a notch every other ¹/₁₆ inch on the straight edge of a round, flexible, plastic storage lid that has been cut in half.

. . . .

Brazil Nut Giandujas

30 to 35 chocolates

7 ounces or 1¹/₂ cups (200 g) Brazil nuts, whole

1 cup (100 g) Powdered sugar

8 ounces (230 g) Chocolate, bittersweet, melted

1 recipe Chocolate Ganache—see p. 42

Equipment Needs

Food processor

Plastic wrap

Metal spatula

In an oven preheated to 350°F, roast the brazil nuts on a sheetpan for 5 to 7 minutes. Set 8 roasted nuts aside and chop with a knife into roughly ¹/₄-inch to ¹/₂-inch pieces.

In a food processor, pulverize the remaining nuts and the powdered sugar until a paste begins to form. Scrape any paste off the sides of the processor and continue to process for 1 minute.

Reserve half the rough-chopped nuts for later use as decoration for the tops of the finished chocolates. Place the other half of the rough-chopped nuts, and the pulverized nut mixture, in a bowl. Pour in half of the chocolate. Using a spatula, mix it thoroughly. Add the remaining chocolate and fold the mixture together until combined. Place in the refrigerator until it cools and begins to thicken.

Stretch a piece of plastic over the back of a sheetpan and spread the gianduja into a ¹/₂-inch-thick rectangle, smoothing the top as evenly as possible. Chill until firm.

Spread a ¹/₈-inch-thick layer of ganache over the top of the gianduja. Smooth the surface with a slightly warm spatula. With a serrated or slicing knife, lightly mark approximately 1-inch by 1-inch diamond shapes to be cut, then press a piece of brazil nut into the soft ganache top of each chocolate.

Allow the ganache to harden somewhat, then remove the gianduja rectangle from the sheetpan and peel the plastic from the bottom. Cut the rectangle into the premarked shapes with a warm knife, cleaning it with a cloth each time.

You may refrigerate the giandujas in an airtight container for 1 week, but they are best if consumed within a few days.

Chestnut Chocolates

25 to 30 chocolates

1 recipe Candied Chestnuts—see p. 47
1 tablespoon (15 ml) Water
6 ounces (170 g) Chocolate, bittersweet, melted
1 recipe Tempered Milk Chocolate—see p. 41

Equipment Needs
Food processor
Chocolate thermometer
Parchment-lined sheetpan

Puree half the chestnuts with their remaining syrup and the water. With a paring knife, cut the remaining whole candied chestnuts roughly into quarters. Reserve for the tops of the chocolates.

Place the puree in a bowl and pour in half the melted chocolate. Using a spatula, mix it thoroughly. Add the remaining chocolate and fold the mixture together until combined. Transfer the mixture to a pastry bag fitted with a ½-inch plain tip.

On a parchment-lined pan, pipe 1-inch-diameter mounds. Settle each chestnut quarter into the top of each mound of chestnut ganache. Refrigerate until they are set.

Dip the bottom of each mound of ganache into the tempered milk chocolate by lowering individually on a fork. Place them on a parchment-lined sheetpan until the milk chocolate sets.

Serve at once, or you may refrigerate in an airtight container for several days.

Espresso Profiteroles

30 to 35 profiteroles

1 recipe Espresso Choux Batter—see p. 29
1 recipe Rich Shortdough—see p. 20
2 tablespoons (10 g) Espresso beans, finely ground
1 recipe Espresso Bavarian—see p. 39

Equipment Needs
Pastry bag with ½-inch and ¼-inch plain tips
Parchment paper
1½-inch-diameter Pastry cutter
Sheetpan

Preheat the oven to 400°F. Fit a pastry bag with a ½-inch tip and fill it with the choux batter.

Lightly dust your work surface with flour and roll half the shortdough to 1/16 inch thick. Sift a thin layer of the espresso over the shortdough. Pass the rolling pin over the dough to make the espresso grounds stick to the dough. With a 1½-inch-round pastry cutter, cut 30 circles.

On a sheetpan lined with parchment, pipe ¾-inch-diameter mounds of choux batter, 2 inches apart. Place 1 shortdough circle on top of each choux mound, espresso side up. Bake for 10 minutes. Reduce the temperature to 350°F and continue baking for an additional 5 minutes. Allow to cool.

With the tip of a paring knife, poke a small hole in the bottom of each profiterole. Fill a pastry bag fitted with a ¼-inch plain tip with the espresso bavarian and fill each profiterole.

Serve at once, or refrigerate for 1 hour.

Ginger Chocolates

30 to 35 chocolates

1 recipe Chocolate-Ginger Ganache—see
    p. 42
1 recipe Candied Ginger—see p. 55
1 recipe Tempered Chocolate—see p. 41

Equipment Needs
Chocolate thermometer
Plastic wrap
Sheetpan
Parchment paper

Finely chop the candied ginger and stir into the ganache. Stretch a 16-inch-long piece of plastic wrap over the back of a sheetpan. Set the bowl of ganache over a bowl of ice. Stir the ganache as it thickens. When the ganache begins to hold its own shape, transfer it to the center of the back of the sheetpan and spread it out with a spatula into a 1/2-inch-thick rectangular shape. Refrigerate for 15 minutes.

Turn the rectangle over onto a cutting board and peel the plastic off the top. Cut into 1-inch squares by wiping and warming the knife between cuts. Return the squares to the refrigerator until final assembly.

Place a ganache square on a fork and dip it into the chocolate. Tap the fork on the edge of the bowl. Pull the bottom of the fork across the edge of the bowl to remove the excess chocolate. Slide the chocolate off the fork onto a parchment-lined sheetpan. Diagonally dip a prong of the fork into the top of the chocolate to leave a line across the chocolate. Continue the process, dipping and scoring all the squares.

You may refrigerate the chocolates in an airtight container for 1 week, but they are best if consumed within a few days.

Chef's Hint

Leftover scraps of ganache could be melted down and reformed into squares or other shapes.

Hazelnuts in Apricots

30 petit fours

15 Apricots, dried
1 recipe Hazelnut Paste, chilled—see p. 45
1 recipe Tempered Chocolate—see p. 41

Equipment Needs
Food processor
Chocolate thermometer
Parchment-lined sheetpan

With a paring knife, slice the apricots in half sideways. Spread them out on a work surface, cut side facing up.

Between 2 hands, roll the paste out into 30, 1/2-inch-diameter oval shapes. Place them on the apricot halves. Roll the dried apricot around the paste.

Dip the ends of the apricots at an angle into the tempered chocolate and place them on a parchment-lined sheetpan.

You may refrigerate the petit fours in an airtight container for 2 days, but they are best if consumed within a few hours.

Macadamia-Orange Cookies

30 to 35 cookies

Cookie Dough

½ cup (115 g) Butter

2 tablespoons (30 g) Sugar

1 teaspoon (5 ml) Vanilla extract

1 cup (140 g) Flour

1 cup (170 g) Macadamia nuts, roughly chopped

Candied Orange Rind

4 cups (960 ml) Water, for blanching

2 Oranges

1 cup (200 g) Sugar

1¾ cups (420 ml) Water

4 ounces (115 g) White chocolate, melted

Equipment Needs

Parchment paper or stickless sheetpan

Prepare the Cookie Dough

Preheat the oven to 350°F. Cream the butter with the sugar and the vanilla extract. Add the flour and the nuts. Mix until combined. Chill the dough in the freezer for 10 minutes.

Using your hands, roll pieces of the dough into ¾-inch-diameter rounds. Place them 2 inches apart on a parchment-covered sheetpan.

Bake for 15 minutes, or until just beginning to lightly brown.

Prepare the Candied Orange Rind

Place the water for blanching in a saucepot on high heat. Cut the oranges in half crossways, and scoop out the flesh with a spoon. Slice the rinds into ⅛-inch- to ¼-inch-thick strips. Put them in the saucepot. Boil for 25 minutes and drain.

Rinse the strips and place them in another saucepot with the sugar and the remaining 1¾ cups (420 ml) of water. Simmer over medium to low heat for another 25 minutes. Strain the strips from the syrup, allow to cool, and save for final assembly.

Assemble the Cookies

Place a macadamia cookie on a fork. Dip the bottom of the cookie and ¼ inch up the sides into the white chocolate. Tap the fork on the edge of the bowl and then pull the bottom of the fork across the edge of the bowl to remove any excess chocolate.

Slide the cookie off the fork onto a parchment-lined sheetpan. Press an orange-rind strip around the bottom of each cookie, adhering it to the cookie where the chocolate coats the sides.

Chill and serve within a few hours.

Mango Linzers

20 to 25 linzers

1 recipe Three-Nut Linzer Dough—see
    p. 22
Flour, for sprinkling
1 Mango
1 tablespoon (15 g) Sugar

Equipment Needs
Parchment paper or stickless sheetpan

Generously sprinkle the work surface with flour. Roll a piece of the linzer dough to 8 inches by 8 inches by ¼ inch thick. Using a French knife, cut the dough into equal triangles measuring 1¾ inches on each edge.

Transfer the triangles to a parchment-lined sheetpan. Chill in the refrigerator for 10 minutes.

Preheat the oven to 400°F. Peel the mango and cut the flesh from each side of the pit. Set the 2 pieces aside. Trim all the remaining flesh from the pit and puree it in a food processor with the sugar. Pass the puree through a strainer.

Spread the puree on each linzer triangle. Cut the mango halves into ⅛-inch-thick lengthwise slices, then cut crossways in 1-inch increments. Arrange the mango slices on the linzer triangles, 2 to 3 pieces feathered across each. Bake for 12 to 14 minutes.

Serve within a few hours.

Mincemeat Turnovers

30 to 35 turnovers

Mincemeat Filling

7 ounces (200 g) Bartlett or d'Anjou pear,
   approximately 1, peeled, cored, diced

4.25 ounces (120 g) Orange, approximately
   ½, pith removed, diced

2.5 ounces (70 g) Raisins, approximately
   ½ cup, chopped

Juice of ½ lemon, zest finely chopped

1 ounce (30 ml) Brandy

1 tablespoon (15 g) Sugar

¼ cup (60 ml) Water

½ teaspoon (.5 g) Cinnamon, ground

½ teaspoon (.5 g) Cloves, ground

Black pepper, a grind

Salt, a dash

1 sheet Puff Pastry—see p. 18

Egg wash

Equipment Needs

Saucepan

Pastry wheel

Parchment paper or stickless sheetpan

Prepare the Filling

In a saucepan over low to medium heat, cook all ingredients, stirring occasionally until reduced in volume by ¼ (about 15 to 17 minutes). Allow to cool and reserve.

Assemble the Turnovers

Preheat the oven to 400°F. Spread out the sheet of pastry and dust it lightly with flour, rolling as necessary to make an even ⅛-inch thickness. Allow it to rest for 15 minutes.

Using a pastry wheel, cut the sheet into 2-inch squares. Lightly brush the edges of 1 corner of each square with egg wash. Spoon a small mound of the filling in the center of each square. Fold a corner of the square over the filling and seal it to the egg-washed opposite corner.

Place the turnovers on a sheetpan lined with parchment. Egg wash their tops. Bake for 7 to 9 minutes.

Serve warm from the oven.

Nougatine Cones

25 to 30 cones

Cones
³/₄ cup (160 g) Sugar
½ ounce (15 g) Almonds, blanched

1 recipe Chocolate Ganache—see p. 42 —see p. 42
4 ounces (115 g) Fruit, seasonally available,
    such as bananas, mangos, or strawberries
¼ cup (30 g) Almonds or other nuts, lightly
    roasted, rough-chopped

Equipment Needs
Food processor
Metal pastry horn mold
Pastry bag with ¼-inch plain tip

Prepare the Cones
Preheat the oven to 350°F. Using a metal pastry horn as a guide, cut a pattern from a piece of paper in the shape of a small coronet and reserve for later use.

In a saucepan over high heat, cook the sugar. When it begins to melt and caramelize, stir with a spoon. When the sugar is light amber in color and completely melted, immediately remove from the heat and stir in the almonds.

Pour the mixture out onto a lightly oiled sheetpan and allow to cool. Pulverize in a food processor until it is very fine.

Lightly oil the sheetpan again and transfer the pulverized mixture to a sifter. Shake the sifter over the oiled sheetpan to evenly cover its surface, about ¹/₁₆ inch thick. Place the pan in the oven and bake the brittle for about 6 minutes, or until it melts and the nuts turn light brown.

Place the paper coronet pattern on the brittle. Using a paring knife, cut around the pattern, returning the pan to the oven, if necessary, to make the nougatine pliable enough to cut without breaking. Peel the nougatine piece from the pan and quickly shape it around the end of the pastry horn. Remove it as soon as it cools somewhat and retains its shape.

Continue warming the brittle, cutting and forming the coronets until you have 25 to 30.

Assemble the Cones
Adjust the temperature of the ganache by stirring it in a bowl over ice water or simmering water in order to bring it to a smooth, piping consistency. Cut the fruit into shapes and sizes small enough to fit into the coronets.

Fill a pastry bag fitted with a ¼-inch plain tip with the ganache. Pipe it into the nougatine coronets to fill them up halfway. Fill the coronets the rest of the way with the fruit, sticking it into the ganache in each coronet, along with a few pieces of the roasted nuts.

Serve at once or within 1 hour.

Praline Moons

30 to 35 moons

1 recipe Praline Chocolate—see p. 45
1 recipe Chocolate Ganache—see p. 42

Equipment Needs
Flat sheetpan
Food processor
2-inch-diameter Pastry cutter

Lightly coat with oil the back of a perfectly clean, flat sheetpan. Pour the praline onto the oiled surface and cover it with a large piece of plastic wrap. Spread it first with your hands, pressing it outward from the center, then with a rolling pin to an even ³/₁₆-inch thickness.

Allow the praline to cool and harden by placing the pan in the refrigerator for a few minutes. Then peel the plastic wrap from its surface. Spread the ganache to an even ⅛-inch thickness over the praline. Chill for 15 minutes.

Using a 2-inch-diameter pastry cutter, press the cutter through the chocolate, starting at 1 edge, and pull the cutter toward you. Set the uneven chocolate piece aside and wipe the cutter off with a cloth. Place the cutter overlapping the round edge of the first cut to make a half-circle moon shape, ½ inch thick at the widest point. Press the cutter through the chocolate layers and pull the cutter toward you.

Wipe the cutter off with a cloth each time and continue cutting moons until you have 30 to 35.

Refrigerate in an airtight container for 1 week. The moons are best if consumed within a few days.

Spice Tuiles

30 to 35 tuiles

¼ cup (60 g) Butter

½ cup (60 g) Powdered sugar

2 Egg whites

⅓ cup (40 g) Flour

½ teaspoon (.5 g) Cumin

½ teaspoon (.5 g) Ginger, ground, dried

½ teaspoon (.5 g) Allspice, ground

¼ teaspoon (.25 g) Cloves

¼ teaspoon (.25 g) White pepper

Salt, a dash

Equipment Needs
Stickless sheetpan or parchment paper

Metal spatula

Cream the butter with the sugar. Add the egg whites and mix until smooth. Sift the flour with the spices and salt. Add the dry ingredients to the butter mixture. Mix until smooth.

Preheat the oven to 375°F. On a stickless pan or a pan lined with parchment and brushed with butter, spread the batter into 2½-inch circles, ¹⁄₁₆ inch thick and 1 inch apart from each other. Bake for 6 to 8 minutes, or until they are lightly browned. Peel from the pan 1 by 1 and wrap them around a 1-inch- or 2-inch-diameter round form, such as a rolling pin, or simply form them by hand into desired shapes. Reheat as necessary throughout the molding process to make them pliable enough to form.

Continue spreading the circles, baking and forming them until you have as many as needed.

Store in an airtight container at room temperature and serve them at once, or within a few hours.

Temperature Conversions

Fahrenheit	Celsius		Fahrenheit	Celsius
32°F	0°C		245°F	118°C
40°F	4°C		250°F	122°C
50°F	10°C		260°F	127°C
60°F	16°C		270°F	132°C
70°F	21°C		280°F	138°C
80°F	26°C		290°F	143°C
90°F	32°C		300°F	149°C
100°F	38°C		310°F	155°C
110°F	43°C		320°F	160°C
120°F	49°C		330°F	166°C
130°F	54°C		340°F	170°C
140°F	60°C		350°F	175°C
145°F	63°C		360°F	183°C
150°F	65°C		370°F	188°C
160°F	71°C		380°F	193°C
170°F	77°C		390°F	199°C
180°F	82°C		400°F	205°C
190°F	88°C		410°F	210°C
200°F	94°C		420°F	216°C
210°F	99°C		430°F	222°C
212°F	100°C		440°F	226°C
220°F	104°C		450°F	230°C
230°F	110°C		500°F	260°C
240°F	115°C			

To Convert Celsius to Fahrenheit
Multiple by 9, divide by 5 (Celsius × 9/5), then add 32.
Example: 190°C × 9/5 = 342 + 32 = 374°F.

To Convert Fahrenheit to Celsius
Subtract 32, multiply by 5, then divide by 9 (Fahrenheit × 5/9).
Example: 400°F − 32 = 368 × 5/9 = 204.4°C.

Index

C